THE ARK,
THE SHROUD,
AND MARY

PHILIP GARDINER

best-selling author of *Gnosis* and *The Serpent Grail*

THE ARK, THE SHROUD, AND MARY

THE UNTOLD TRUTHS ABOUT THE RELICS OF THE BIBLE

NEW PAGE BOOKS
A division of The Career Press, Inc.
Franklin Lakes, NJ

THE ARK, THE SHROUD, AND MARY
EDITED AND TYPESET BY ASTRID DERIDDER
Cover design by Dutton & Sherman
Printed in the U.S.A. by Book-mart Press

To order this title, please call toll-free 1-800-CAREER-1 (NJ and Canada: 201-848-0310) to order using VISA or MasterCard, or for further information on books from Career Press.

The Career Press, Inc., 3 Tice Road, PO Box 687,
Franklin Lakes, NJ 07417
www.careerpress.com
www.newpagebooks.com

Library of Congress Cataloging-in-Publication Data

Gardiner, Philip.
    The ark, the shroud, and Mary : the untold truths about the relics of the Bible / by Philip Gardiner.
        p. cm.
    ISBN-13: 978-156414-924-4
    ISBN-10: 1-56414-924-2
        1. Relics. 2. Bible—Antiquities. I. Title.
BV890.9—dc22

2006038040

DEDICATION

To those who know themselves.

ACKNOWLEDGMENTS

I would like to acknowledge the input,
whether directly or indirectly,
of Crichton Miller, Graham Phillips,
Graham Hancock, Ian Wilson,
Stuart Munro-Hay, the late Gopi Krishna,
Gary Osborn, Warren Croyle,
the music of George Harrison,
my wife, my children,
and the spirit of oneness.
My thanks, as ever, go to my
wonderful editor, Astrid deRidder.

CONTENTS

INTRODUCTION

I had no intention of writing a book about the Ark of the Covenant, let alone the Shroud of Turin or Mary. The thought never crossed my mind. In fact, I thought the subjects had been pretty well covered. But something happened that changed my mind.

But first, a little of my own history will probably help you understand where I'm coming from. I want you to be fully aware that I have no ax to grind, no faith to uphold, and no academic reputation to protect.

I am an ordinary man. I went to school, graduated, joined Her Majesty's Army, and then found a proper job in the printing industry. I began taking management courses, and eventually got myself qualified as a marketing man. But it was not enough. I had a strong, inner drive, and still do. This drive, when unfocused (as it was in my youth), has caused me many problems. Thankfully, today I can clearly see who I am, what I want, and where I want to be. But this was not always the case.

I was working as a man of business, running a company with a business partner, and I should have been happy. But I wasn't. You see, I had met several people who influenced me, without even being aware of it. One of these men was in a kind of club, called the Sealed Knot. Those who live in England may be aware that the Sealed Knot is an English Civil War re-enactment society, and members spend their weekends camped out at various locations, sticking long pikes into each other and getting hilariously drunk at night. All in all, it's great fun and a wonderful spectacle for the audience. This particular gentleman was fascinating to talk to, and we spoke for hours and hours about history. We debated about historical fact and fiction, which inspired me to amass a great quantity of books. My inquiring mind and competitive appetite was whetted.

The author on a research trip to Rome.

The second influential man I met was deeply interested in poetry and philosophy. He was equally intelligent to the first influence, but opposite in a number of ways. He was a member of another club, the Lord Byron Society, and anybody who knows of the mad, bad Lord Byron will be aware of the strange and beautiful language that surrounded him. This new world of thought was opening up before me as a blossoming rose, but I wanted the whole bouquet.

For the next 10 years I studied history, religion, philosophy, alchemy, and science, as though possessed. Every waking moment was spent with my head in a book. I had a book in the car, a book in the bathroom, a book in the bedroom, and so on. I felt it was a waste of my time to do anything other than read and absorb information.

Eventually though, the books were not enough. I was reading the same things over and over again. I recognize a great deal of what I read as political and religious propaganda, due to my marketing expertise. I also knew that an equal amount was information repeated from other books. So, I took my knowledge on symbolism, the occult, cults, religion, alchemy, history, architecture, and so much more, and went out into the world to see it in real life. The timing was perfect. The company was doing well and I could now afford to see the world. I saw sites that astounded me. My thirst for knowledge was becoming more refined, similar to a wine taster. The coarse, standard history books no longer satisfied my taste buds; they were as home-brewed ale to me. I needed fine wines from exotic locations around the globe.

I spent many hours in the British Library, the Bodlein, and many other well-stocked libraries. I had various book buyers scattered across the world keeping their eyes out for special books on magic, rituals, or any other arcane texts. I spent too much money on books, that much is sure!

Through my research, I discovered several inaccuracies in the historical record, and I decided to write my own book. I launched the book under my own imprint, and with my marketing skills I managed to get it to best-seller status. I followed this with a book published by a professional publishing company, and it too sold incredibly well. Then I decided it was time for a life change. The business was doing well, but it was running me down both physically and emotionally. I had no desire to be a business leader anymore. I enjoyed researching, writing, and the delight of discovery much more. So I sold my half of the business and took a leap of faith into the big wide world of authorship—which leads me back to where I was when I became interested in the Ark of the Covenant.

I was writing *Gnosis: The Secret of Solomon's Temple Revealed*, and I suppose the intricacies of the esoteric wisdom literature, linked with the fables of the Bible and other texts, must have been quite prominent in my mind.

On one particular day I was out and about looking for images for my book. I was in Winchester, England, and I was taking in the wonderful medieval cathedral. I had my new digital camera clutched firmly in my grasp and was walking around, staring at the floors, walls, windows, and ceiling, all the while trying desperately not to miss anything. I was even quite impressed to find that a (probable) ancestor, Stephen Gardiner, had been the last Roman Catholic bishop there in the 16th century, during the reign of the ill-fated Queen Mary I.

The Ark of the Covenant being carried from Egypt. Note the pyramids in the background, with their triangular shape, and the water beneath the feet of the porters. This relief is carved at Winchester Cathedral in England.

I noticed a beautiful stone image of Prudence, with the face of a woman on the front and a bearded male on the back. I smiled and told myself that this was a physical representation of the union of opposites—whereby our Gnostic ancestors believed that true understanding could only be found in uniting the two elements of our psyche. Nearby I noticed another beautiful carving: an image of Moses leading his people out of Egypt. In the center, the people of Israel are carrying the Ark of the Covenant on large poles, and in the background are the pyramids at Giza. The Ark looked similar to a small reliquary box I had previously photographed at the Kykkos Monastery in Cyprus. In fact, it was exactly the same, but obviously much larger—even though hundreds of miles and years separated the two. On the other side of the beautifully carved mausoleum was another wonderful image: of Jesus is emerging from a coffer, which looked remarkable similar to the Ark. Jesus is holding the cross and is flanked by two praying angels as the Vesica Piscis, or almond shape, radiates light from behind him.

It struck me that these designs were interrelated, and were telling a story of the New Covenant or Testimony. The Ark was the old Covenant, now lost, and Jesus was emerging from the Ark as the resurrection of the Testament. At that point, I suddenly realized the truth of the Ark, the Shroud, and Mary. The rush to my head made me feel nauseous, and it was all I could do to take a few photographs before making for the exit to get some air.

Christ rising from the tomb (or Ark).

It is moments such as this that make the role of the author and researcher worthwhile. It is uncovering an ancient and sacred treasure that has been lost for centuries. Unlike *Indiana Jones*, there are no fires, rats, rolling balls, or guardians with guns trying to take a shot at you, but during the research for this book I uncovered truths that brought me closer to secret societies than ever before. There were moments when I feared for my life, and moments of pure elation; moments when I became unnerved by power, and moments when I thought I was at a dead end. In each case, something would happen to alter my course, and always, just around the corner, I was completely surprised.

I decided to pursue the intriguing ideas about the Ark, the Shroud, and Mary. I scoured the book shops, the Internet and even had someone from a little old bookstore in Lincoln pass the word around. Eventually I gathered around me every book ever written on the Ark and most of those on the Shroud and Mary. I was shocked when I examined the various books on the subject. As I sat in my office I must have resembled a crazy wizard, surrounded by piles of fusty old books. Where to begin? Which book to read first? I closed my eyes placed out my hand and came back with an old book about sacred geometry. My journey was about to begin.

Throughout my research I have never tried to force the facts to fit the theory. I have allowed the story to come out. I have written of the evidence (or lack of it) as I have found it. And I have kept my silence all these years while researching and writing this book. Out of all the books I have written, this has been the most draining, because of its complexity and intrigue. All the time I have been coming up against dogma, doctrine, bigotry, and religious intolerance. Everybody, it seems, has a theory on the Ark, whether they are Jewish, Muslim, Christian, or Freemason. To add to this burden, I also needed to investigate the Shroud. (I was inviting the world of science down on my head.) And then, to make matters even worse, Dan Brown released his novel *The Da Vinci Code*, which altered everybody's perception of who or what Mary was—and all the time this new, growing, popular perception was directly opposite to the truth I knew I was uncovering.

The facts were so startling, so at odds with the base, cultural, and current popular beliefs. I would rage at the lack of understanding of almost everybody I spoke to. Even many authors seemed to want to view the world according to how many books they could sell, regardless of the truth. Sadly, I could not tell the whole story to anyone (short of my own wife) for fear of giving too much away. I have, in the past, been plagiarized, and it is not a nice thing. The torment of the tale of the Ark is one I am sure I share with a great many researchers, authors, and thinkers out there in the wide world—but I can now rest my soul and say that I am happy with what I have written. It is not until the last word is down on paper that this feeling of elation can be allowed to roam free—but now I set my beast of burden loose upon the world, and all I ask is that you spend time trying to understand the words and ideas I've written. Allow the words to have their say, without attacking them with any preconceived ideas.

Think about what it is we search for. Think about the people who wrote the ancient texts. Were they really reporting on ancient alien technology? Were they really seeing and hearing the word of Yahweh between the Cherubim? Or is there more to the whole story than we could even imagine? I tell you now: Be prepared to expand your mind—because our ancestors were much more complex, intelligent, and intuitive than we ever imagined.

A reliquary box that looks strikingly similar to the box depicted in the relief at Winchester Cathedral (see page 16). This box is on display at the Kykkos Monastery in Cyprus.

CHAPTER 1
THE ESOTERIC ARK

The word *esoteric* is derived from the Greek *eis*, meaning *into* or *within*. According to most dictionaries, the word means *something taught to the few*, or *initiated*. The word is associated with elements of secrecy and inner traditions. Examples of the esoteric elements of the world are those books you read where you know there is more depth; the teachings of secret societies, and the many layers of understanding them; the hidden truths of the Bible and other religious texts; wisdom literature; mystery religions; and, of course, the Gnostics.

The truths of the esoteric world all seem to revolve around the spiritual perspective, although it could be said that many societies have their esoteric traditions—special words, handshakes, nods, and winks—those things only the initiates understand. In this book I want to concentrate on the inner truths of the mind, and do so with a distinctly spiritual perspective.

The world we are going to explore has many different nations, beliefs, and cults. Not all are the same, but there are similarities we shall discover. These similarities exist because we are all human. We all have the same basic genetic pattern; we all live on the same physical plane; we all eat and drink similar things; we are all part of the beautiful electromagnetic world; we all have dreams and desires; and we all hope for something better. This world we are about to explore is also occupied by a strange breed of humans who appear different from others, and who have, throughout history, spoken out and made their voices heard. They have often been given power and responsibility, and they have sometimes abused it. However, there were once some among them who wanted their higher knowledge to become known to others, and so left their experiences in writing or in symbols. These people can be found in many places and under many titles. Among them are the mystics.

THE MYSTICS

If the mystical experience were fleeting, then we would have little information upon which to base our knowledge. However, the mystical experience is one that remains with a person forever. It is an experience that changes the individual's attitude to life itself, bringing feelings of oneness with the universe, peace, sometimes calm and sometimes fever, and often a feeling of presence from a divine being.

The mystical experience comes from the inner world of the mind, which is believed by some to be connected with the greater universe, or God. Mystics reveal this Otherworld to our world through the only means they know (such as poetry, art, texts, and even structures). Often these influences from the minds of the mystics are the generative cause of our own religions and belief structures. This is seen directly in the religion of Islam, which is based on the mystical experiences and visions of the Prophet Muhammad.

The world around the mystic becomes one of profanity. Politics, commerce, and human desires are all entirely at odds with the inner reality that the mystic believes he or she is truly connected to. It could even be assumed that the mystical experience often brings balance back to a world that is simply led by the evolutionary desires of greed and lust. The visions of the mystic can, in this way, also cause immense problems for the visionary, as he or she struggles to cope with the new sights and experiences, and sometimes either opts in to the world and out of the Otherworld. Unfortunately, sometimes the pressure becomes unbearable, and the mystic commits suicide. These suicides are often passed over by later religious scribes as unworthy, and the scribes often attribute the mystic's death to some kind of bizarre symbolic act.

Of course, having a mystical experience does not immediately make a mystic of anybody—it simply means that the person has had a unique experience. For example, look at the kundalini. Many in the world today claim to have had this experience, but many of these individuals remain unbalanced and boastful.

People such as the painter Vincent Van Gogh could easily be said to have had mystical experiences, but he was far from balanced in his attitude to life, and it is doubtful that he understood his own experiences. Many people today are placed under psychiatric care due to their inability to cope with mystical experiences, so they only comprehend this ancient union with the divine through drugged eyes.

In times gone by, there were no psychiatrists to try and take away the mystical experience with therapy and prescriptions. Instead there were priests, shamans, and medicine men who understood the role of the experience in the life of man. These special shamans often experienced the mystical element of humanity, and eventually created stories and fables to explain the reason behind the mystical experiences. As most people have no comprehension of the mystical experience themselves, these stories and fables became the dogma and doctrine of religious establishments, and, very soon, *walking on water* became a literal event, rather than a symbolic phrase.

A stained glass image of the Ark from the Cathedral of Lincoln. Notice that the priest has horns, a symbol of illumination or enlightenment. The priest is also almost asleep, illustrating the hypnagogic state that is requred to access the unconscious self.

However, the fact remains that throughout the history of mankind there have been experiences that the mystic has found difficult to explain. These experiences, however you wish to view them, are real and widespread. They are, in fact, almost archetypal. But what is the purpose? As Arnold Uleyn writes, "Perhaps the fundamental meaning of religion is rooted in the enduring human desire for peace and harmony. In the individual's hankering after and quest for reconciliation and union on a cosmic level in which all conflicts and frustrations are removed, for the eternal bliss in which every ambivalence will come to an end."[1]

The mystical experience is a direct result of the evolution of consciousness. The higher the consciousness, the further into this mystical world we seem to go. Consciousness could have been caused by the mystical experience itself. At the end of the day, the mystical experience is a human phenomenon that should not be ignored: "On the one hand, mystical experience, like human love, is not the exclusive privilege of neurosis-free individuals (should any exist) and on the other hand, it offers the human a chance to be more human…. Psychiatry must come to recognise this experience as a psychic phenomenon *sui generis*. Only then will the psychiatrist be in a position to help these people who react in an unhealthy manner, and to show them the way that leads out of the blind alley into a new life."[2] Of course, psychiatrists see the mystical experience as an unhealthy process that takes people away from the real world. Others see the experience as a stepping stone towards higher consciousness. Whatever the truth, our ancestors often enjoyed the experience and did all that they could to return to the inner world. Those who could not or did not have the experience instead worshipped and made gods out of those who did.

By our own desire to explain the world, both outwardly (exoterically) and inwardly (esoterically), we have created a language for others to understand. The esoteric (or mystical) language is an attempt to speak the unspeakable, and thus it becomes a paradox to those who have their feet firmly on *terra firma*.

In *Mysticism: Its History and Challenges*, Bruno Borchert writes that "…the mystic's work is to destroy, to wreck, to annihilate, and at the same time to recreate, to establish, to resurrect; the mystic is marvellously terrifying and marvellously mild; the mystic is miserly and open-handed, chivalrous and jealous, asking for all and giving all."[3] It is because of this duality, these opposites in the mind and life of the mystic, that he or she opens up a *third-state* or *channel*, and it is through this channel that the mystic is able to see in an alternate way. It is similar to what we call an altered state of consciousness, and it is because we all live in one of the opposing worlds that we fail to see the middle way, and thereby fail to understand the language of the mystic. Many of those experiencing the kundalini today are so firmly rooted in their own experience that they fail to see balance. I know of one particular man who was so self-centered about his experience that his wife and children were secondary, and suffered badly as a result. My own extraordinarily balanced father had a similar event, when he had sat in the sun for too long. He tried to understand it, but the love of his wife and children balanced out his yearning to know more, and he remained centered. Over time he understood his vision as a middle way, and knew that there must be more after life. He was calm in his knowledge and his experience, and he did all things in balance. He had no language for his experience, but through my research I have learned the ways of the mystics, and have been able to communicate with him regarding his mystical experience.

Over the course of human history this language has been lost, found, and lost again. This repetitive aspect will now hopefully come to an end with our modern era of widespread information (unless, some time in the future, another religious fervor comes along and they burn all the hard drives). The fact that literalism has overtaken mystical texts has stopped us from being able to see the truth: Literality is only one side of the duality. The ancestors who placed their thoughts on paper for us all to read believed no more in walking on water than you or I, and yet millions of people are told or instructed to believe in it literally as an act of faith. We are told to give credence to God without having to see miracles, but then we are shown his miracles. The whole paradoxical situation of the Bible and other religious texts that are seen as literal events, places, and people, can now be explained properly through the esoteric eyes of the mystic.

The mystical experience was, in ancient times, said to be a gift of God: "Who possibly can describe what He reveals to the loving souls in whom He resides? And who can put into words what He gives them to experience? And, finally, who knows what He makes them desire? No one is able to do this, that is sure. It exceeds the capacity even of those involved; since, for that very reason, it is in a flood of images, comparisons, and symbols that they release something of what they have perceived."[4]

The inexpressible nature of the mystic is due to the all-encompassing knowledge accessed at the point of the vision or experience. It is supposedly the knowledge of all, of God. In the blink of an eye the mystic is overwhelmed with love, hate, greed, and compassion—all the thoughts and emotions possible. The mind is opened to all things, and can access more than we can while fully conscious. The fact that we are conscious most of the time stops us from accessing the deeper parts of our mind that the ancients saw as the gateway to God. Once we control our minds and access the unconscious world we are in a position of power—knowing the things that are archetypal to all men is to know the mind of all men. This control, however, only comes with practice. So we have developed religious rituals and controls. Those who managed to control this altered state are really no longer mystics; they become adepts or shaman. The mystic either experiences altered states spontaneously, or manages to access other realms in prayer or meditation. Control of the Otherworld has been seen as power, and was the role of the shaman, prophet, guide, or Messiah. For the rest of us, we need a priest to explain and give physical order to these peculiar concepts. Using modern psychological thought, we could say that all the religions of the globe are a direct result of mental disorder. However, this would be a statement out of balance. For the sake of equilibrium, we should see and recognize the world between the mental disorder and the divine connection.

This will become clear through in our tale of the Ark. It is both a metaphysical symbol and a physical representation of the inner reality. To search for it is similar to trying to comprehend the mystic's vision. As we shall discover, it is similar to the Grail journey, for those who look for it, will not find it.

THE GNOSTICS

A new concept was developed for understanding the mystical experience. It came to be known as Gnosticism, and was a merging of experience with wisdom. This method of connection to the inner divine developed from Judaism, mystery religions, and Christianity, with a lot of Greek philosophy thrown in. In truth, it has been evolving ever since its birth in ancient Egypt. The rituals of Bacchus (the Roman version of the Greek Dionysus) heavily affected the Gnostic creeds that were seen in the early Christian church. The rituals produced (in the followers of Bacchus) something known as *enthusiasm*, meaning *to have God enter the individual*. The Gnostic adherent believed he or she was becoming one with God by sweeping away the conscious thoughts of passion, greed, and lust by actually (and paradoxically) enacting those very sins. This dangerous element placed the adherent on the very edge between prudence and passion, between greed and generosity. In the end, though, the ritual accomplished the goal of providing the Gnostic with a fixed pattern of finding the third, in-between state.

Whether these rituals actually did anything other than create ecstasy in the followers of Bacchus is debatable, but it does reveal the symbolic elements of the true Gnostic. Balance of the opposites is required in order to know the true middle path. The concept is actually quite simple and yet complex—as it should be. For example, the simple act of walking is actually quite complex. One leg is useless without the other, but when used together they are vehicles for the true body. If we only had one leg, though, we wouldn't get very far. In the same way, we often travel through life with one-sided beliefs, but we should strive to balance our beliefs. The same is true in the brain, where we have a left and a right side. The left side controls our logic, and the right controls our emotions. To be entirely logical causes many problems, as it does to be entirely emotional. If we balance both sides of the mind, then we have achieved a third-state. This process of balance has many levels, and our ancestors developed many stories, fables, images, and symbols to enable us to work through these issues with our own conscious mind. Achieving balance is never the result of a single process, truth, or secret, such as the followers of the kundalini propose.

Many societies have found drugs to be useful to access the third-state, but others knew this to be wrong and said so. The tale of Orpheus, the son of Calliope (meaning *beautiful voice*), reveals that drugs, here symbolized as the Sirens, were a distraction: "His songs could charm wild beasts and coax even rocks and trees into movement. It was said to be Orpheus' music which prevented the crew of the Argos from being lured to destruction by the Sirens— who falsely promised that they would give knowledge, ripe wisdom and quickening of the spirit to every man who came to them."[5] The Sirens are the distraction from the true course, the beautiful music that resides within our mind when in perfect balance. Orpheus himself could visit the Otherworld and so is an archetypal shaman—he is ourselves, the son of the music. The Argos, of course, is the Ark, as it travels the true path, the journey that we must all take to true enlightenment.

At the root of all religions, including that of the early Gnostics, there are issues of balance between the male and female polarities. These issues, as the psychologist Carl Jung and others have pointed out, are to be found in the myths of the world. "Whether we think of the masculine element as being the doer and the feminine element as being the instigator, or whether we think of the former as active and the latter as passive, really does not matter. It is when we achieve a balance between the two energies that we find it easier to think of a 'perfect world'. It is the balance of the physical and the spiritual that is important."[6] In truth, many branches of Gnosticism speak of this balance from the very highest levels, claiming that the Supreme Being is androgynous and can be referenced as either male or female. The concept of male and female as the opposites was as a reference to all opposites that we come across in our lives and that need balance—not just the energy channels of the kundalini.

According to the texts ascribed to Jesus in the Gnostic Gospel of Thomas: "He said to his disciples, 'These infants being suckled are like those who enter the kingdom.' They said to him, 'Shall we then, as children, enter the kingdom?' Jesus said to them, 'When you make the two one, and when you make the inside like the outside and the outside like the inside, and the above like the below, and when you make the male and the female one and the same, so that the male be not male nor the female....'" Even Christ is being ascribed the same Gnostic elements of union of the opposites, and spelling it out quite clearly that we are to be neither positive nor negative, but neutral. This neutral place is also similar to the Grail element, where the searcher must not search, but must simply wait. By trying to force the issue, one is taking oneself away from that neutral place. As Jesus said in the Gospel of Thomas, "On what day will the kingdom come? It will not come while people watch for it."

Gnosticism also emerged from within the realms of the Persian Magi (the Zoroastrians) and from them into the worship of Mithras, who (before he became a Roman deity) was a minor deity within Zoroastrianism known as a *yazatas*. He was the god of the airy light, which is to be found between heaven and earth. He is the light of the sun, not the sun itself. We should become reflections of this light of the one who exists between the worlds. Mithras was also the god of contracts or covenants, and is therefore no different from the Solar Orb, which is between the prows of the Egyptian B'arque (as the metaphysical element of the physical sun) or the light of Yahweh, who resides between the Cherubim on the Ark of the Covenant.

Balance is required to achieve illumination or enlightenment. This stone carving of the scales of justice is an excellent representative of the balance that is required in life in order to truly know God, which is to truly know yourself.

All these principles are the same, and all have the same meaning: Find true balance at every level in your life, and you will be the mirror of the light. Then, and only then—when we have true balance in our lives—will we be able to truly converse with the inner divinity, which is ourselves.

The cult of Mithras had seven layers, something we will discover to be of importance, and can be said to relate to the planets. Each level increases in knowledge and balance, from Mercury to Saturn. The planets are being related to—not separated from—the inner processes of the mind. The first three grades (Mercury, Venus, and Mars) are internal workings and self-improvement techniques, and the final four (Jupiter, the Moon, the Sun, and Saturn) are for adepts who have passed the initiatory tests.

The worship of Mithras in Persia is not the oldest record of Gnosis. Mithras was often depicted as fighting with the bull, which is believed to reveal that the cult was as old as the age of Taurus, or some 2,000 years before Christ. The origins of Gnostic traditions are very old indeed.

The Greeks developed the panoply of cults and creeds into a whole system of major and minor deities. Philosophies after Plato moved away from focusing on the outer world of the planets, and instead concentrated on the inner worlds of the soul. The image of the Messiah character developed from one who saved the planet and the people, to one who would save the soul of man. In essence, Jesus himself was being created by these Greek philosophers, who would then move on to influence the Jews, particularly the Jewish sect of the Essene. The Greeks nurtured the *Gnosis Theou*, the *Knowledge of God*. But what was this knowledge? It was not an intellectual proof of God, but a knowledge of God through Oneness with him—*enthusiasm*. It was complete union, complete fusion of the opposites into the third-state of mind—a mind in balance and harmony. Therefore God was balance and harmony. As long as we walk in balance, we are all sons of God, and we are all God himself.

These Greek elements moved into the Jewish culture. The ancient concepts of the Ark of the Covenant and the Ark of Noah, which were influences from Egypt, Mesopotamia, and India, were updated and resurrected as the Ark of Mary, giving birth to the light.

CHAPTER 2
LOCATING THE ARK

In the preceding chapter, I quickly ran through the basic concepts of the inner teachings of the mind from the perspective of our spiritual ancestors. This primer was important before we try to find the Ark, because there will be clues and trapdoors along the way that may be better revealed if we look with our esoteric vision.

Once my interest in the Ark was peaked, I scoured the world looking for every book about the Ark that I could find. All but one of these books was devoted to locating the Ark, and even the one exception made an attempt to pinpoint its final resting place. And so, with a literal heart, I decided that I too must take up the search of the Ark.

The first thing I had to do was to analyze the discoveries and writings of previous researchers and authors. A great many weird and wonderful theories exist out there, both in published text and cyberspace—from the Ark being alien technology, to it being a gift from some hidden, underworld realm. But there is one theory that a significant number of people seem to cling to: the theory that the Ark was a complex battery or weapon that could cause mass destruction with its power.

THE ARK'S EXISTENCE

But before we can decide whether the Ark was a complex battery or weapon, we have to decide whether the Ark existed at all. For this I want to go back to Randall Price's book, which quotes an archaeologist from the University of Southern California, Jordan Maxwell: "There never was an Ark of the Covenant. It's as fictional as the search for it by *Indiana Jones in Raiders of the Lost Ark.* As serious scholars, we can all stop looking for that lost Ark of the Covenant and leave it to Hollywood, because that's where it belongs, in the realm of fantasy!"

Of course, it is easy to say that the Ark never existed at all, but such an assertion is impossible to prove. The fact remains that there are numerous parallels in history to the Ark, such as the Egyptian b'arques, which carried their deities and their own souls. And so, it would be no surprise if the Israelites did indeed recreate these Egyptian concepts as outlined in the Old Testament. Upon examining the Ark in detail from the biblical statements, it becomes distinctly clear that the Ark was a copy of an Egyptian portable ceremonial shrine known as a b'arque. But instead of crossing the sky or the waters, this Ark had to cross land and desert.

THEORIES ABOUT THE ARK

Believe it or not, the ancient Jewish box we call the Ark has been claimed to be an ancient battery with such immense power that it could wipe out whole armies. In *Searching for the Ark of the Covenant*, author Randall Price asks the question, "Is the Ark a superweapon?"[1] Well, of course my answer would simply be no, but Randall Price says that this kind of imaginative theory requires no refutation, because he says there is no evidence for it. Models have been made on a reduced scale to the proportions laid out in the Bible, and none of them have produced significant electrical charges. In addition to this, many Egyptian relics duplicate the Ark's design and prove that this style was typical of the period.

I decided I would examine the battery theory, so drove up to my local university to see a resident electrical expert I knew from school, named Bob. He proved to be a valuable individual in this research. We sat for hours and mused over the dimensions and conductivity of the Ark from the biblical records. Bob could see why people assumed that it may have been a battery or, as Bob said, "based upon an original battery design," but as it was in the Bible, the charge created was simply not enough to light a bulb.

I insisted that Bob take into account all the possible electrical and electromagnetic influences upon the Ark, such as the tectonic plate movement in the original location—Jerusalem. And so, we ventured into the geography department on the other side of the complex, stopping for a coffee on the way. We spoke to several geography experts who kindly allowed us to use a very complex computer model they had been developing that revealed ground electrical charge in various locations, and influences that may alter these charges. It was a fascinating exercise, and it was lucky I had brought some research material with me, because we needed to lay out the structure of the buildings in the correct alignments to be able to ascertain a charge level. We finally managed to place the Ark *in situ*, but it still couldn't light a bulb.

I left the research with Bob, who promised to keep thinking about the problem. Several weeks later, Bob phoned me and said he managed to get the Ark to light a bulb by simply leaving it alone. He found that the Ark collected an electrical charge over time and stored it. It was an amazing conclusion. However, when I asked how long it would take before the Ark had a sufficient charge to wipe out armies or strike people down, he said that such a thing was impossible. It would never store enough energy, no matter how long the Ark sat.

From our little experiment, it seems quite natural to conclude that the Ark will collect a charge if placed in Jerusalem, but that it could never be enough to kill. But Bob's notion that the Ark could have been based on an original battery design was still interesting to me. The fact remains that there were many arks in Egypt that had the concept of light—the Solar Orb—placed between the prows of the ship. I had to wonder, on a physical level: Could the magicians of Egypt (or elsewhere) really have created a battery vessel that lit up the dark places with the light of the sun, and thereby mirrored the light of Ra?

It may be that several Hebrew Arks were created over the course of time, and that this could answer the many different viewpoints arrived at by various authors. I decided now to turn my attention towards Ethiopia itself, as this country, ever since Graham Hancock's bestselling book, *The Sign and the Seal*, was released, has been the one place the majority of the world believes the Ark to reside.

ETHIOPIA

Stuart Munro-Hay writes in his book, *The Quest for the Ark of the Covenant*, that "Graham Hancock, the only writer to study the tradition of the Ark in Aksum at any length, perceived the Ark's presence there as a reality: it was 'the single ancient and recondite truth concealed beneath the layers of myth and magic' of the KN. Ironically, despite Hancock's affirmation of the incredible legend of the Ark at Aksum, I have never yet met an Ethiopian who commends his book."[2] Munro-Hay, in my opinion, had no ax to grind other than his own deep knowledge and love of Ethiopia. I have also spoken to other people who have been to Axum/Aksum in Ethiopia about the culture of the people. It does appear that, unless you speaks the language of the land, then little will be revealed. However, those who do take the time to learn the local ways are often rewarded with the truth, which is that the Ark at Axum is a *tabot*.

The truth of the Ark in Ethiopia must circumvent various problems—the least of which is the fact that the one at Axum isn't the Ark of the Covenant. One of these problems is the age of the story of the Ark. The path that leads to the Ark, says Munro Hay, is well over 1,000 years before the emperors of Aksum raised their obelisks, and 1,500 years before the Christian king named Ezana is said to have built the church in which the supposed Ark was to be placed.[3]

This is an immense period of time, and absolutely anything could have happened to the Ark. In all this time, it's highly likely that there would have been a text written, somewhere, revealing the location of the Ark. It would have been spotted by somebody. But there was nothing. In all this time there has been nothing but a belief. What we do have as far as sightings go are slabs of stone or wood, known as *tabot*. It has been suggested that these slabs are either the original tablets of stone from the Ark (placed there by Moses), or that they are copies of the same. They could also be original (or copies) of the first set of tablets that Moses threw to the ground when he saw the people of Israel worshipping the golden calf.

As Stuart Munro-Hay, one of the world's leading experts on Ethiopia, says, the second set of stone tablets that Moses made at Sinai to replace the original broken tablets may have survived, but there is certainly no evidence of them in Ethiopia, or anywhere else, for that matter. The object hidden in the Chapel of the Tablet at Aksum is "[i]mbued through a complex and esoteric symbolism with the holy aura of the Ark in which the tablets once rested, and bearing the same name, it is the substitute that receives the reverence and adoration of the Ethiopian Christians—not for a 'real', scientific, reason, but through its mystical identity with Zion, the Ark of the Lord.... The KN itself explains how the Ark is actually a heavenly thing, and that even the Ark of Moses was nothing more than an authorised likeness made by the hand of man."

The actual Ark, if it ever existed, would now be more than 3,000 years old. Even if it had been cared for, or kept hidden in some hermetically sealed chamber, time would have caused serious issues with the wood. Munro-Hay was adamant that the Ark, as the larger perceived chair or box, was never at Aksum. So we can be perfectly clear from the opinions of our expert friends that if the Ark did exist, it certainly isn't—and has never been—in Ethiopia. So exactly what is it that draws the crowds to this special place? What is the tabot?

THE TABOT

The *tabot*, made popular by the investigations of Graham Hancock, is seen today as a representation of the Ark itself, specifically as the tablets of the law as brought down Mt. Sinai by Moses. There are thousands of tabot in Ethiopia; almost every church has one. The ultimate version is the one at Aksum, which is believed by some to be both the tablets of the law as well as the Ark itself. All the other tabot are copies of this one. It is probable that the tabot is derived from the Coptic Church's use of the *maqta'*, an altar board developed during the increasing isolation of the Egyptian Church. The Egyptian (or Coptic) board serves the same purpose as the tabot, in that it is used for supporting the bread and wine of the eucharist.

Of course, we should remember that the Hebrew term used for Noah's Ark was *tebah*, and not *Aron*, the word used for the Ark of the Covenant. Thus we have an interrelationship of terms appearing in Ethiopia. This is the first tantalizing link between Noah's Ark and the Ark of the Covenant. The term *arc* is simply a device of the representation of the shape of a bow, similar to the crescent moon, which is also associated with the Ark of the Covenant and the vessel of Mary. The crescent moon reflects the light of the sun.

The tabot is an intimate and ritualistic device or tool of connection to God in the Ethiopian Church. The use of the term *tabot* in the way the church uses it is slightly incorrect in physical terms, but in ritual terms it just doesn't matter. "The word tabot strictly implies a container for something, a chest or coffer."[4]

The Ethiopian church appears to have copies of the tablets of stone, but not the Ark container. Obviously there was some misinterpretation between the words for the tablets and for the container. One thing is clear: The priests of the Ethiopian church understood that there was a great deal to be learned from their 3,000-year-old box. Munro-Hay asserts that the conceits are very much part of what is known as the *dabtara*, or lay canon, in which the poetry known as the *qene* enfolds this double meaning. It is known as the *samenna warq*, or *wax and gold*, whereby the wording conceals behind the banal significance of the wax or surface layer another (esoteric) meaning of gold.[5]

True, esoteric language is revealed in the teachings of the lay canon: Behind the wax (the banal) lies gold, or true knowledge. This poetry is revealing, as are the dabtara, for they speak of God being in the stone, as if it were the stone of the Philosophers. In this way, the use of the tabot is no different from the original Ark. It is paraded, it is worshipped, it is revered, and it contains God. The concepts are the same, the beliefs are the same, and so it may be said that the Ark does indeed exist in the church of Mary Zion in Axum. But it isn't the physical Ark, so we must turn our attention elsewhere.

The Arch of Titus was built by the emperor Domitian to commemorate the capture and sacking of Jerusalem and A.D. 70. Due to the arch's depiction of the destruction of the Temple, many Jewish people refuse to walk beneath it.

A close examination of the Arch of Titus, which is located along the Via Sacra in Rome, shows several porters carrying a heavy box or reliquary. Although it is not labeled, this could be an image of the Ark being carried out of Jerusalem.

MOSES AND MOUNT SINAI

Known as the Mountain of God, because the Israelites believed this to be where their God resided, Mount Sinai is where Moses encountered the burning bush, and also from where he descended with the tablets of law. Are there any clues in the stories about this mountain? Mount Sinai is one of the few places that God is said to have physically appeared.

> And the Lord said unto Moses, Lo, I come unto thee in a thick cloud, that the people may hear when I speak.... And mount Sinai was altogether in a smoke, because the Lord descended it in fire: and the smoke thereof ascended as the smoke of a furnace, and the whole mount quaked greatly.... And the glory of the Lord abode upon mount Sinai, and the cloud covered it six days: and the seventh day

he called unto Moses out of the midst of the cloud. And the sight of
the glory of the Lord was like devouring fire on the top of the mount
in the eyes of the children of Israel.

We could interpret this passage from Exodus 19:9 in several ways. We could easily say that this is the folk memory of a volcanic deity, and that the priesthood interpreted their volcanic deity through the actions of the sacred volcano. However, there is another side to this peculiar connectivity with the Israelite deity, and one that seems to have a golden thread throughout time. This may be symbolic language, which has a way of stating connection to the deity. Enlightenment is often represented as fire, or sometimes as the serpent or solar fire. We can see this in Acts 2, when the enlightened apostles receive the fire on their heads: "And when the day of Pentecost was fully come, they were all in one place. And suddenly there came a sound from heaven as of a rushing mighty wind, and it filled all the house where they were sitting. And there appeared unto them cloven tongues like as of fire, and it sat upon each of them."

This is similar to the *bindu* or *seventh chakra* of the Hindu kundalini system. This seventh chakra element may also be seen in the phrase *and the seventh day he called to Moses*, or even the seven planets or levels of Mithras. This is the true spiritual point of awakening that was supposedly achieved by such avatars as Moses and Buddha. If India was the origin of many beliefs and traditions in Egypt, Mesopotamia, and Israel (as I believe), then it would make perfect sense that an ancient system (similar to the kundalini, but not exactly the same) was the origin of these various uses of the number seven. In truth, our ancestors related the light to the sun and the stars, and so our own inner light is related to the seven planets, as well as to measurement and navigation. This explains the all-encompassing use of the ship as a symbol, such as the Ark. It is symbolic language such as this that clouds true vision, and it takes a clear explanation to truly see the glorious (and yet terrible) fire of God: the inner duality in balance.

In one interpretation, we have Moses connecting to his inner self (the Inner Sun or light of the sun). He is doing this via the law (which is mathematics developed for navigational purposes in ancient times) of chaos and creation as well as the wisdom of Thoth, and emerging (as in the Hebrew meaning of his name) as the enlightened one with shining horns and an illuminated countenance. Only by connecting the ideas in this way will we know the path ahead.

Of course, there is another clue. According to Graham Phillips in *The Templars and the Ark of the Covenant*, Mount Sinai is also the place where Jeremiah supposedly buried the Ark. In attempting to try and locate the Mount Sinai, we are attempting to find something that may never have truly existed.

We are encouraged to believe that the mountain of Sinai was somewhere in the Sinai Wilderness—or the wilderness of the moon god (Sin or Thoth). Let's look at Exodus 19:1-2 for a clue: "In the third month, when the children of Israel were gone forth out of the land of Egypt, the same day came they into the wilderness of Sinai. For they were departed from Rephidim, and were come to the desert of Sinai, and had pitched in the wilderness; and there Israel camped before the mount." Where is the town or place of Rephidim from where they departed? It is not a true location. Instead, it means *place of rest*. The children of Israel camped in the wilderness after they had departed from rest. Quite simply, the place of rest in the wilderness is the point between awake and asleep, between this world and the next, between the pillars. It is the twilight zone in the land of the moon god, and only here could they contact their God. Of course, the moon god is important because the moon is lit by the reflecting light of the sun.

In *The Ark of the Covenant*, by Roderick Grierson and Stuart Munro-Hay, when speaking of the literal wilderness and the area around the Jebel Musa or Mountain of Moses, the authors state that the wilderness is harsh and barren, and that it seems unlikely that anybody stood in this place with a reassuring sense of their own place in creation.[6] Sinai, they say, is not the easiest of places to enjoy a vision of the oneness of life or a revelation of its bounty and fruitfulness. It is a place that is dead and empty.

This is the location—the real place—where thousands of people claim the aged Moses climbed 3,000 steps in searing heat to meet his God. If there is literal truth in any of the biblical story of this place, then we must overcome these issues of this location. Those who believe (literally) in the Bible circumnavigate these issues by simply moving the location to any number of other places. There is, however, a place where archaeological exploration has uncovered significant evidence.

The excavation by Valerio Manfredi was on Har Karkom—a place many archaeologists believe to be the real Mount Sinai. It is located on the Sinai Peninsula and is part of an ancient trade route in the Negev Desert. It has taken more than 20 years of excavations (and hundreds of experts) to uncover the desert's amazing finds. One such discovery was an ancient *tumuli* on the eastern edge of Har Karkom. The profile of this tumuli can be seen for many miles around as a man-made mountain, and it was once thought to contain a burial of some great ancestor. But nothing of the sort was found. Instead, what was discovered has puzzled archaeologists. Lying on a large rectangular boulder was a white stone shaped as a semi-circle (similar to the moon). This was a mountain of the moon-god Sin, and the object was placed in the very center of this man-made mountain. In fact, the stones used to cover and protect the white stone were perfectly black, just as the night sky. This was an exciting discovery.

Further down the mountain, researchers discovered ibex cult scenes painted on the rock. The horns of the ibex symbolize the moon god Sin. In Deuteronomy 1:2, the Bible states: "There are eleven days journey from Horeb by the way of Mount Seir unto Kadeshbarnea." Kadeshbarnea is Ain Kudeirat, or Ain Kadis, both nearby Har Karkom. It takes 11 days to walk the distance from one to the other. Mount Sinai is said to be nearby Kadeshbarnea. In Exodus 24:4, we read: "And Moses wrote all the words of the Lord, and rose up early in the morning, and builded an altar under the hill, and twelve pillars, according to the twelve tribes of Israel."

This hill is Mount Sinai, and archaeologists found 12 standing stones beneath Har Karkom. It seems this (and more) evidence may suggest a real location for the biblical Mount Sinai, and evidence that Sin should indeed be equated to Sinai, and thereby also to Moses (and Sin or Thoth). Many scholars refute this evidence, but their refutations are grasping at straws. I have no associations or links to universities, and my job does not rely on my stated position. I follow where the evidence leads me, and in this case, it appears to be leading me up a mountain called Sinai. I decided it was time to take a look at the word *sin*, to see if there could be any clue in the name to help me confirm the location of Mount Sinai.

Sin

The word *sin* comes from a Syriac term meaning *to shine*, and comes to us as *sin* via the Babylonian *sinu*, for *the moon*. Of course, the term *to shine* will have those who have read my previous book, *The Shining Ones*, sitting up, as this is a celestial Shining One come down to earth. This shining aspect also comes through because the Desert of Sin was so named because of the glare from the white chalk. It seems that the moon is named *Sin* because it shines by the light of the sun. This shining glare was also reflected upon the earth as a connection to the light of the sun, which can still be seen as alive in night. Even in darkness we ourselves may shine, or so say the Gnostics. This element also comes true when we consider that Mount Sinai was also known as *Horeb*, meaning *place of desolation*. It was a place of duality, and a place to find balance.

There may also be tangential evidence found in the biblical tale of Moses, who rescued a Hebrew slave by killing an Egyptian and then escaped to Midian territory. This tale parallels a story from Egypt, in which a court official escaped to live in Syria-Palestine. The court official was known as *Sinuhe*.

A statue depicting the Ark of the Covenant located in St. Peter's Cathedral in Rome. Note the Cherubim in the place of the Cherubs, as well as the Agnus Dei in the center. The Agnus Dei is the lamb of God, or Christ.

TRACING THE ARK

If we try to accept for the moment that there was a real Ark (even if we believe this to be a copy of some ancient Egyptian b'arque or Mesopotamian throne of God), then we must attempt to trace this treasure. According to many, we must look to the prophet Jeremiah and to the second book of Maccabees. This apocryphal book was written sometime between 100 B.C. and A.D. 70, around the time of Herod's Temple. The writer, we are told by biblical scholars, was a Jew with Pharisaic leanings and who only wrote in Greek. This suggests that this Jew would have been able to read other tales and fables that were also written in Greek. We must remember that these Jewish writers were not mere chroniclers of history. They were, in fact, creating history. Bringing together a vast wealth of knowledge and using elements from around the known world made perfect sense to their own culture, and aided them in breading a new Jewish spirit.

Let's take a quick look at the second book of Maccabees, where we find that the prophet Jeremiah was being warned about the impending doom of the Temple of Solomon by an oracle and forced Jeremiah to give "…instructions for the tabernacle and the Ark to go with him when he set out for the mountain which Moses had climbed to survey God's heritage. On his arrival Jeremiah found a cave dwelling, into which he brought the tabernacle, the Ark and the altar of incense, afterwards blocking up the entrance." Hundreds of authors have jumped on this tradition, and claim that it must point to the location of the Ark (hidden by Jeremiah in a magical cave). But we have to take this theory apart to understand its true meaning. First, Jeremiah is supposed to have lived between 650 and 580 B.C., and yet 2 Maccabees was written 100 B.C. to A.D. 70. There are several reasons why Jeremiah and the Ark were used at this time. Most simply, the story is pure propaganda. The Greeks and Romans were in the land of the Israelites during these periods, and the Israelites (especially the Pharisees, of which the writer of 2 Maccabees was one) were against these intrusions. Hugh Schonfield points out in *The Essene Odyssey* that we: "have, I hope, sufficiently clarified that early in the second century BC the Jewish people were caught up in a Hellenising process, which was corrupting the chief priests, and seemed likely to bring about the extinction of Judaism."[7]

We find at this time that the Essene and others escaped or migrated to Damascus, to the region known as Haura, and remained in exile while they developed their New Covenant ideas and began the Jesus fable. The individual these groups looked up to was called the True Teacher or Lawgiver. This is none other than Thoth, which is merely a title. This powerful individual is also none other than God himself, as it was God who gave the law to Moses on the mountain of the moon, and the moon is Thoth, who gives his name to the first part of Tutankhamen's name (*Tut* is *Thoth*). You probably won't be surprised to learn that in Tutankhamen's tomb, archaeologists discovered a great many arcs. Tutankhamen is the Lawgiver incarnate as man. The Essene would create the greatest Lawgiver of all, and would call him the New Covenant, or Jesus. This is the same Jesus who is represented by a great and powerful light in the Shroud of Turin or the Veil of Veronica. Jesus' goal was, in effect, to bring the new law to mankind.

Now, we must return to Jeremiah, who is also identified as one who constantly speaks of the covenant or law: "It was Jeremiah also who had spoken of God's perpetual covenant with the Levitical Priesthood, as well as with the House of David."[8] This phrase links the guardians (the Levites) of the Ark with the family of the Ark (David). But I want to step back a little, so we can see the process of wrongdoing in the sight of the Lord, and discover what inspired Jeremiah to hide away the Ark. In the apocryphal First Book of Esdras, also known as Nehemiah or Ezra and to be found in 2 Chronicles 35 onwards, we find the accounts about the laying up of the Ark in the Temple:

> 1:1 And Josiah held the feast of the passover in Jerusalem unto his Lord, and offered the passover the fourteenth day of the first month;

> 1:2 Having set the priests according to their daily courses, being arrayed in long garments, in the temple of the Lord.

> 1:3 And he spake unto the Levites, the holy ministers of Israel, that they should hallow themselves unto the Lord, to set the holy ark of the Lord in the house that king Solomon the son of David had built:

> 1:4 And said, Ye shall no more bear the ark upon your shoulders: now therefore serve the Lord your God, and minister unto his people Israel, and prepare you after your families and kindreds,

> 1:5 According as David the king of Israel prescribed, and according to the magnificence of Solomon his son: and standing in the temple according to the several dignity of the families of you the Levites, who minister in the presence of your brethren the children of Israel,

> 1:6 Offer the passover in order, and make ready the sacrifices for your brethren, and keep the passover according to the commandment of the Lord, which was given unto Moses.

Here we have Josiah instructing the Levites to place the Ark in the Temple of Solomon. However, all did not go well for Josiah, and he did badly in the eyes of the Lord:

1:25 Now after all these acts of Josiah it came to pass, that Pharaoh the king of Egypt came to raise war at Carchamis upon Euphrates: and Josiah went out against him.

1:26 But the king of Egypt sent to him, saying, What have I to do with thee, O king of Judea?

1:27 I am not sent out from the Lord God against thee; for my war is upon Euphrates: and now the Lord is with me, yea, the Lord is with me hasting me forward: depart from me, and be not against the Lord.

1:28 Howbeit Josiah did not turn back his chariot from him, but undertook to fight with him, not regarding the words of the prophet Jeremiah spoken by the mouth of the Lord:

1:29 But joined battle with him in the plain of Magiddo, and the princes came against king Josiah.

1:30 Then said the king unto his servants, Carry me away out of the battle; for I am very weak. And immediately his servants took him away out of the battle.

1:31 Then gat he up upon his second chariot; and being brought back to Jerusalem died, and was buried in his father's sepulchre.

In essence, Josiah's death is his own fault, because the Egyptian Pharaoh made it plainly clear that the Lord God was with him: "I am not sent out from the Lord God against thee; for my war is upon Euphrates: and now the Lord is with me, yea, the Lord is with me hasting me forward: depart from me, and be not against the Lord."

In *The Legends of the Jews* by Louis Ginzberg, we find that Josiah was following in his father's footsteps, Amon, and that he tried to outshine his father by being virtuous. But he was informed that this would not be enough to satisfy God and so he hid the Ark and treasures for what he and his ancestors had done:

Amon, the son of Manasseh, surpassed his father in wickedness. He was in the habit of saying: "My father was a sinner from early childhood, and in his old age he did penance. I shall do the same. First I shall satisfy the desires of my heart, and afterward I shall return to God." Indeed, he was guilty of more grievous sins than his predecessor; he burned the Torah; under him the place of the altar was covered with spiderwebs; and, as though of purpose to set at naught the Jewish religion, he committed the worst sort of incest, a degree more heinous than his father's crime of a similar nature. Thus he executed the first half of his maxim literally. For repentance, however, he was given no time; death cut him off in the fullness of his sinful ways.

That the full measure of punishment was not meted out to Amon his evil deeds were such that he should have forfeited his share in the world to come was due to the circumstance that he had a pious and righteous son. Josiah offers a shining model of true, sincere repentance. Though at first he followed in the footsteps of his father Amon, he soon gave up the ways of wickedness, and became one of the most pious kings of Israel, whose chief undertaking was the effort to bring the whole people back to the true faith. It dates from the time when a copy of the Torah was found in the Temple, a copy that had escaped the holocaust kindled by his father and predecessor Amon for the purpose of exterminating the Holy Scriptures. When he opened the Scriptures, the first verse to strike his eye was the one in Deuteronomy: "The Lord shall bring thee and thy king into exile, unto a nation which thou hast not known." Josiah feared this doom of exile was impending, and he sought to conciliate God through the reform of his people.

His first step was to enlist the intercession of the prophets in his behalf. He addressed his request, not to Jeremiah, but to the prophetess Huldah, knowing that women are more easily moved to compassion. As Jeremiah was a kinsman of the prophetess their common ancestors were Joshua and Rahab the king felt no apprehension that the prophet take his preference for Huldah amiss. The proud, dignified answer of the prophetess was, that the misfortune could not be averted from Israel, but the destruction of the Temple, she continued consolingly, would not happen until after the death of Josiah. In view of the imminent destruction of the Temple, Josiah hid the holy Ark and all its appurtenances, in order to guard them against desecration at the hands of the enemy.

Josiah lost more than just his own life; he lost the rule of Judea and Jerusalem, which was now in the hands of the Egyptians. The Egyptians decided to place a puppet king on the throne, a man named Joachim, who was the brother of the Pharaoh, and who also did badly in the sight of the Lord. This time the treasures of the Temple were taken by the Babylonians.

1:37 The king of Egypt also made king Joachim his brother king of Judea and Jerusalem.

1:38 And he bound Joachim and the nobles: but Zaraces his brother he apprehended, and brought him out of Egypt.

1:39 Five and twenty years old was Joachim when he was made king in the land of Judea and Jerusalem; and he did evil before the Lord.

1:40 Wherefore against him Nabuchodonosor the king of Babylon came up, and bound him with a chain of brass, and carried him into Babylon.

1:41 Nabuchodonosor also took of the holy vessels of the Lord, and carried them away, and set them in his own temple at Babylon.

1:42 But those things that are recorded of him, and of his uncleaness and impiety, are written in the chronicles of the kings.

1:43 And Joachim his son reigned in his stead: he was made king being eighteen years old;

1:44 And reigned but three months and ten days in Jerusalem; and did evil before the Lord.

1:45 So after a year Nabuchodonosor sent and caused him to be brought into Babylon with the holy vessels of the Lord;

1:46 And made Zedechias king of Judea and Jerusalem, when he was one and twenty years old; and he reigned eleven years:

1:47 And he did evil also in the sight of the Lord, and cared not for the words that were spoken unto him by the prophet Jeremiah from the mouth of the Lord.

1:48 And after that king Nabuchodonosor had made him to swear by the name of the Lord, he forswore himself, and rebelled; and hardening his neck, his heart, he transgressed the laws of the Lord God of Israel.

1:49 The governors also of the people and of the priests did many things against the laws, and passed all the pollutions of all nations, and defiled the temple of the Lord, which was sanctified in Jerusalem.

1:50 Nevertheless the God of their fathers sent by his messenger to call them back, because he spared them and his tabernacle also.

1:51 But they had his messengers in derision; and, look, when the Lord spake unto them, they made a sport of his prophets:

1:52 So far forth, that he, being wroth with his people for their great ungodliness, commanded the kings of the Chaldees to come up against them;

1:53 Who slew their young men with the sword, yea, even within the compass of their holy temple, and spared neither young man nor maid, old man nor child, among them; for he delivered all into their hands.

1:54 And they took all the holy vessels of the Lord, both great and small, with the vessels of the ark of God, and the king's treasures, and carried them away into Babylon.

1:55 As for the house of the Lord, they burnt it, and brake down the walls of Jerusalem, and set fire upon her towers:

1:56 And as for her glorious things, they never ceased till they had consumed and brought them all to nought: and the people that were not slain with the sword he carried unto Babylon:

1:57 Who became servants to him and his children, till the Persians reigned, to fulfil the word of the Lord spoken by the mouth of Jeremy:

1:58 Until the land had enjoyed her sabbaths, the whole time of her desolation shall she rest, until the full term of seventy years.

Again and again the rulership of Jerusalem fails and does not listen to the will of the Lord. If we do not listen, we cannot hear and we cannot oblige that which speaks to us—even if it is ourselves. However, the next thing we hear is that Cyrus is now king, and he returns the treasures to Jerusalem. His spirit is raised up and he attempts to accomplish those things the Lord wishes. But the Ark is not among the treasures returned:

2:1 In the first year of Cyrus king of the Persians, that the word of the Lord might be accomplished, that he had promised by the mouth of Jeremiah;

2:2 The Lord raised up the spirit of Cyrus the king of the Persians, and he made proclamation through all his kingdom, and also by writing,

2:3 Saying, Thus saith Cyrus king of the Persians; The Lord of Israel, the most high Lord, hath made me king of the whole world,

2:4 And commanded me to build him an house at Jerusalem in Jewry.

2:5 If therefore there be any of you that are of his people, let the Lord, even his Lord, be with him, and let him go up to Jerusalem that is in Judea, and build the house of the Lord of Israel: for he is the Lord that dwelleth in Jerusalem.

2:6 Whosoever then dwell in the places about, let them help him, those, I say, that are his neighbours, with gold, and with silver,

2:7 With gifts, with horses, and with cattle, and other things, which have been set forth by vow, for the temple of the Lord at Jerusalem.

2:8 Then the chief of the families of Judea and of the tribe of Benjamin stood up; the priests also, and the Levites, and all they whose mind the Lord had moved to go up, and to build an house for the Lord at Jerusalem,

2:9 And they that dwelt round about them, and helped them in all things with silver and gold, with horses and cattle, and with very many free gifts of a great number whose minds were stirred up thereto.

2:10 King Cyrus also brought forth the holy vessels, which Nabuchodonosor had carried away from Jerusalem, and had set up in his temple of idols.

2:11 Now when Cyrus king of the Persians had brought them forth, he delivered them to Mithridates his treasurer:

2:12 And by him they were delivered to Sanabassar the governor of Judea.

2:13 And this was the number of them; A thousand golden cups, and a thousand of silver, censers of silver twenty nine, vials of gold thirty, and of silver two thousand four hundred and ten, and a thousand other vessels.

2:14 So all the vessels of gold and of silver, which were carried away, were five thousand four hundred threescore and nine.

2:15 These were brought back by Sanabassar, together with them of the captivity, from Babylon to Jerusalem.

It appears that the Ark simply disappeared during its sojourn into Babylon, and was never seen again from that day forth. However, as I mentioned earlier, there is a fable that says that Jeremiah hid the Temple treasures (as spoken of in *The Legends of the Jews* by Louis Ginzberg), and it is thought that Jeremiah was doing this on the instructions of Josiah or God:

> The task laid upon Jeremiah had been twofold. Besides giving him charge over the people in the land of their exile, God had entrusted to him the care of the sanctuary and all it contained. The holy Ark, the altar of incense, and the holy tent were carried by an angel to the mount whence Moses before his death had viewed the land divinely assigned to Israel. There Jeremiah found a spacious place, in which he concealed these sacred utensils. Some of his companions had gone with him to note the way to the cave, but yet they could not find it. When Jeremiah heard of their purpose, he censured them, for it was the wish of God that the place of hiding should remain a secret until the redemption, and then God Himself will make the hidden things visible.

> Even the Temple vessels not concealed by Jeremiah were prevented from falling into the hands of the enemy; the gates of the Temple sank into the earth, and other parts and utensils were hidden in a tower at Bagdad by the Levite Shimur and his friends. Among these utensils was the seven-branched candlestick of pure gold, every branch set with twenty-six pearls, and beside the pearls two hundred stones of inestimable worth. Furthermore, the tower at Bagdad was the hiding-place for seventy-seven golden tables, and for the gold with which the walls of the Temple had been clothed within and without. The tables had been taken from Paradise by Solomon, and in brilliance they outshone the sun and the moon, while the gold from the walls excelled in amount and worth all the gold that had existed from the creation of the world until the destruction of the Temple. The jewels, pearls, gold, and silver, and precious gems, which David and Solomon had intended for the Temple were discovered by the scribe Hilkiah, and he delivered them to the angel Shamshiel, who

in turn deposited the treasure in Borsippa. The sacred musical instruments were taken charge of and hidden by Baruch and Zedekiah until the advent of the Messiah, who will reveal all treasures. In his time a stream will break forth from under the place of the Holy of Holies, and flow through the lands to the Euphrates, and, as it flows, it will uncover all the treasures buried in the earth.

Although the Ark disappeared during captivity, it did not fall into the hands of the enemy, but was safely hidden by the prophet Jeremiah, where no man would be able to find it again until the advent of the Messiah. This Messiah is now spoken of as if he were Jesus, but this is a Christian assumption. The Messiah concept is much older and more widespread than Christianity.

In this beautiful stained glass image from a church in Southwell Minster, England, an Angel appears before the Ark of the Covenant as it sits in the Temple in Jerusalem.

THE MESSIAH

The Messiah was a man of light, a vision of true mysticism, called by *Daniel* in the Book of Daniel, or the Son of Man: us. Indeed, many early Gnostics believed that Jesus was an ordinary man, within whom the Messiah or Christ emerged from the Otherworld. This divinity is (or was) realized through meditation or prayer, as Bernard Simon suggests in *The Essence of the Gnostics*: "The idea of the need for meditation, a kind of bridge between the material world and the Divine is not such a strange one, for it is found in all major religions in one form or another. It is only when the individual has achieved a certain level of awareness or knowledge that he can function as a mediator, as a Way."[9]

The Ark—the connection device to the supernatural or mystical world of the divine—will be lost to us until the return of the Messiah, which is the Son of Man, which, in turn, is ourselves. In this way we can all rediscover the Ark of the Covenant. It is within us.

But there is more. It may not have been the Ark that Jeremiah hid away in a cave. This is a subtle clue to the real treasure. Hugh Schonfield tells us in *The Essene Odyssey* exactly what the literal items were that Jeremiah supposedly hid: "[I]n the context of these passages, we find Jeremiah buying a piece of ground, and, in the hearing of those Jews who were with him in prison, instructing his disciple Baruch to have the purchase documents put 'in an earthern vessel, that they may continue many days'. This was to be a sign from God."[10]

Baruch is another word for *Ark*. In essence, Jeremiah was placing the documents of law in a vessel in a cave, in exactly the same way as stated in 2 Maccabees. This was the story told by those scribes of the various biblical documents: the Essene. It is also the same thing that occurs in the New Testament during the burial of Jesus. Hugh Schonfield points out the link between the Essene and the later Knights Templar, who have been linked again and again to the Temple and the Ark. These Templars, as "repositories of unorthodox and esoteric teachings," had contact and very close links with their Jewish and Islamic brothers in the Middle East. It is Hugh Schonfield's assertion that the: "Templars would have been able to gain access to much Essene teaching"[11] and that this must therefore be the hidden legacy uncovered by the Templars on their journeys into the true Temple. It is no surprise therefore to find that the Essene, as with Jeremiah, also deposited their wisdom in vessels in caves, as uncovered by the wonderful discovery of the Dead Sea Scrolls. I was not prepared at this point to uncover the true origin of the Templars, but later I was to discover that Schonfield and other authors were on the right track.

WRITING THE ARK

I wanted to see if this idea or concept of the word *ark*, as written on parchment or *skin* and hidden as a treasure, could be taken any further, and if there were any links to the real Ark. There was a Greek legend of the *Argo*, which has been linked to the Ark as a ship bearing a deity. This ship and its crew were on a journey, a voyage of discovery, led by Jason. The word *Argos* derived from the maker or creator of the vessel, *Argus*, which also means *guardian* or *watcher* in Greek. In a text titled *Aureum Vellus* (by the German philosopher Salomon Trismosian) we discover that the fabled Golden Fleece, for which the Argo and her valiant crew sailed, was really *vellum* and not the fleece of a ram. *Fleece* originates in the Germanic word *vlus*, meaning *sheep's skin*. It was Trismosian's assertion that the Golden Fleece was the secret of the Philosopher's Stone. In fact, Trismosian was quite right. The journey of the Argonauts is the journey of the alchemist, Gnostic, mystic, and exponent of the esoteric. And so, in the true sense of the word, this ark, the *Argo*, was the guide or guardian to the deeper secrets of the mind. To discover the secret, we have to journey inwards. We have to explore the link between Greece and the Hebrew, Egyptian, Indian, and Ethiopian arks that I knew (at this point) to exist. Then I discovered the *Cabiri*.

CABIRI

Originally, the Cabiri were Phrygian fertility deities linked with Mother Goddess worship and were protectors of sailors and excellent navigators. The Cabiri were mysterious demons with ritual cults, and they numbered only two male gods, Axiocersus and his son Cadmilus, and two later two females, who are mentioned as balance, named Axierus and Axiocersa. Pausanius described them as a race. It is thought that the two male Cabiri were initially sacred meteorites that fell from the stars and were kept within sacred containers—becoming stellar arks. The rest of the Cabiri were the stars in the sky. Pinning down the exact worship of the Cabiri is difficult, because the rites and customs were so clouded in secrecy that a clear view of them is just not possible. The exact etymology of the word *Cabiri* is also much debated, and so I decided to take a look.

The correct spelling was *Kabeiroi*, but the origin is unknown. There have been many guesses, such as *kabir*, meaning *great* in the Semitic tongues, or the Hittite *habiri*, meaning *looters*. But neither of these has satisfied etymologists, and my hunch was much older and more Sumerian in origin. *Kaabar* in Sumerian means *copper*, which struck me for two reasons. First, because of the brazen serpent in the wilderness held up by Moses and that is associated with Jesus, and because brass is a copper/zinc alloy. But the other thing that struck me was the falling meteorite aspect. All of Islam worships a sacred stone, said to have been a meteorite that Allah sent down as a sign. It is known as the *Kaaba*, and (I believe) must be related etymologically to the Cabiri. As I was to discover, the Kaaba itself has incredible links to the Ark.

THE STONES

In "The Trail of the Serpent" published by *Inquire Within* (circa 1940s) we find the following statement written by a man named Rabbi Drach: "Our fathers, sons of Sem, preserved in the sanctuary of the Temple of Jerusalem the Beth-el Stone of Jacob, and in this Stone they worshipped the Messiah. This cult was imitated by our neighbours of Phoenicia, sons of Cham, who had a common language to us. From thence spread the cult of the Stones called Betyles or Beth-el, which the race of Japhet called also lapides Divi, divine or living stones, and these Betyles were similar to the animated stones of the Temple of Diana in Laodicea."

It seems the worship of these fallen stones, or *Beth-el's* (*House of God* or *Shining House*), needed some kind of casket or container, similar to a b'arque or ark, and that the worship of them spread. Phoenicia was also home to the Cabiri, which we've now related to the Kaaba. What were the stones that Moses brought down from Mount Sinai but meteorites? Jewish tradition states that the tablets themselves were formed by using the sapphire, or *Schethiya*, which God removed from his throne in heaven (the sky) and had cast down into the abyss. This would have relationship to the law, as the stars themselves were considered responsible for measurement on earth (we navigate and measure by their positions). It is also upon these sacred stones that God stamped his will on the very face of Nature—the law of nature. Next, we read from the same book that: "...they then enclosed them in Tree-Betyls, such as the ancient Oak, with its spring, worshipped at the Temple of Dodona, representing I.A.O.— the creative principle...."

This creative principle is the Betyl of Osiris, or the phallus (the divine spark) seen to fall from the sky as if in a battle of the deities, and based in a literal and physical event—a falling god or part of a god—who was then encased in a tree or casket. This aspect of the tree would then take on great significance in the tales of Osiris, and even Vishnu. Proof of this comes from the Masonic writer Albert Pike, who speaks of the ceremonies of the: "Cabiri, slain by his brothers, who fled into Etruria, carrying with them the ark that contained his genitals; and there the Phallus and the sacred ark adored."[12]

It now makes complete sense to ponder the tablets of stone that Moses brought down from Mount Sinai, where the Ark would be created to hold the sacred stones. Sinai is known as the cosmic mountain, or the location that connects heaven and Earth. It is the place where Moses would have gone to collect the meteorite stones of the Lord (from heaven). The stones (the meteorites) are the sperm, the creative principle, the law of the universe. It is this law that was written upon the stones, and not the Ten Commandments as we know them today. The two stones represent the superior and the inferior worlds; both governed by law, both seen and unseen, both oral and written. They were male and female, the creative principles.

There were initially two stones (the lesser stones) and then two more, as Moses went back up the mountain to collect additional stones after he broke two in anger. The male Cabiri were two in number, but there were also two lesser Cabiri, the females, and these Cabiri were meteorite stones, similar to the Kaaba—which is believed to have two stones also! This breaking of the stones and their casting down to earth represents the division of the superior and inferior worlds—often depicted as male and female, positive and negative— thus forming a world between above and below.

My good friend (and author), Alan Alford, also pointed out in his tremendous book, *When the Gods Came Down*, that the pot of manna, said to also have been in the Ark, was, in fact, a meteorite.[13] The Ethiopian *Kebra Nagast* explains that the Ark did contain this pot of manna, and that it was a gold vessel containing a "measure of the manna which came down from heaven." Alford also explains that the word *manna*, when broken up, gives us *man*, meaning *what is this?*, and *na*, meaning *stone*. So *manna* resolves into *what is this stone?*

It could be true that these meteorites, if large enough, could have caused electrical and radioactive activity, giving rise to many of the more spectacular myths surrounding the Ark. Stories of fiery discharges, and even that the Ark caused bleeding, could be generated by the radioactive nature of meteorites placed into a sealed container with conducting poles, which basically takes on the form of a unique battery.

This last thought hit me as if it was a bullet, and so I telephoned my university colleague, Bob, one last time. Could the Ark we had programmed earlier actually create a greater amount of electrical charge if there were a radioactive meteorite (or two) encased within? The answer was yet another question regarding the properties and nature of the radiation. We researched known meteorites and their radioactive properties and took an average, and Bob did the calculations. It turns out that there would be no difference. We decided that the evidence was inconclusive on that front. However, as I have come to know, no matter how many so-called physical or literal elements to ancient tales I have uncovered, there is always an esoteric tradition layered on top.

An image of the Ark of the Covenant with the Divine Glory, as described in Exodus.

Manas, mensch, mens, or man is readily associated with the manna that came down from heaven. It is the human spirit that descended from our Father above for a pilgrimage through matter, and the Golden Pot wherein it was kept symbolises the golden aura of the soul body.... Christ also explained at that time in mystic but unmistakable language what that living bread, or manna, was, namely, the Ego. This explanation will be found in verses thirty-three and thirty-five, where we read: "For the bread of God is he which cometh down from heaven and giveth light unto the world - I am (ego sum) the bread of life." This, then, is the symbol of the golden pot of manna which was found in the Ark. This manna is the Ego or human spirit, which gives life to the organisms that we behold in the physical world. It is hidden within the Ark of each human being, and the Golden pot or soul body or "wedding garment" is also latent within every one. It is made more massive, lustrous, and resplendent by the spiritual alchemy whereby service is transmuted to soul growth. It is the house not made with hands, eternal in the heavens, wherewith Paul longed to be clothed, as said in the Epistle to the Corinthians. Every one who is striving to aid his fellow men thereby garners within himself that golden treasure, laid up in heaven, where neither moth nor rust can destroy it.[14]

This passage from Max Heindel wonderfully portrays the complexity that has become the story of the Ark, for it has ended up meaning so many things to so many people. To Alan Alford, the manna is the stone that fell from the sky. To the philosopher, it is a stone of a different ilk. On the one hand it is a literal meteorite falling to the ground, but on the other it is the very creative spark, the semen of god impregnating Mother Earth. It is our own life-essence. Of course, the truth resides in both camps. Meteorites were often worshipped as creative stones, and thereby the union of the physical and metaphysical is made. Unfortunately, it is the mind of man, which must split things apart and create destructive dualities that creates mysteries. Our ancestors saw all things—physical and metaphysical—in union.

AN INSPIRATIONAL FABLE

As much as this was an interesting diversion, I needed to return to Jeremiah and Graham Hancock, who takes us back nicely with the statement from the Jerusalem Bible about the hiding of the Ark within a cave, where he says that in the opinion of the scholars who first produced the English translation of the Jerusalem Bible, Jeremiah's expedition to hide the Ark was nothing more than an inspirational fable or myth devised strategically by the author of the second book of Maccabees as part of a deliberate attempt to reinvigorate the interests of the expatriate Jews in their homeland. Hancock points out that even the editors of the Oxford Dictionary of the Christian Church regarded this passage as being "of no historical value."[15] And yet, dozens of books, hundreds of research Websites, and countless magazine articles still use this one scrap of evidence to pinpoint the location of the real Ark. It was contemporary propaganda as pointed out by biblical scholars—an "inspirational fable."

Do not be disheartened. I was on the most famous of treasure hunts the world has ever known—and one with the biggest failure rate. Here I was, having uncovered the true esoteric secrets of the Ark of the Covenant, to find that it may never in fact have been a real item. But, as ever with internal psychological or religious matters (what we call the esoteric), mankind cleverly manifests these things into reality. That is, they make the items, artifacts or prophecies come true.

In Hebrews 8:1 we find some remarkable clues: "Now this is the main point of the things we are saying: We have such a High Priest, who is seated at the right hand of the throne of the Majesty in the heavens, a Minister of the sanctuary and of the true tabernacle which the Lord erected, and not man." The first point here is this, that the Lord erected, not man. This tells us that by the time of writing the New Testament, it was beginning to dawn that there needed to be another explanation for the lack of evidence for the tabernacle, Temple, and Ark. We move on:

> For every high priest is appointed to offer both gifts and sacrifices.
> Therefore it is necessary that this One also have something to offer.
> For if He were on earth, He would not be a priest, since there are
> priests who offer the gifts according to the law; who serve the copy
> and shadow of the heavenly things as Moses was divinely instructed
> when he was about to make the tabernacle. For He said, "See that
> you make all things according to the pattern shown you in the

mountain.... For this is the covenant that I will make with the house

of Israel after those days, says the Lord: I will put My laws in their

mind and write them on their hearts."

It seems that we have New Testament confirmation that the Ark of the first Covenant and the Tabernacle were copied from those that were already in heaven, and that the new covenant will be placed directly in the mind of mankind. The first has become obsolete, and so disappeared from the planet. The second appeared in Jesus Christ, to instil it directly into our hearts. Indeed, "it was commonly held by the ancient rabbis that the Ark would be found at the coming of the Messiah,"[16] which is exactly what Hebrews is attempting to confirm— that it came in the form of the new Ark—Mary, who carried the law within her. So, all we have to do is find Mary, and we can find the second Ark. But Mary is almost impossible to find, because there is absolutely no evidence of her existence (or that of her son). But there is a church from the late-19th to early-20th century called Our Lady Ark of the Covenant Church, or Monastery on Notre Dame Street, at the entrance to Abu Gosh (Kiriath-jearim) in Israel, between Tel Aviv and Jerusalem.

ABU GOSH

Abu Gosh, or Kiriath-jearim, was the biblical city where Abinadab held the Ark from the time of Samuel to the time of the Messiah-King David—making the location a power place on earth. The present church stands on top of a fifth-century Byzantine church discovered by a farmer in 1905. He discovered mosaics, columns, and a semicircular wall. In around 1911 to 1924, Sister Josephine Rumebe of the Sisters of St. Joseph of the Apparition organized the building of the present edifice, with a statue of Mary and child. I decided to get on a plane and see for myself.

The site is Roman Catholic, and the statue of Mary holding the Christ child at the pinnacle is paramount for all to see. It is not the most beautiful of places, but it does feel special. From the front, Jesus is obviously a child. However, when viewed from behind, the image transforms, and the child grows into a man—Mary and Christ standing tall and equal. They both stand on top of a Shroud-covered Ark, with Christ holding the contents: the manna and the tablets.

Basically what we have here is the overlaying of Mary on one of the very locations that the Ark resided. We also have a correlation between Mary as the Christ carrier and the Ark as the carrier of God, as written in the pamphlet "Sister Josephine and the Ark of the Covenant," which was written by the Sisters of St. Joseph of the Apparition and sold on site:

> [T]he Church looks to Mary, Ark of the New Covenant…she like the Ark, was the repository of God's presence…Mary…became the repository not simply of the tablets of the Law, but of the Law-giver Himself; not simply of the desert manna, but of the Living Bread from heaven.. Hence they called her by such titles as Abode of the King, Tabernacle of the Lord, Ark of Holiness, and Ark of the Covenant…as the David danced before the Ark, so the child in Elizabeth's womb leapt for joy…. She is the Inmost shrine, the Holy of Holies.

What we have here clearly laid out and unopposed by the Catholic authorities is the statement that Mary is the *new* Ark of the Covenant—in that she represents the exact same thing: the connection and gateway to God. This, of course, makes Jesus the Law or Lawgiver—he was the tablets of stone within the Ark. If Mary is the World Mother Goddess, also known as Isis, Astarte, and many more, then they also must be seen as arks too. So is Mary also Isis?

MARY AS ISIS

In many depictions of Mary, we find her suckling the baby Jesus. Similar images have been found of Isis and various other virgin goddesses. In fact, many early Christians mistook these images of Isis as those of Mary, and brought them back to Europe, where they also became the Black Madonna. There is a wonderful depiction of one of the oldest Mother Goddess images from Sumeria suckling her baby serpent at her breast. She also bears a remarkable resemblance to a serpentine lady. It seems the serpent association stretches back over thousands of years and is something we shall find to be of paramount importance in India.

Isis was the consort and sister of Osiris. Horus (as the reincarnated Osiris, and therefore the son of god and god) was the son of Isis, and so Isis is both sister, mother, and wife to Osiris. In biblical tales, we find that we have a Mary as the mother, sister, and proposed wife of Jesus, who is the son of God and also God on earth. In truth then, the biblical record is nothing other than a retelling of an ancient and symbolic tradition. If these people—Mary and Jesus—existed at all, then it was in title only, and they were following the rules written by earlier generations. Just as Osiris was carried in the b'arque or Ark of Isis, so too would be Jesus carried in the womb of Mary—the new Ark. It may be true to say that these titles were passed on from generation to generation, and that this could be the true lineage spoken of by other authors.

Isis, many years before the Marian creation, was usually seen at the location where Moses descended from Mount Sinai. As Moses came down for the first time he saw that Aaron and the Israelites had built a sacred cow, which forced him into a rage. The Israelites were punished, and the original tablets of the law were broken. So Moses had to go back up the mountain and make them again. The cow that was worshipped by the Israelites may have been the sacred Apis bull of Memphis—the son of the Isis-cow or great sow of Heliopolis—the depiction that Isis was often seen. *Hathor* means *House of Horus*, and she gave birth to the sun each day. This House of Horus is therefore nothing more than the womb of the son of god—the same as Mary and the Ark. Today, people confuse Hathor and Isis as separate deities, yet they are simply different aspects of the same goddess, just as the various Mary's in the Bible are different aspects of the same ancient Mother Goddess.

Now that we understand this ancient link, we can see certain other symbolic elements that relate to various images of the Ark across the ages. Hathor, for instance, was often depicted with the Solar Orb rising between the upraised horns of the cow—this is the shining One element, the son of the sun, resurrecting between the dual horns in balance from the mind, just as the Solar Orb rises between the prows of the Solar B'arque. It is the presence of the Lord between the cherubim of the Bible upon the Mercy Seat. It is the entrance between the pillars in the Masonic Lodge. It is the route to God and the Otherworld. It is the divine location between the opposites. The symbol is as old as man and can be found many thousands of years ago in some of the most ancient structures and imagery in the world as we shall see.

MARY AND THE SHROUD

This association led me now onto an amazing link with the Shroud of Turin. I had recently read Ian Wilson's excellent book *The Blood and the Shroud*, where Wilson writes about the Edessa Cloth, which he links strongly as the Shroud of Turin. August 15, 944, he says, was chosen specifically because it was the Feast of the Assumption—"symbolically, Mary Mother of Jesus was regarded as a 'vessel' of Jesus and the Edessa cloth repeatedly associated with her." [17] The cloth was transported by boat across the Bosphorus to St. Mary at Blachernae, where it was viewed and venerated by Byzantine's royals.

When I read this, several things immediately struck me. First, that a Feast Day of Mary had been chosen in relationship to the veneration of the Shroud. Second, that the Edessa Cloth itself had repeatedly been associated with her. Were the Ark, the Shroud, and Mary all one and the same in symbolism? There may have been many replica Arks, there may have been many Marys and

Mother Goddesses, and there may indeed have been many Shrouds, but the only distinct conclusion I drew from all of this was that they all meant the same thing. They were all symbols of the higher state of enlightenment available to mankind, which has been perceived as contact with the divinity, which is always shown to be residing within. The Ark contained the deity. Mary contained the same, as did the Shroud. We are all these things.

All the issues and problems that have arisen from the search for these enigmatic objects and people could now be answered. Objects and things may very well have existed as symbols of the inner world of illumination, but they were all incidental. The message to us is simple and perfectly in line with the later Gnosis that the Catholic Church attempted to wipe out: God is inside us.

CHAPTER 3

WISDOM OF THE ARK

The Ark of the Covenant was supposedly kept in the center of Solomon's Temple, in what is known as the *Sanctum Sanctorum.* Sir Isaac Newton related this to a perpetual fire of light radiating in a circular fashion, and yet also falling back towards the sacred center. "In line with this thinking, a point within a circle was indeed a symbol for Light in ancient Egypt and, in the lodge ritual of Freemasonry, there is a related conversation which takes place between the Worshipful Master and his Wardens concerning the lost secrets. The Master asks the Question: 'How do you hope to find them?' Answer: 'By the center'. Question: 'What is a center?' Answer: 'That point within a circle from which every part of its circumference is equidistant'... a point within a circle is the most important of all masonic devices."[1]

The dot within the center of the circle has been symbolic of the sun from the very earliest of times, and some suggest that the dot is the sun in the center of the solar system. The symbol can cover a great many things, and I have personally seen it used in rituals for both physical and metaphysical purposes. If you were to take a pole with a string attached to the top, you could draw a perfect circle on the ground. Thus begins our sacred geometrical structure, which is a perfect union of the esoteric and exoteric. Seen from above, the pole would appear as a dot in the center of a circle, which resembles a conical hat. A hat of this shape was often seen in the ancient world as symbolic of enlightenment and wisdom. Today it is most commonly associated with a witch or wizard hat.

The dot could also represent the inner sun, or the enlightenment within. This is sometimes seen as the center point of all things, collecting to a singularity, similar to a black hole drawing in all matter or knowledge. It is the place that possesses all the energy required for the creative spark, similar to atomic structure, which mirrors our own solar system. The dot resides in the void or empty space from which (our ancients believed) all thought was derived. This inner concept of the self, of the deity, and of all knowledge is clearly seen in the mark Hindus place upon their brow—this is the dot at the center of the true Temple. The symbol is symbolic of so many perfect things.

The fact that this symbol is so old and is seen so widely as encompassing many physical and metaphysical concepts reveals one thing: Our ancestors were not fools; they understood a great deal more than they have previously been given credit for. We are only just beginning to comprehend the true wisdom of the ancients, and I want to concentrate on this aspect so that we may get to the center of the Temple ourselves, and look outward instead of always trying to look in. First we must erect the Temple. In modern times, this is the role of the Freemasons.

Concentric rings are meditative devices that direct you toward the center, as illustrated on this jug on display at the Kykkos Monastery in Cyprus.

THE NUMBER 7

"The Liberal Arts were, in effect, perceived as routes towards personal enlightenment in the finer things that were the keys to harmony and justice. In the 2nd degree of Craft masonry (the Fellow Craft degree), it is explained to the candidate that there are seven levels to the winding staircase that leads to the middle chamber of Solomon's Temple. They are important aspects of the journey to wisdom...."[2] In this extract from Laurence Gardner's book *The Shadow of Solomon*, we find that the center point is accessed by a spiral staircase. This spiral itself is seen across the globe in visions brought on by altered states of consciousness, linked inextricably to the process of divine wisdom. The processes, known by different methods and names across the world, send the adept into a vision trance, whereby he or she believes he is actually contacting the spirits or the divine in another world. The spirals are seen across the world in rock art, carved into stone, and in the drawings and fables of our ancestors (sometimes appearing as serpents). Serpent fire is also seen to rise from the peak of the Great Pyramid as energy spirals, looking remarkably similar to the double helix of the DNA strand. This may be the reason that the word *pyramid* actually means *fire in the middle*. In this symbol, the Freemasons are physically depicting the inner (and thereby esoteric) concepts, creating art, texts, and even structures to manifest this fire; hence God appears within the pillar of smoke, just as he does above the Ark. They also reveal another level of truth: the number seven.

There are a great many reasons for the number to have been used by our ancestors. One thing we will always find when researching the past is that, unlike us, the universe (and life, in general) is not separated into dogmatic sciences. Religion is not that different from astronomy or astrology; it is not separate from plants and animals. Nature itself is in harmony with our own internal and mental world. All things are and should be seen as being interrelated. Whether the number seven indicates the planets, the days of the week, or the levels of heaven, they are also related to a process that man developed to achieve enlightenment, and gain access to the divine. In the kundalini system, the number seven became the number of chakra points that reside on the axis of the body, from the sacral regions to the brow, and even above that, to the *bindu* point above the head. By raising energy levels within the body in a process of self-improvement, one can supposedly achieve enlightenment. If the Ark is at all related to the wisdom traditions of the globe, then it will also reveal the use of this number, just as many other fables and folktales from across the globe do. The kundalini is just another one of these processes.

When speaking of a tale from Ethiopia regarding the Ark, the authors Roderick Grierson and Stuart Munro-Hay relate (in their book, *The Ark of the Covenant*) a moment when the Emperor Iyasu displays his devotion towards the object called the Ark of the Covenant. The authors state that nothing can prepare the reader for the events of the next morning, when the emperor enters the sanctuary, commanding the priests to bring forth the Ark of Zion. The priests have no choice but to comply, but the Ark is encased in a chest with seven seals. It can only be opened by a special key in a special manner. The keys are brought in and the priests start the task of unlocking the seals. The chronicler explains how each of the seven levels is opened. However, when the priests reach the seventh level, they struggle in vain. The seal cannot be broken. In the end they have no choice but to bring the chest to the emperor with the seventh seal still unopened. As they stand before him, the seal opens as if by magic, and everybody is astonished, believing it to be an act of the God of the Ark of Zion, who himself resides above the Ark itself. "He knows that the emperor is pure in spirit and devoted to the Orthodox faith."[3]

Here we have similarities with the Grail and wisdom lore, in that only those who are pure of spirit can access the wonders of the Grail. In this case, it is the Ark, and the wonder is the connection to the divine. It is extremely interesting to note that the level on which the emperor accesses the divine is the seventh level, meeting the symbolic elements of the Grail and the various enlightenment processes.

But now we must prepare ourselves for the true temple. "According to 1 Kings 6:1, it was 480 years after the Exodus that David's son Solomon began to build his temple on Mount Moriah. Seven years later the temple was ready to receive the Ark."[4] Again, what we find here is that the Temple will take seven years to erect—the Temple of man will take seven stages to be perfected, similar to the Alchemical perfect man. And once made perfect, this Temple will hold the truth, the secret, which within the Holy of Holies at the very center of the Temple. As with all things, we cannot simply hope that perfection will arrive. We cannot blindly follow the path laid out in the various wisdom traditions. We must always remain balanced. In many traditions, this balance is perceived as two serpents, or the symbols of opposites. This union of opposites is spoken of again and again in gnostic and esoteric schools, and can be found on every level of our lives. The male and female opposites are obvious physical dual natures, but these opposites can also be seen within us. Opposite sides of the mind continually struggle unless they find common ground, which is a neutral state. We cannot strive to find the Grail, we must be neutral first.

The Ark itself is the center, this neutral ground known as the mid-point in the Holy of Holies. It is a spiritual realm or substance:

> This spiritual substance is neither heavenly nor hellish, but an airy,
>
> pure, and hearty body, midway between the highest and lowest,
>
> without reason, but fruitful in works, and the most select and beautiful

of all other heavenly things. This work of God is far too deep for understanding, for it is the last, greatest, and highest secret of Nature. It is the Spirit of God, which in the Beginning filled the earth and brooded over the waters, which the world cannot grasp without the gracious interposition of the Holy Spirit and instruction from those who know it, which also the whole world desires for its virtue, and which cannot be prized enough. For it reaches to the planets, raises the clouds, drives away mists, gives its light to all things, turns everything into Sun and Moon, bestows all health and abundance of treasure, cleanses the leper, brightens the eyes, banishes sorrow, heals the sick, reveals all hidden treasures, and, generally, cures all diseases. Through this spirit have the philosophers invented the Seven Liberal Arts, and thereby gained their riches. Through the same Moses made the golden vessels in the Ark, and King Solomon did many beautiful works to the honour of God. Therewith Moses built the Tabernacle, Noah the Ark, Solomon the Temple.[5]

In this passage, by one of my favorite alchemists, mystics, and philosophers (Paracelsus), we have the absolute conviction that whatever it was that allowed Solomon to build the Temple (or Moses to construct the contents of the Ark), it was something that was in balance. It was something that was neither good (heavenly) nor bad (hellish). It was neutral. Paracelsus also tells us that this is the highest and most concealed of God's secrets. It is no wonder then that mankind has sought this truth ever since he became aware of it.

This neutral position can also be found in architecture, placed there by Freemasons, who once understood the concepts. Graham Hancock, speaking of his sight of the Ark at Chartres Cathedral, sees this duality standing on the front steps of the Cathedral in the columns, which (he explains) were situated midway between Melchizedek and the Queen of Sheba: "Indeed I found that I could draw a neat triangle connecting up all three pieces of sculpture—with Melchizedek and the Queen of Sheba at either end of the long base and the Ark of the Covenant at the apex of the two shorter sides."[6] Hancock sees the sacred geometry of the Freemasons at play, revealing the divine balance in physical structures. The Ark is seen between the old male wisdom of the Old Testament, Melchizedek (the lawgiver or true teacher), and the young Queen of Sheba, who would go on and give birth to the Ethiopian messiah-king in union with Solomon.

The triangle Hancock could draw was a sacred symbol of the divine trinity. The esoteric shape of the tablets of stone that Moses placed within the Ark also illustrate the divine triangle. This left Hancock with a more exciting outcome to think about. Perhaps, he says, the people who were responsible for the north porch of the cathedral had drawn a "cryptic map" for the future generations to follow. Indeed, as Hancock asserts, this north porch was also known as the "door of the initiates."[7] Indeed, the door of the initiates provided (Gnostic) guidance in the Latin inscription found there. Graham Hancock claims that the inscription is incorrect, which he, with his "schoolboy Latin," could readily identify as wrong. But it was not incorrect at the time of its carving. In the medieval time, Latin was often misspelled, which has caused many misinterpretations to occur throughout history. The original text, as Hancock points out in *Archa Cederis*, very roughly translates as "you are to work through the Ark." This is exactly what the medieval Masons were trying to say. The Ark, as the center point between male and female opposites, is the place where we must be to produce the good work. It is the center of the void and is the access point to the Otherworld, where peace and heaven can be found (within the mind of the adept).

The true union is also often portrayed as being divided or split in two. This is an indication of the truth, the enlightenment itself, and the access to the divine. Graham Phillips, in his book *The Templars and the Ark of the Covenant*, tells us about the Ark, and reveals this symbolism: "As there is no further mention of it [the Ark] being used again, either as a weapon or for communing with God, the general inference among biblical scholars is that its power was lost when the Israelites displeased God by dividing into two separate kingdoms after Solomon's death."[8] Of course, this is both true and untrue. It is true that the Ark disappears, and we almost never hear of it again. It is not true to say that it was lost because God was displeased at the division of the tribes. The tribes were symbolically divided because the power holding them together was the last vestiges of the wisdom of Solomon. Without this final strength, the tribes could no longer hold together.

PHILO OF ALEXANDRIA

Luckily, none of this really happened. It is pure Gnostic language speaking to us across the pages of religious and historical teaching. The truth is that the connection to God (our true self), imaged here by the Ark, is lost when we divide our minds and lose our balance. I am not the first to come to these conclusions regarding the Ark. Philo of Alexandria, born approximately 20 years before Christ, was a Jewish philosopher. He is one of the only non-biblical sources to mention the Ark at all, implying it was not widely known as a Jewish concept.[9] Although coming from a wealthy family, Philo was keen to see the inner (and almost pagan) traditions of spiritualism come to light. He did not remain focused on the fate of the physical Ark, but instead developed his belief that the Ark was the true key to real enlightenment.

Philo spent a considerable part of his life attempting to reconcile the differences that emerged between Judaism and the Greek philosophers in Alexandria. He tended to pagan viewpoints, and believed that one day his spirit would escape the flesh and return once more to the deity—in the same fashion as the Egyptians. He said that the very Ark itself was the essence of the presence of God and everything sacred to the Jews. It was the answer to the mysteries of divinity itself. Amazingly, because of Philo's cosmopolitan religious viewpoint, he even saw the Ark as having seven parts:

▶ the Ark itself

▶ the Law

▶ the mercy seat

▶ the two Cherubim

▶ the voice of the divine

▶ the presence of the divinity

Each of these parts had mystical significance to Philo, and each level ascended until it reached the actual presence of the Absolute Being, which, in Greek beliefs, radiated the same divine light as the Ark.

The Ark was seen as the symbol of union or access to God. It was a gateway: Just as Mary was the portal for Christ into this world, so too the Ark was a portal for God to speak to us from the Otherworld. In a return fashion, we could also ascend to the Otherworld through the Ark. Our ancestors would use this Ark, this boat to heaven, as a method of esoterically reaching the divine (with all manner of requests and sacrifices). The dead were often placed on sacred boats and floated out to sea, either literally or on the sea of the Otherworld.

In Ethiopia, where many claim the Ark resides, the *dabtara* are the lay clergy. The tabernacle of the law (the Ark) represents many things to these esoteric dabtara, and one of these things is the gateway: "It is the mercy seat, a place of refuge, the altar, a place of forgiveness of sins, salvation, the gate of life...."[10] In another of Stuart Munro-Hay's works, *The Ark of the Covenant*, we find confirmation of the gate to God aspect: "What are we hoping to find as we begin our search for it? What should it look like, and why should it matter? In even the most austere accounts of it, the Ark is the moral heart of the universe, containing the Law given by God. In more mystical or cosmic visions of it, the Ark is the navel of the earth, a microcosm or universe in miniature. It is a door to a higher world, an assurance of the presence of the divine."[11] Here we have the phrases "a door to a higher world" and the "presence of the divine." This is similar to the *vesica piscis*, Mary, the Grail, and so many other esoteric devices. In fact, the Grail itself has even been equated to the Shroud of Turin, due to the link between Joseph of Arimathea, who was involved with the burial of Jesus and who supposedly caught the blood of Christ from the Cross.

This image depicts Mary being visited by the Angel Gabriel. Note the dove and the Shroud above the buildings. This relief is on display at the Kykkos Monastery in Greece.

THE SHROUD AND THE CHALICE

As Ian Wilson in *The Blood and the Shroud* points out, researcher Dan Scavone looked into the earliest roots of the Grail legends and came away with some remarkable results. He first asked the question as to why Joseph of Arimathea was also associated with the Grail legends in the 12th and 13th centuries. He found: "...a little-known Georgian manuscript of the sixth-century that quite specifically and unmistakably described Joseph as collecting Jesus' blood, not in any chalice or dish, as in the later stories, but in a shroud. In the words of the manuscript, in which Joseph speaks in the first person: 'But I climbed Holy Golgotha, where the Lord's cross stood, and collected in the headband and a large sheet the precious blood that had flowed from his holy side.'"[12] It seems the Shroud and the chalice (often seen as a crescent moon), and the Ark (also imaged as the crescent moon), are all related. The crescent moon is the point between visible and invisible; between empty and full; it is between the opposites—similar to the gateway.

The gateway, of course, is between the Alpha and Omega, the beginning and end, the creation and destruction, the way in and out. And yet it is also the very center of all things, because the true gateway lies at the very center of ourselves; at the center of the atom; and at the center of the universe. Jewish Rabbis often attest to this fact: "[T]he Ark was in the exact center of the whole world...standing on the starting point of the creation."[13] The Ark was at the very center of Eden, and the Tabernacle (or, later on, the Temple) was a representation of Eden, where the Ark was located. If we are indeed at the center, we can see all things by simply looking around. Our vision is flawed if we have to look from opposing sides. From a psychological point of view, being centered is the same as being balanced. The same is true of the ancient gnostic and esoteric beliefs.

Another clue to the gateway struck me when I was reading Graham Phillips's entertaining book, *The Templars and the Ark of the Covenant*. Phillips points out that King David ordered the Ark to be kept in a house of a Levite priest by the name of Obed-Edom, where it remained for three months. The author's previous knowledge of Obed-Edom led him to assume that the four supposedly separate men named Obed-Edom in the Bible were all one man, and he was a Levite priest. Phillips points out that this priest was a Gittite or a Philistine of the city of Gath, to which the Ark in 1 Samuel 5:8-9 and 6:17 had brought disaster:

> King David conquered Gath (2 Samuel 8:1) and probably brought these Gittites with him back to Jerusalem. These Gittites worshipped Dagon who was the son of El, the Shining One and Asherah, the serpentine goddess found again and again in the Temple of Jerusalem throughout the Bible. Dagon of course is Odakon, Jonah or Oannes— all of which are fish-deities from which the Christian fish symbol, Bishop's hat and associations of the Jesus with the fish, originates.

> Even Herman Melville mentions Dagon in his infamous Moby Dick chapter LXVIII, "In fact, placed before the strict and piercing truth, this whole story will fare like that fish, flesh, and fowl idol of the Philistines, Dagon by name; who being planted before the ark of Israel, his horses head and both the palms of his hands fell off from him, and only the stump or fishy part of him remained."[14]

Of course, what Melville reveals is that the Ark stripped away all the additions, all the parts of the deity which were not him, and revealed the true fish deity beneath. The Ark can see straight through you and get to the truth. It is at the center. *Moby Dick* is a tale full of symbolic language that reveals the journey of the Ark to capture and kill the nemesis of the Captain, only to discover it is the self that is the true enemy. The fish (or whale) is the animal our ancestors saw that could journey into the Otherworld through water, the same water that a boat (or b'arque) could sail upon.

What is it about Obed-Edom that is so remarkable that only he could be the one to guard the Ark? We know that in 1 Chronicles 13:13-14 the Ark is said to have brought great blessings to the house of Obed-Edom, and that afterwards David was able to move the Ark with great gladness to Jerusalem, where it remained in the Tabernacle pending the erection of Solomon's Temple. So Obed-Edom's house was obviously something that was seen as beneficial to the Ark, and the term *house* generally meant whole family and tribe, rather than mere dwelling place. In 1 Chronicles 16:5 and 16:38, Obed-Edom is called a Levite musician who ministers before the Ark, and is given another important role: "And he [David] appointed some of the Levites to minister before the ark of the Lord, to commemorate, to thank, and to praise the Lord God of Israel: Asaph the chief, and next to him Zechariah, then Jeiel, Shemiramoth, Jehiel, Mattithaiah, Eliab, Benaiah and Obed-Edom...and of Obed-Edom with his sixty-eight brethren, including Obed-Edom the son of Jeduthun, and Hosah, to be gatekeepers." This last role, of gatekeeper, is one of the most important roles for any Levite. According to standard biblical dictionaries, the gatekeeper was somebody who collected offerings and cared for the temple grounds. But this denies the esoteric meaning and neglects to question whether any of this was meant to be interpreted literally. The truth is that the *temple* (meaning *place of time*), was the gateway to God, and, as the gatekeeper, Obed-Edom was the guardian of the gateway to God. In this respect he was able to protect the Ark, which was the portable gateway. The Ark somehow disappeared in *Babylon*, which means *Gate of God*. Later on, in the reign of King Amaziah, another man by the title of Obed-Edom was the treasure keeper at the temple, in a similar role.

THE COPTIC CLUE

The Copts believe the Ark to be a wooden container for a chalice containing wine mixed with water during the liturgy. Called the *maqta'*, this chest occupies the central position on the altar and is known as the throne for the crucified Christ, and as a saving device similar to the Ark of Noah or the blood of Christ. It also represents the Ark of the Covenant and the Virgin Mary, thus encompassing all three symbols of the carrier: the chalice (carrying the blood of Christ), the Ark (carrying God), and the Virgin (carrying the Son of God).[15] The contents of the Ark, whether New or Old Testament, are: divine power, energy, and food, all of which equate to life. They are the food of the Otherworld, the nectar of the gods, sustaining us both physically and spiritually—similar to the ba and ka of the ancient Egyptians.

MARY AS THE VESSEL

Mary, as the Theotokos, was the God-bearer. She was the sacred vessel of the Son of God. In the Litany of Loretto from the 16th century she is known as the spiritual vessel or the vessel of honor. More importantly, she is seen as the *arca foederis*—the Ark of the Covenant. "In the twelfth century, the redoubtable Saint Bernard of Clairvaux had also explicitly compared Mary to the Ark of the Covenant—indeed he had done so in a number of writings."[16] Of course, Bernard is richly interwoven in the historical tapestry of the Knights Templar, who seem to crop up in almost all of the medieval mysteries. Bernard certainly understood the Gnostic and esoteric elements of folk tales and biblical traditions, the most profound of which were his connections to the recreation of the Grail myths, something Graham Hancock points out in his book, *The Sign and the Seal.*

The association of the Ark with Mary also reveals why the Ark in Chartres Cathedral was seen by Hancock to be "moving towards Sheba." Sheba is nothing more than the pre-Marian female principle balancing Solomon's male principle.

I wanted to find original texts speaking of Mary as the Ark, just to convince myself that what Hancock and others were stating was true. After hours of hunting, I came across sevreal liturgical texts (*Menaia*) translated by the Monastery of Saint Andrew the First Called in Manchester, England. These texts speak of the Mandylion, or the image of Christ or Shroud, which is amazingly related to the Ark and Mary. At Vespers, tone 2 is spoken "With garlands of praise," which goes this way:

> With what lips shall we, poor and worthless, call the Mother of God
>
> blest? She is more honoured than creation and holier than the
>
> Cherubim and all the angels; she is the unshaken throne [mercy seat]
>
> of the King, the house in which the Most High made his dwelling;
>
> the salvation of the world; the hallowing of God, who on her godly
>
> feast richly grants the faithful his great mercy.

What songs of awe did all the Apostles of the Word offer you then, O Virgin, as they stood around your death-bed and cried aloud with wonder: The Palace of the King departs, the Ark of hallowing is exalted. You gates be lifted up, that the gate of Gate may enter in great joy....The company of the Disciples is gathered from the ends of the earth in Gethsemane's field, Mother of God, to bury your body which held God. Arise, O Lord, to your rest: you and the Ark of your holiness.

In this Greek text (taken originally from the Apostoliki Diakonia in Athens) we have confirmation that Mary is indeed seen as the Ark of Holiness. But why was this Menaion written? To commemorate the moving of the cloth of Edessa (Antioch), also know as the Mandylion or Icon of the Lord Jesus Christ. The words for Mary were spoken in commemoration of the image of Christ, whom she had carried, as the Ark of Holiness.

This statue is of Mary, the Mother of God. However, Mary could be a reinterpretation of a much older myth: the legendary Isis.

Mary was the vessel of Christ; she was the vessel of enlightenment. She is not enlightenment itself, but the vessel of it, just as we ourselves are vessels of the light. Mary passed the light of the Old to the New; she is the womb of wisdom. If we are to follow the Bible and believe that Christ is all and in all, then we too should manifest our own Mary, our own vessel of grace, and let Christ—as the enlightenment—be born within us.

Christ is the light aspect, the shining element of the sun, similar to Horus of Egypt, who is both the son of Isis (Mary) and Osiris (who is both the father of Horus and Horus reborn). This light must be reborn as Ra, the sun, each day for the creative spark to continue and for life to carry on. This is the light of wisdom, not just the solar rays of the sun in the sky. We must find the creative spark within us to enable life to be born anew each day. It is a concept older than the Gnostics themselves. It is related to the sun because the sun gives life to everything.

THE LIGHT OF WISDOM

"In this day, they that are submerged beneath the ocean of ancient Knowledge, and dwell within the ark of divine wisdom, forbid the people such idle pursuits."[17] The Ark is a symbol for the light of wisdom, according to certain philosophers from our past. It is for this reason that it sheds light so bright that all shall be blinded. In the following Rosicrucian text we find the Ark explained from this perspective on many levels:

> In the westernmost end of this apartment, the western end of the whole Tabernacle, rested the "Ark of the Covenant." It was a hollow receptacle containing the Golden Pot of Manna, Aaron's Rod that budded, and the Tablets of the Law, which were given to Moses. While this Ark of the Covenant remained in the Tabernacle in the Wilderness, two staves were always within the four rings of the ark so that it could be picked up instantly and moved, but when the Ark as finally taken to Solomon's Temple, the staves were taken out. This is very important in its symbolical significance. Above the Ark hovered the Cherubim, and between them dwelt the uncreated glory of God. "Three," said He to Moses, "I will meet with thee, and I will commune with thee from above the Mercy Seat, from between the two Cherubim which are upon the Ark of the Testimony."

The glory of the Lord seen above the Mercy Seat was in the appearance of a cloud. The Lord said to Moses, "Speak unto Aaron thy brother that he come not at all time into the Holiest Place within the veil before the Mercy Seat which is upon the Ark, that he die not, for I will appear in the cloud upon the Mercy Seat." This manifestation of the divine presence was called among the Jews the Shekinah Glory. Its appearance was attended no doubt with a wonderful spiritual glory of which it is impossible to form any proper conception. Out of this cloud the voice of God was heard with deep solemnity when he was consulted on behalf of the people.

When the aspirant has qualified to enter into this place behind the second veil, he finds everything dark to the physical eye, and it is necessary that he should have another light within. When he first came to the eastern Temple gate, he was "poor, naked, and blind," asking for light. He was then shown the dim light which appeared in the smoke above the Altar of sacrifice, and told that in order to advance he must kindle within himself that flame by remorse for wrongdoing. Later on he was shown the more excellent light in the East Room of the Tabernacle, which proceeded from the Seven-branched Candlestick; in other words he was given the light of knowledge and of reason that by it he might advance further upon the path. But it was required that by service he should evolve within himself and around himself another light, the golden "wedding garment," which is also the Christ light of the soul body. By lives of service this glorious soul-substance gradually pervades his whole aura until it is ablaze with a golden light. Not until he has evolved this INNER illumination can he enter into the darkened precincts of the second Tabernacle, as the Most Holy place is sometimes called.[18]

The Temple and the Ark are a kind of initiation into the deeper mysteries of God, and that this results in our own inner illumination. Then what point is there then in searching for the real thing? In truth, even those authors who have claimed to have discovered the Ark have stumbled onto this ancient wisdom tradition. As Graham Hancock points out in his book, he was excited to find that a number of ancient Jewish traditions had "asserted" that the Ark itself was the "root of all knowledge." He points out that the golden lid itself, surmounted by the Cherubim, revealed the gift of knowledge, for: "...the distinctive gift of the cherubim was knowledge...."[19] This, of course, is reference to the words of the philosopher and writer Philo of Alexandria, who did not know what these cherubim looked like, only that they must somehow be symbolic of knowledge.

Because the existence of the Ark is taken literally, the elements of light emissions have brought all manner of wonderful theories. Graham Hancock, however, was much closer to the truth when he hit on the inspirational notion that the Ark was similar to the Holy Grail. What Hancock discovered was that the image of the Ark and that of the Grail were said to give off a luminescence, and when lost, the holy of holies (and even the land) was plunged into darkness. [20]

Isis or Mary, from the Cathedral D'Aix La Chappelle. She is seen here in control of, or sustaining, the Ark.

This "place of thick darkness" reminded me of the pile of black stones that covered the image of the crescent moon from Har Karkom. But similarities with the Grail were also obvious. Chretien's Grail was fashioned from pure gold, and the Ark was overlaid with pure gold. However, it seems that the gold was not the reason for the glowing light, which can be traced to the contents of the Grail as blood of Christ, or the Ark being the tablets of the law. It is supposedly the power and energy of God; it was God's hand that inscribed the tablets, and it was God's blood in the chalice. It was God's power that made Moses' face shine, and it was the God within that made Mary the light bearer. It was also the shining light of Christ resurrected that imaged the Shroud. In truth, the secret of the Ark, the Grail, Mary, and the Shroud is nothing more than the power of the divine within. And we are told where to find this divine: within ourselves. It is in the midst, between man and woman; it is positive and negative in balance.

Now, of course, all of this shining and luminescence relates to the process of illumination as I have outlined in *The Shining Ones* and *Gnosis*. It answers one of the most peculiar enigmas of the Ark: the death rays. These rays were said to have affected the two sons of Aaron, who was the brother of Moses. Nabad and Abihu, as they are named, entered the Holy of Holies carrying metal incense burners in their hands, where, according to the book of Leviticus they offered a "strange fire" to the Lord. But because they had previously been commanded not to do so, a great flame leapt out from the Ark and devoured them.[21] If the Ark was never really made, then this story must have another meaning. That meaning could be spontaneous human combustion.

KING TUTANKHAMEN

From where did this symbolic imagery derive? The answer can partly be found in the barges or b'arques found in the infamous tomb of Tutankhamen— the boy Pharaoh who lived around 1352 B.C., just before the time of Moses. I already knew that the Israelites were clever at reusing the fables, images, and symbols of other nations, so it would be no surprise to find similar motifs and elements within the biblical accounts. Literally dozens of ark-shaped chests, boxes, and coffers, carrying deities of light, were found in Tutankhamen's tomb. Made of wood and plated inside and out with gold, they were certainly similar to the biblical Ark, almost as if "…the mind that had conceived the Ark of the Covenant must have been familiar with objects like these."[22]

In addition to this imagery, there were twin mythical figures with wings both on the doors and at the rear of Tutankhamen's burial chamber, thought to be Isis and Nephthys as angels of vengeance. These images reminded me of the Cherubim that protect the Ark of the Covenant, and especially as their wings spread upwards in the same fashion. These Cherubim are, in effect, protecting the presence of the divine in balance.

SACRED GEOMETRY

The placing of certain objects in certain locations, and in buildings with strict mathematical dimensions, is of course the result of sacred geometry. Protagoras once said that "Man is the measure of all things, of being things that they exist, and of nonentities that they do not exist." Geometry is the measurement of lines and angles, and of curves and shapes. Our ancestors tell us that order was derived from chaos, and that it was the creator gods who ordered the universe. This order is divine. In addition, man found that he himself was in perfect mathematical relation to the universe around him. From the smallest atom or virus to the largest whale or galaxy, certain patterns emerge. These patterns are even found in the laws of nature, to which we unknowingly adhere. These laws are the underlying principles of everything, and because man is the measure of all things, then we are created in the image or pattern of God. This is the sacred law that Moses brought down Mount Sinai to include within the Ark: the law of nature, the law of the divine. The same sacred geometry we find in the outer world, can also be found in the inner world of the mind, and both worlds have sets of correspondences. However, the inner world can sometimes appear to be chaotic. This is where man believed he was getting close to the creative spark.

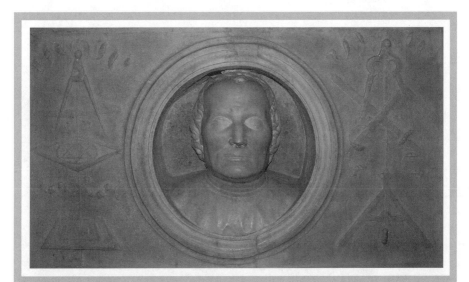

Sacred geometry can be seen in this image, which is carved on a tomb in St. Peter's Cathedral in Rome.

Sacred geometry lays out the law on the earth for all. It is a way of keeping creation alive and not returning to chaos. From the earliest of times this system of planning has been in effect around the world. In remote times, structures followed nature and the cosmos in general, but as time moved on they became more complex and included profound psychological meaning. The ability to lay out the land in such a perfect, natural, and ordered way is almost magical. It was the secret of the priesthood, who were the ones who could bring back the wisdom of the gods and open portals to the mathematical world of the divine. This was a great power and also a great knowledge, which was guarded closely by the adepts. Knowledge of the sacred ratios has come down to us today within the secret society of the Freemasons and the Lodge. The symbols and artifacts of the Freemasons reveal the arcane knowledge of their ancient priesthood.

These same priests also controlled the access to the divine, as magic, science, mathematics, and religion were inseparable. These were the men who made the Temple of the inner man—the divine—a reality on earth. How can we spot sacred geometry in use? The answer is more simple than you think. Numbers are the creation of man, but ratio is the creation of nature, and it is in ratio that we find the secrets of sacred geometry. These ratios reveal forms, such as squares, circles, and triangles.

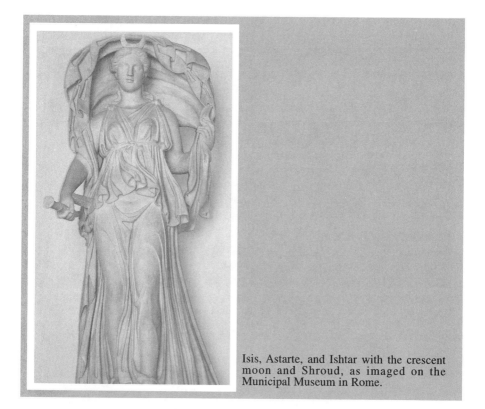

Isis, Astarte, and Ishtar with the crescent moon and Shroud, as imaged on the Municipal Museum in Rome.

TEMPLES IN SACRED FORM

Early temples were often built in the square form, which represents the microcosm and are symbolic of stability. Structures such as pyramids, ziggurats, and stupas were based on this principle, and often include other forms such as the triangle (pyramid), or circle and semi-circle (stupa). These foursquare structures are symbolic of the world-mountain, or *axis mundi*. The mountain rises upwards from the earth upon which man lives, into the sky or heavens where the gods live. By physically building this world-mountain, man is able to access the divine.

Location and ratio were incredibly important to manifest the law in the structure to enable it to work. But the ratios did not always have to be used on permanent structures—they were also used on artifacts such as the Ark, and moveable temples such as the Tabernacle. These moveable structures would then have to be given sacred sites on which to rest. One of the most important ratios is known as the Golden Section, and it has been used in sacred architecture from ancient Egypt onwards. In essence, the Golden Section or Ratio is all about the division of space, and is originally derived by drawing a square.

Imagine a square in front of you. Now place a pole in the bottom left-hand corner. Attach a string to the pole and tie a marker to the other end at the length of the top right-hand corner of the square, so that the marker can touch to top right-hand corner. Now draw an arc from this corner downwards, and you will find that you have added to the square an extra length known as the Golden Section. Make the square into a rectangle from the new point you have just made in the bottom right, and repeat the process, this time with the rectangle corners. You will be adding to the square (or building) with the Golden Section ratio. The exact ratio is 1:1.618. Eventually you will have created a double square, which is the Temple of Solomon. The secret of this sacred geometry recurred in Europe when Leonardo Bigollo Fibonacci traveled to Algiers and brought the Arabic concepts back with him. But even before this, Plato had stated in his work (*Timaeus*) that the ratio was the key to the physics of the cosmos. Fibonacci showed (with the mathematical series now named after him) that this was true, and that shells, leaves, and many other beautiful structures from nature incorporated this divine ratio. The Fibonacci Sequence runs in a numbered sequence by adding together the previous two numbers in the series, such as 0, 1, 1, 2, 3, 5, 8, 13, 21, 34, 55, and so on. When this wonderful Golden Ratio is used in buildings, we create the most beautiful sights in the world. When it is ignored (as so many of our modern architects do) then the result is an eyesore.

MEASURING THE ARK

Sacred geometry involves the use of ratios that are found in nature, and are deemed to be the result of the order brought about by the divine creator. In Exodus 25:10-22, the measurements for the Ark of the Covenant are laid down for all to see. The unit of measure is the cubit, which is 18 to 22 inches, so working in inches and assuming 18 inches per cubit, the measurements for the Ark are as follows:

- length: 45 inches (113 cm)
- width: 27 inches (68 cm)
- height: 27 inches (68 cm)

The exact measurements (whether 18 inches or 22 inches to a cubit) simply do not matter. What is important is the ratio, which works out to a remarkable width to height to length ratio of 1:1.666, which is incredibly close to the infamous Golden Section ratio. Again, the Mercy Seat (*kapporeth*), which was said to be placed on top of the Ark as a kind of lid, also has the ratio of 1:1.666 (2.5 × 1.5 cubits). Incidentally, this *kapporeth* was also known in Hebrew as *kiseh chesed*, where *chesed* means *wisdom* and *kiseh* means *seat of power*. As far as the esoteric interpretation goes, we have *a seat of powerful wisdom*. The *Kebra Nagast* of the Ethiopians states thusly:

> 104. More concerning the Ark and the Talk of the Wicked. For it is
> called "mercy-seat", and it is also called "place of refuge", and it is
> also called "altar", and it is also called "place of forgiveness of sins",
> and it is called "salvation", and it is called "gate of life", and it is
> called "glorification", and it is called "city of refuge", and it is called
> "ship", and it is called "haven of salvation", and it is called "house
> of prayer", and it is called "place of forgiveness of sins for him that
> prayeth in purity in it", so that [men] may pray therein in purity and
> not defile their bodies.[23]

The Ark, according to the *Kebra Nagast* of the Ethiopians, is all things to all men. Many of these ideas can be found in ancient Egypt. This influence upon the Hebrews was derived from those great builders of temples, the Egyptians and the Chaldeans, and anybody who takes the time to look closely at the ancient structures in these places will discover the Golden Section widely in use. The same is also true of India.

The porters of the Ark from the baptismal font at the Cathedral D'Hildesham. Note the Ark is balanced, and the porters walk through the waters of the Nile.

One of the earliest uses of the ratio we find in the Hebrew canon is in the dimensions of Noah's Ark. We also find that the Ark is actually man. According to Genesis 6:14: "Make thee an ark of gopher wood; rooms shalt thou make in the ark, and shalt pitch it within and without with pitch. And this is the fashion which thou shalt make it of: The length of the ark shall be three hundred cubits, and the height of it thirty cubits. A window shalt thou make to the ark, and in a cubit thou shalt finish it above...."

The length of the Noah's Ark was to be 300 cubits, the breadth 60 cubits, and the height 30 cubits—all following the sacred Golden Section, just as the body of man does. But in the kabbalistic belief, Noah's Ark is also divided into three storeys with 11 sections, making the sacred number of 33. Why is this number so important? Because the axis mundi is the spine or backbone, and it has 33 vertebrae. I am not the first to notice the remarkable resemblance of the Ark of Noah to the human form. Cornelius Agrippa beat me to it:

> Seeing man is the most beautiful and perfect work of God, and His
>
> image, and also the lesser world; therefore he by a more perfect
>
> composition, and sweet harmony, and more sublime dignity doth

contain, and maintain in himself all numbers, measures, weights, motions, elements, and all other things, which are of his composition; and in him, as it were, is the supreme workmanship.... Moreover God Himself taught Noah to build the ark according to the measure of a man's body, and He made the whole fabric of the World proportionable to man's body. Therefore some who have written of the microcosm, or of man, measure the body by 6 feet, a foot by 10 degrees, every degree by 5 minutes; from hence are numbered 60 degrees, which make 300 minutes, to which are compared so many geometrical cubits by which Moses describes the Ark; for as the body of a man is in length 300 minutes, in breadth 50 and in height 30; so the Ark was 300 cubits long, 50 broad and 30 high.[24]

In fact, the ratio of the Ark is not just similar to man. William Stirling, in his book *Canon: An Exposition of the Pagan Mystery Perpetuated in the Cabala as the Rule of All the Arts*, states that the measures of the Ark make a correspondence to the planet Earth itself. But more than that, Stirling actually draws a parallel with the greater cosmos: "If this explanation be correct, we must conceive, by the proportions of the ark, the vast figure of a man, in the likeness and the image of God, whose body contains the measure of the sun's path in the ecliptic, the circuit of the Earth, and the orbits of the seven planets."[25] Similar ratios were in fact prevalent in the Ark of the Covenant. The Ark in length was 2.5 cubits and the breadth 1.5 cubits, and Stirling again gives us his interpretation: "It measured 2.5 cubits long, or 3.25 feet, or 45 inches; its breadth and height were 1.5 cubits, or 2.5 feet, or 27 inches. Its perimeter was therefore the mystic number of 144 inches. If the Ark were rather more than an inch thick, which would be sufficient for a box of this size, its contents would amount to 24860 cubic inches, or the number of miles in the circumference of the Earth."

What had I discovered on my search for the wisdom of the Ark? I had discovered that throughout the esoteric history of the Ark (and all that surrounded it), there was a secret and sacred knowledge, reflecting the inner self. This inner wisdom is manifested physically as objects and structures, and also as Mary, as a divine woman. In all ways the Ark was a portal to a higher plane of existence, to a higher consciousness. By manifesting the axis mundi or world-mountain in proportions according to the natural world, mankind is reaching upwards physically and metaphysically. The devout devoured the landscape for the divine and divided it into sacred ratios. When man was nomadic he chose to create objects with sacred ratios. When he finally settled, he did so on sacred locations. In all these ways mankind was perpetuating his search for the divine and for inner peace and wisdom. Today we see this search in the beautiful ancient and medieval structures erected for us by the aged brotherhood of the Freemasons, who have kept alive the arcane knowledge of the sacred Golden Section.

CHAPTER 4
ORIGINS OF THE ARK

W hen looking for the origins of the Ark, I had to begin with Moses. After all, he was given the commandments of God and created the Ark. It was on Mount Sinai (or Mountain of the moon god Sin) that Moses met with his God. Of course, the Egyptian equivalent of Sin is Thoth, who was venerated across Egypt as a moon god. Both Thoth and Osiris were gods of the moon and the dead, and both were lawmakers. Sin as the Sumerian lunar deity was related to Thoth of the Egyptians as the lawmaker and measurer of time.[1]

In Egypt, Osiris and Thoth (according to the Book of the Dead) worked together to bring about the great flood—Osiris being saved from the flood in a similar fashion to that of Noah. Osiris then went around the world taking his law for mankind, but a plot was hatched against him by 72 members of his court, who were led by Set. A coffer or ark of wood and gold was offered to anyone who could fit within it. Because this ark was made for Osiris, not surprisingly, he fit within. As soon as he did so, the lid was shut, and the ark was cast adrift upon the Nile, but Isis and Thoth found the ark and placed it in a secret location. Eventually, Set found the ark and opened it, cutting Osiris

89

into 14 pieces and scattering them. Isis and Thoth worked hard together and brought the pieces together. Osiris was resurrected as king of the Underworld, from where he occasionally returns to walk the earth. If nothing else, the similarities in the Egyptian and Christian tales are astounding, and reveal that the location of the Ark may never be found, as the Christian story appears to be a copy of an earlier Egyptian myth.

FINDING MOSES

But who was Moses? Was he also a copy of an Egyptian ruler or administrator, as so many authors have claimed? To answer that, I first had to make the switch of names or titles, such as Sin to Thoth. The moon God Sin, associated now with Sinai, is the equivalent of the Egyptian Thoth, and he appears in the title of Tutankhamen (Thoth ankh Amen), the boy pharaoh, who had dozens of arks in his tomb, many in similar fashion to those of the biblical Ark.

Exodus 2:19 refers to Moses quite specifically as an Egyptian: "And they said, An Egyptian delivered us out of the hand of the shepherds." Later in Exodus 4:10 and onwards we find that Moses has difficulty communicating with the Semites, because he doesn't know their language: "And Moses said unto the Lord, O my Lord, I am not eloquent, neither heretofore, nor since thou has spoken unto thy servant: but I am slow of speech and slow of tongue." Even the chronicler and adviser to Ptolemy I, Manetho, in his *The Aegyptiaca* recorded Moses as being an Egyptian. Exodus 11:3 also tells us that Moses was "very great in the land of Egypt."

Can we discover any clues from his name? In Hebrew, *Moses* is *Mosheh*, because it is not an original Hebraic name title. If Moses truly was of Egyptian origin—either the title/name or the real person—then we should be able to find the name elsewhere, in Egypt. The name *Moses* may derive from the Egyptian *Mose*, which means *heir*. The use of this can be found in some important people, Tuthmose (Thoth-*moses*) for instance, which means *heir of Thoth*.

Could the character of Moses be based on a real Egyptian of great importance? There is one person who has always taken hold of my imagination (and millions of others interested in Egyptian history): Akhenaten, whose son was the ill-fated Tutankhamen. Otherwise known at Amenhotep IV (*Amenophis* in Greek), in Greece he is identified with the god Mercury, the scribe and messenger of the gods, due to his association with Thoth (Mercury).

In the very first year of his reign, Akhenaten declared his allegiance to the Solar Orb known as the *Aten*. This cult religion is said to have worshipped the sun itself, and Egyptologists believe that Aten was an amalgamation of a trinity, namely Ra, Amen, and Horus. Akhenaten was not the first to worship, as others had done so before him. But he was the first to worship Aten as a merged trinity, bringing them together in one form. Unlike the popular misconception that Akhenaten destroyed the other deities, the truth is that he worshipped a pre-existing trinity. The whole basis of the new religion was life and light—the purity of the shining orb in the sky, born again each day at Akhetaten (Aten on the Horizon), now known as *Amarna*. This location itself gives us a clue, as across the Nile is a city now called Mal-lawi. Laurence Gardner in *Lost Secrets of the Sacred Ark*, tells us that: "Mal-lawi (Malleui)…means, quite literally, City of the Levites, and the High Priest of Akhenaten's Amarna Temple was Meyre. His name was equivalent to the Hebrew Merari: one of the sons of Levi (Genesis 46:11)."[2]

With the name *Akhenaten*, the pharaoh was the effective spirit of the Aten—he was the spirit of light itself. As I showed in *The Shining Ones*, this Aten was more than the life-giving sun we see in the sky. As many of you will be aware, it is our modern world that must reduce all things down into compartments—such as religion, science, and art—and then we reduce these down even further. By the time we have finished reducing, nothing seems to relate to anything else anymore. There is no unifying element left. However, our ancient ancestors did not see things this way. Instead, there was a Oneness to everything. The whole universe was manifest in various ways: their God or gods were seen everywhere, and they were all part of the greater whole. The same applied to their internal world, including the world of the mind, which to our ancestors was a miniature version of the universe. Therefore, the true Aten was also the inner sun—the center point of light within the mind, accessed through processes of trance and altered states of consciousness. To become a true Shining One was to become Aten. He was the dot at the center of the circle.

Akhenaten was following his internal religious impulse and exoterically worshipping the Solar Orb as himself. He was a shining one. Moses, with his resplendent horns, was also an image of enlightenment and also worshipped the solar deity—the moon deity being a reflection of that. Akhenaten's son merged the wisdom of the lunar god Thoth (Tut) with the Solar Orb (Aten) and became *Tutankhaten*, but was forced to alter this by the vengeful priests of Amen to Tutankhamen, even though he didn't actually destroy Aten worship. The sun and the moon are different sides of the same coin, as the moon is only lit by the power of the sun—so it is only right that Ra and Thoth or Aten and Thoth, or even Amen and Thoth, be joined in union.

According to Ahmed Osman in *Moses, Pharaoh of Egypt*, Akhenaten was banished from Egypt in around 1361 B.C. with his followers, who regarded him as the true heir or *mose*. Akhenaten, Nefertiti (his wife), and Tiy (his mother) all disappeared without a trace, and were eradicated from Egyptian history.

Akhenaten, his wife, and his mother could never have journeyed alone from Egypt, so it seems to make sense that he would have escaped with those who were seen as monotheists. The historical fact remains that it was at this very time that Israel is first formed. A Greek writer of the Ptolemaic era, Strabon, said that Moses had been a great ruler who intended to create a new religion in Egypt. Strabon even pointed out that he had built a new city (Amarna) to worship the one solar god. Could this be why early Christian Gnostics claimed that Jesus had also been to Amarna, and had been taught there? Was Jesus really of the cult of Aten, going home to be reborn? The biblical and extra-biblical texts themselves often reveal how Jesus and Moses were merged together, as if they were men of the same title. If this is all the true, then the Jewish chroniclers would later utilize this pharaoh in their Old Testament texts, and Moses would become the follower of the one God, the lawgiver, and the one whose countenance shone—just like Akhenaten. However, there could be another who fits the description.

Akhenaten's father, Amenhotep III, had another son. He may fit the description of Moses even better. We know, for instance, that Moses received his commandments from the Mountain of the moon god Sin, otherwise known in Egypt as Thoth. Moses appears to have gained his law from Thoth. He is therefore the *heir of Thoth*, which is written as *Thothmose* or *Tutmose*. At this time in history, this was the name of Akhenaten's brother, Prince Tutmose. There is however, precious little information about this prince of the realm, other than he disappeared, as did Akhenaten, in the 23rd year of Amenhotep's reign for no discernible reason. Two years later, Amenhotep was dead, and Akhenaten claimed the throne.

According to Josephus (in his *Jewish Antiquities*), Pharaoh commanded Moses to lead the army against the Ethiopians. Coincidentally, the one thing we do know about Tutmose is that he commanded an army against the Ethiopians. According to Josephus, Moses commanded the army so well that Pharaoh became jealous and ordered his arrest. Not wanting to spend the rest of his life in jail, Moses escaped the country. Years later, Akhenaten also disappeared. The stories of Tutmose and Moses may have merged, or Akhenaten and Tutmose may emerge as the intertwined brothers of the Bible, Moses and Aaron.

There is evidence that a Semitic rebellion took place in Avaris. How is this important? Well, quite simply, it is written by Manetho that the revolt was caused by the High Priest of Ra from the temple at Heliopolis. Both Tutmose and Moses were said to have been the High Priest. To add to that, Amenhotep was advised to banish the rebellious individuals from the country in a fashion similar to that described in biblical accounts.

To simplify, what we have here is evidence that the originator of the Hebraic Ark, from the Mountain of Thoth/Sin, was Moses or Tutmose of Egypt. His brother Akhenaten was also Aaron. Moses did not speak the Semitic tongue; he was a high priest; he commanded the army; and he was in charge of the law of Ra. The writers of the Old Testament simply adapted the stories and altered things slightly to bolster their own ethnic and cultural traditions, just as any good government throughout time has done. But what about the Ark? Does this also have Egyptian origins?

A carving of an Egyptian b'arque.

THE ARK IN EGYPT

Graham Phillips, in *The Templars and the Ark of the Covenant*, makes it clear that he believes the Ark originated in Egypt.[3] There have been many festivals involving the use of the arks, from Abydos to Medinet Habu. The parading of the b'arque of Amun occurred twice a year during the Opet and Valley Festivals. There were also two versions of the boat of Amun, one for parading and another for refurbishment. It did not seem overly important for there to be just the one sacred ark. One of the versions, however, was specifically smaller than the other, and this was carried in procession by the priesthood using long poles, similar to the biblical Ark. The second version was floated down the Nile with the statue of Amun placed amidships—in the center of the boat—to maintain balance.

It has been the opinion of many that the Ark of the Covenant was copied almost directly from the Egyptian:

> The temples of Egyptian mysticism (from which the Tabernacle was copied) were—according to their own priests—miniature representations of the universe. The solar system was always regarded as a great temple of initiation, which candidates entered through the gates of birth; after threading the tortuous passageways of earthly existence, they finally approached the veil of the Great Mystery—Death—through whose gate they vanished back into the invisible world. Socrates subtly reminded his disciples that Death was, in reality, the great initiation, for his last words were: "Crito, I owe a cock to Asclepius; will you remember to pay the debt?" (As the rooster was sacred to the gods and the sacrifice of this bird accompanied a candidate's introduction into the Mysteries, Socrates implied that he was about to take his great initiation.)

> Life is the great mystery, and only those who pass successfully through its tests and trials, interpreting them aright and extracting the essence of experience therefrom, achieve true understanding. Thus, the temples were built in the form of the world and their rituals were based upon life and its multitudinous problems. Nor only was the Tabernacle itself patterned according to Egyptian mysticism; its utensils were also of ancient and accepted form. The Ark of the Covenant itself was an adaptation of the Egyptian Ark, even to the kneeling figures upon its lid. Bas-reliefs on the Temple of Philæ show Egyptian priests carrying their Ark—which closely resembled the Ark of the Jews—upon their shoulders by means of staves like those described in Exodus.[4]

Even the very Temple itself, as with those of Egypt, were copies of life and the journey we must all take. There are clues that reveal this process, which is hidden in symbolism for the initiate to work through and become an adept. These are the great mysteries of the Egyptians and Hebrews.

There is no doubt that the Tabernacle, its furnishings, and ceremonials, when considered esoterically, are the same as the structure, organs, and functions of the human body. At the entrance to the outer court of the Tabernacle stood the Altar of Burnt Offerings, which was 5 cubits long and 5 cubits wide, but only 3 cubits high. Its upper surface was a brazen grill upon which the sacrifice was placed, and beneath was a space for the fire. This altar signified that a candidate, when first entering the precincts of sanctuary, must offer upon the brazen altar not a poor bull or ram, but its correspondence within his own nature. The bull, being symbolic of earthiness, represented his own gross nature, which must be burned up by the fire of his divinity. The sacrifice of animals and humans, seen in temples across the world, is in reality nothing more than a misinterpretation of this, or at worst a replacement of this truth.

Further west, in the Tabernacle, in line with the Brazen Altar, was the Laver of Purification. This signified to the priest that he should cleanse not only his body but also his soul from all stains of impurity to enter the presence of Divinity. Beyond this laver was the entrance to the Tabernacle, which faced east towards the rising sun. The concept was to enable the light to enter so that nobody could hide in darkness. The light of sun would be able to light the Ark of the moon, which was in complete darkness, just as in nature.

In the very center of the room, close to the partition that led into the Holy of Holies, was the Altar of Burnt Incense. This is believed to be symbolic of the human larynx, where the voice of man is generated and should be directed upwards to God, just as the smoke from the burnt incense would take our prayers to the Lord. Within the inner sanctum itself would be found the Ark of the Covenant, the mind within the head. It was this place where direct communication with God occurred, and therefore it is within the mind of man that this gateway exists. The light of the sun reached this inner sanctum, just as we should allow light to enter our darkest recesses. This is not, however, a new interpretation. This is an ancient one, held secret by the mystery schools. Even Josephus, the infamous historian of the period, stated that the Temple itself was symbolic of many things, including the planets, the Earth, the sun, and the moon.

These same things are true also of the temples, shrines, and b'arques of ancient Egypt, as we would expect if it were true that the Hebrews assumed the role of the priests of Egypt. How long the boat aspect or b'arque had been held sacred in Egypt is anybody's guess:

> Sacred boats were not new. They seem from early times to have had
>
> an important symbolic and ritual role. What the New Kingdom did
>
> was to lavish great attention on certain of them (especially the barge
>
> of Amun of Karnak called Userhat-Amun, "Might of prow is Amun"),
>
> and to develop the smaller, portable version. One "Superintendent of

Carpenters and Chief of Goldsmiths" called Nakht-djehuty, who lived in the reign of Ramses II and evidently specialised in making them, was repeatedly commissioned to make new ones for a variety of temples, probably up to a total of twenty-six. Both the riverine and the portable boats were put at the center of temple design and temple celebrations. The portable boat shrines were made of wood, but ornately gilded and decorated and equipped with a closed cabin in which the image of the deity sat. Long carrying-poles on each side or set laterally and up to five in number bore the shrine along on the shoulders of priests.[5]

To add to Kemp's informative description of a gold-covered ark carried by poles, we should also state, that more often than not, sitting either side of the deity would be some form of winged animal, similar to the descriptions of the Cherubim on the Ark of the Covenant. Often these were Isis and Nepthys, the female sisters for balance.

An Egyptian arc being carried in a procession. Note the winged Cherubim on either side of the center, providing balance.

COVERED IN GOLD

I wanted to know a little more about gold. I was already aware from my previous researches and conversations with authors such as Crichton Miller[6] that gold was used as a currency because it was seen to be part of God, or the Solar Orb. This was also the reason for the circular shape. The dots around the edges were the stars. In essence, ancient gold coins represented the solar system. I pondered these very real and physical elements, and I discovered this: Gold was actually used as a covering for the Ark for spiritual and psychological reasons that would have made perfect sense to our ancestors:

Philadelphus: All that is compounded of Elements must be more or less corruptible. And though certain elementary bodies may have arrived at some degree of incorruptibility, yet it is but a degree, it being impossible for them to be ever perfectly freed from corruption, but by a dissolution and a resuscitation. For this is a most assured maxim, that all things must be perfected upon the cross and all things must be tried by Fire. Without passing through the Cross there is no resurrection, without passing through the Fire there is no Fixation or Incorruption, no Purification or Spiritualization. Hence the messenger of the Covenant of Immortality is by a certain prophet compared to a refiners Fire, who saith of him that he shall purify the Priesthood and purge them as Gold that they may rightly offer the sacrifice of Minha to Jehovah. Hence also a great and wise King saith, the word (or outflowing emanation of the Lord is refined; and again he cries out Thy Word is exceedingly refined most fine and pure. And likewise this very Word of the Lord or the Word the Lord saith to the shepherds of Israel: I will refine them as Silver is refined, and will try them as Gold is tried. And elsewhere he saith, I have refined thee melted thee down, and then brought thee out of the furnace. For this cause the precious Sons of Zion are compared to fine gold, and the Angelical man who appeared to Daniel had his loins Girded with fine Gold of Ophir. From this also an account may be given why the Altar of Incense was made of refined Gold, together with the Ark and the Cherubims, also why Wisdom's oracle is so often compared to fine

> Gold; and lastly why the Shulamite describes both the head and the
> feet of her beloved to be as of fine Gold, that is such an indivisible,
> indiscernible and incorruptible substance, as being extended is
> therefore a body, and as possessing all the properties of the material
> and gross Gold, is therefore a spiritual body, or immaterial and celestial
> gold.[7]

In this remarkable text (now out of print), we discover that the gold of Ophir (Gate of the Sun) is something we need to gild our loins with. As this cannot possibly be literal, then neither can the other statements, and we end up with a truly enlightening substance, one that is symbolic of light, symbolic of our own balance, and symbolic of the purity we achieve once we have been through the fire. These are Gnostic concepts covering the acacia wood of the Ark.

BUILDING THE BARGE

Nobody is exactly sure when the first Egyptian barges were built, but it is now known that as early as the First Dynasty (2950–2775 B.C.) they were being used in large numbers. Egyptologists believe that simple light rafts made from bundled papyrus reeds may have been among the first vessels used by the Egyptian hunter-gatherers who moved into the Nile valley during the Upper Paleolithic era (30000–10000 B.C.). However, nothing remains of these vessels, and there is precious little in the way of evidence. There is some evidence of boats in the Naqada II culture (3500–3100 B.C.) around 12 miles north of Luxor. Archaeologists have found red painted pottery from the era showing designs including boats as important symbols, and some scholars interpret many of these as religious. More evidence was discovered on tomb reliefs, where ship-building yards are depicted. Model boats have also been found dating from pre-Dynastic times.

Even papyrus rafts appeared to have gained sacred significance as far back as the First Dynasty, due to what the Egyptologists term "the association with the Sun God." In fact, the earliest of depictions of the Sun God show him travelling on a reed float made from bound papyrus—supposedly predating the Egyptian knowledge of wooden boat construction. This association with the Sun God remained with the boat from the earliest of times through all the Dynasties. Eventually the different aspects of the boat were more clearly specified, with specific ritual barges becoming the God carrier, and reed rafts becoming more hunting vessels than ritualized boats. There was one kind of boat, though, that maintained its connection to the gods through its continued symbolic use of the papyrus plant. This ship is known as the papyriform boat, and is made in the same manner as the wooden boats, but with the shape of an elaborate papyrus raft. These papyriform boats were for the use of royalty, in pleasure, and for funerals and pilgrimages. These became the ritualized boats of later years. A beautiful example was found in Tutankhamun's tomb, with the boy-king standing erect while sailing—similar to the *linga* (phallus) and *yoni* (vagina) vessels in India.

Not surprisingly, the boat became extremely important to a culture built on a river; for transportation of people and goods, for worship and processing their gods, and for warfare. Indeed, Ramses III wrote this to Amen, his god: "I built you ships, freight ships, arched ships with rigging, plying the Big Green. I manned them with archers, captains and innumerable sailors, to bring the goods of the Land of Tyre and the foreign countries at the end of the world to your storage rooms at Thebes the Victorious."

It seems that many of the papyriform boats were never intended to float on the river. They were instead used for transporting deities. The image or statue of the god would be placed (just as with the Solar Orb) in the center of the boat. The papyriform boat would be gold-encrusted (just as the Ark of the Covenant) and studded with gems. It would have been carried upon the shoulders of priests, who would then transport it from one location to the next. Indeed, should this journey require the god to travel upon the Nile, the papyriform boat was simply placed on another boat.

In addition to this kind of ritual procession of the gods, boats were also used to transport the dead in a symbolic fashion. From the boat pits of Abydos and Cheops, researchers have discovered full-sized boats buried with the dead to take them further along their journey into the afterlife. However, due to the massive expense of constructing full-sized boats to bury, the practice fell away by the 12th dynasty, and replica models replaced the boats in tombs and burial places.

There were also boats that were religious symbols. The B'arque of Ra, for instance, would carry a host of deities across the sky each day, mirroring the Sun God Ra's actions. These boats were simply copied and placed in the inner sanctums of various temples, awaiting the next outing. In this way, the symbolism of the Ark in the Bible may also have been made real—following the symbolic, esoteric language of the text, and creating duplicate arks, thus giving rise to the many appearances and disappearances throughout history that seem to contradict each other. This also explains the many and varied *tabot* that are still found in Ethiopia.

To fully understand that the Hebrew Ark tale takes many of its elements from the Egyptian concept, we have to also briefly understand the Temple. The b'arque shrine was the sacred location where these boats were kept. In many temples, such as the one at Karnak, an alley of Sphinxes were on guard—looking both towards tomorrow and yesterday, guarding the place of now, the in-between. Next we find the pylons, massive rectangular jambs tapering inwards, and known as the portal. Linking these pylons was a lower lintel, creating a gateway. Through this, and we come to the second section of the temple, opening out into a central region covered in colonnades. At the far end of this great court, we would see the hypostyle hall with a ramp leading up to it. This hall would have a stone roof, supported by massive pillars throughout the hall. Now we would come to the most important element: the Holy of Holies, the inner sanctum. This is the precinct of god. A small chamber at the very center would hold the sacred b'arque of the deity—just as with the Holy of Holies in the Temple of Solomon, where supposedly the Ark of the Covenant lay. Only the king and the priests were allowed anywhere near this place.

There is no difference between the Hebrew Temple and Ark and the Egyptian Shrine and B'arque. We see the exact same process occurring. Not only that, but we also find that the very walls of the hypostyle hall were often carved with the waves of the abyss—thus imitating the watery Otherworld of our own unconscious state and mirroring the journey of that other Ark of Noah. In *Rebel in the Soul: An Ancient Egyptian Dialogue between a Man and His Destiny* by Bika Reed, we find the following statement:

> The nameless, hieractic papyrus 3024, from the Berlin Museum, was translated for the first time in 1896 by the German scholar Adolph Erman, under the name A Man Tired of Life in Dispute with His Soul…. The evolution of consciousness, symbolised by the B'arque of the Sun, moving through the Underworld (the unconscious), is the main theme of Ancient Egyptian sacred writings. Stages of this evolution were often treated individually on the walls of tombs and in papyri. In this voyage, at a certain "hour" (stage), we meet the Rebel in the Soul. I have given this new title to the papyrus because it speaks of that hour of spiritual transformation. Rebel in the Soul is an initiatic text, dedicated to this critical stage: intellectual rebellion. It was meant for students of the Temple, whose highly developed intellect was approaching this crisis. Here the crucial role of the intellect in spiritual survival is assessed in its most deeply paradoxical nature. Egypt often expresses man's inner conflict by the image of the field and the plougher. There is no instant liberation, no other solution to our problems, except cultivation, a balanced development of man's spiritual potential. At the peak of its evolution, like mature fruit, intellect has to face its inevitable transformation, to be able to perpetuate its seed, life itself.[8]

Our Egyptian ancestors were wiser than we thought. They established esoteric traditions, and used clever metaphor and analogy to describe them. Elements of this can be seen in the burial attire of Tutankhamun. On friezes in the tomb of Tutankhamen we find images relating to the boy-king's journey and preparation for death. Tutankhamen is seen lying upon a deathbed, which is upon a b'arque. The golden mask worn by the king has the following inscription: *"Royal is thy face. Your right eye represents the solar b'arque and thy left eye represents the lunar b'arque."* If the sun and moon (the eyes of Horus), or opposites, are represented on the face of the king (on the very eyes, no less), then could we have an esoteric belief? Of course we do, as most of the Egyptian religious pantheon was set up with esoteric intentions—not just following the patterns and cycles of exoteric life, but also those of the internal world.

OUT OF EGYPT

There is another way that the Egyptian b'arque concept could have arrived in Jerusalem, other than as an esoteric concept melting into the mindset of the Hebrews. It could have arrived physically, and it could have been one of the most important of all b'arques ever to have existed: the B'arque of Amun.

Thutmose III has been described as the Napoleon of Ancient Egypt, and for good reason. To quote from David Rohl's magnificent book, *A Test of Time*: "Thutmose III walks into the spotlight of history to begin his prolonged, vigorous military assault upon the city-states of the Levant."[9] Thutmose III was a warrior pharaoh with a will to expand his nation states and great power to do so. This included Jerusalem, and Thutmose III is revealed within the Bible as the king of Egypt, possibly as Shishak, although some claim that King David was Thutmose III.[10]

The Egyptians saw Jerusalem as a sacred location, and when Thutmose III conquered the land, he brought with him to Jerusalem the B'arque of Amun, carried on poles, similar to the Ark of the Covenant. Normally this B'arque was kept in the Holy of Holies in the Shrine of Amun at Karnak; however, this time the B'arque travelled into war, just as the sacred Ark of the Israelites *would later on.*[11]

What interested me most of all with this filtering of religious artifacts from Egypt to Jerusalem was the fact that the B'arque of Amun had been carried across land with poles, in the same manner as the Ark of the Covenant, and it appears this was a pretty common practice. The Harris Papyrus is the largest extant Egyptian papyrus dating from the early part of the reign of Ramasses IV. The document is more than unique for its large size, and it is also highly useful for its historical content. In one particular section, we find the following words when speaking of the Solar B'arque: "I wrought upon its great carrying-poles, overlaid with fine gold, engraved with thy name." Of course, this reveals that golden poles, just as those spoken of in the Bible were used: "And thou shalt make staves [poles] of shittim wood, and overlay them with gold."

Amun was a solar deity, as was Ra, who also had a Solar B'arque. There is but one god of Egypt, and that all the other gods are different manifestations of him. Often these boats were seen in Egyptian imagery as a semi-circular or half-moon shaped, with the Solar Orb in the center (the sun and moon in union), and two winged creatures either side. It is not surprising to find that the neighbors of the Egyptians, the Abyssinians (or, less specifically, the Ethiopians) have this same symbolic reference in their Ark. The *Kebra Nagast*, or Book of Kings (used so extensively by Graham Hancock in his *Sign and the Seal* book to prove that the Ark was in Ethiopia), actually states that the sun disk was a symbol for the Ark. This solar orb or sun disk seems to have arrived in Ethiopia as a symbol of the Ark, not from Judaism, but from Egypt. Therefore the Ethiopian traditions can be shown to be a mix of the different cultures, not merely as a direct influence from Judaism. In fact, it reveals that the Ark, with the sun disk, could actually have pre-dated the Judaism influence by hundreds of years.

An Egyptian image showing a ceremonial b'arque being carried on poles, in a manner similar to that of the Ark of the Covenant.

MESOPOTAMIAN ARKS

In fact, the Ark goes back to ancient Mesopotamia, as can be seen here from The Schweich Lectures given by Leonard W. King in 1916 at the University of London. King was the assistant keeper of Egyptian and Assyrian antiquities in the British Museum.

> It may be worth while to pause for a moment in our study of the text, in order to inquire what kind of boat it was in which Ziusudu escaped the Flood. It is only called "a great boat" or "a great ship" in the text, and this term, as we have noted, was taken over, semitised, and literally translated in an early Semitic-Babylonian Version. But the Gilgamesh Epic, representing the later Semitic-Babylonian Version, supplies fuller details, which have not, however, been satisfactorily explained. Either the obvious meaning of the description and figures there given has been ignored, or the measurements have been applied to a central structure placed upon a hull, much on the lines of a modern "house-boat" or the conventional Noah's ark. For the latter interpretation the text itself affords no justification. The statement is definitely made that the length and breadth of the vessel itself are to be the same; and a later passage gives ten gar for the height of its sides and ten gar for the breadth of its deck. This description has been taken to imply a square box-like structure, which, in order to be seaworthy, must be placed on a conjectured hull.

What we find is a ridiculous situation where the house of God is actually a box shape that must be placed on a semi-circular prow to float. It is God manifesting in the center of the opposites and with sacred geometrical units and shapes (circle and sqaure) as a magical precursor of a later and more complex symbolism.

The esoteric concepts of the Ark also came through into the Ark of Noah, which we know to be a development of more ancient Mesopotamian stories. The following is the Genesis version of Noah's Ark:

6:13 And God said unto Noah, The end of all flesh is come before me; for the earth is filled with violence through them; and, behold, I will destroy them with the earth.

6:14 Make thee an ark of gopher wood; rooms shalt thou make in the ark, and shalt pitch it within and without with pitch.

6:15 And this is the fashion which thou shalt make it of: The length of the ark shall be three hundred cubits, the breadth of it fifty cubits, and the height of it thirty cubits.

6:16 A window shalt thou make to the ark, and in a cubit shalt thou finish it above; and the door of the ark shalt thou set in the side thereof; with lower, second, and third stories shalt thou make it.

6:17 And, behold, I, even I, do bring a flood of waters upon the earth, to destroy all flesh, wherein is the breath of life, from under heaven; and every thing that is in the earth shall die.

6:18 But with thee will I establish my covenant; and thou shalt come into the ark, thou, and thy sons, and thy wife, and thy sons' wives with thee.

6:19 And of every living thing of all flesh, two of every sort shalt thou bring into the ark, to keep them alive with thee; they shall be male and female.

6:20 Of fowls after their kind, and of cattle after their kind, of every creeping thing of the earth after his kind, two of every sort shall come unto thee, to keep them alive.

6:21 And take thou unto thee of all food that is eaten, and thou shalt gather it to thee; and it shall be for food for thee, and for them.

6:22 Thus did Noah; according to all that God commanded him, so did he.

This Genesis story reveals quite a few esoteric truths. First, that the Ark is the tool used to establish a new Covenant with the Lord's people. Second, that Noah is to take two of every living creature both *"male and female."* This union of duality is required to ensure good balance—the union or fusion of opposites. And third, the dimensions of the Ark conform to sacred geometrical measurements, used extensively in the Ark of the Covenant and the Temple of Solomon.

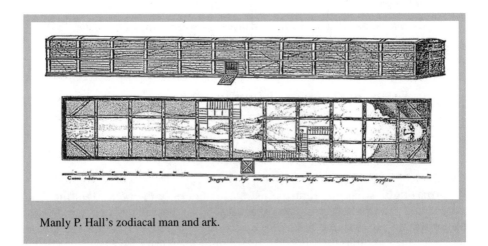

Manly P. Hall's zodiacal man and ark.

The diagram shown above is also reproduced in The Rosicrucians, by Hargrave Jennings. This author adds to the original diagram appearing in Antiquitatum Judaicarum Libri IX the signs of the zodiac, placing Aries at the head and continuing in sequential order to Leo, which occupies the fifth cross section of the ark. Jennings assigns the panel containing the door to the undivided constellation of Virgo-Libra-Scorpio (which is continued into the first subdivision of the second section) and the remaining four cress sections to the constellations of Sagittarius to Pisces inclusive. A study of the plate discloses the ark to be divided into eleven main sections, and along the base and roof of each section are shown three subdivisions, thus making in all the sacred number 33. Occupying the position corresponding to the generative system of the human body will also be noted the cross upon the door of the central section. Two openings are shown in the ark: one—the main door representing the orifice through which the animal lives descend into physical existence; the other a small window proximate to the crown of the head through which the spirit gains liberty according to the ancient rites. "When the androgenic Scorpio-Virgo was separated and the Balance or Harmony made from Scorpio, and placed between Scorpio, i.e., male, and Virgo, i.e., female, then appeared the 32 constellations or signs, as we now have them." The ark is three stories high (perhaps to symbolise Heaven, Man, Earth). In the figure of the Man, notice the parting of the hair in the middle of the forehead and the arrangement of the beard, whiskers, moustache and the hair, on the back of the neck and shoulders.[12]

Amazingly, what this figure illustrates is not only the belief that the Ark represented man, but that he was the vehicle, or vessel through which the divine works. He was the Ark. The base nature, entering through the lower nature area (or genitals) is worked upward until the spirit (dove) escapes from the top of the head and out of the small window in the Ark. This is similar to the kundalini, whereby the adept must rise energies from the lower natures to the bindu point above the head. It is the secret teaching of the esoteric cults—that man himself has the power to raise up. The Ark is portrayed as the vessel, a symbol of the process of the course of the inner light. This symbolism was taken on and fostered by the secret societies, as evidence by the 33 degrees of the Masonic order reflecting the 33 vertebrae of the Ark.

Indeed, Freemason, mystic, writer of more than75 published works, and philosopher Manly P. Hall wrote in *Old Testament Wisdom*:

In most of the ancient writings, Noah's ark did not actually or literally mean a boat. Its name signified rather some peculiar form of enclosure, a superior place to which men could go for refuge, and the idea of a boat floating on the waters of the universal night was a poetic form developed by later theologians as a symbol of the ship of salvation. Philosophically speaking, the ark symbolised a spiritual sphere or over-state, above the material world, which survived the disintegration of the physical universe. Briefly, then, the ark of Noah, with its three decks, represents the three parts of the divine world, or the archetypal region. The Ark, as its symbolism develops, is evidently a miniature of the universe.[13]

The Ark, therefore, is an enclosure for everything. To access it, one is accessing the knowledge of everything: Gnosis.

The Solar Barge of Khufus is on display in a specially built museum at the south face of the Great Pyramid in Egypt. It was found in a boat pit and reassembled from 1,224 pieces. Photo courtesy John Bodsworth.

Celtic Arks

Of course, in Mesopotamia we have the moon god Sin, who may have given us the Mount Sinai of the Bible and the crescent shape for the prow of the b'arque. These are things we find mirrored in Egypt, with Thoth as the moon god. But are there any similarities elsewhere, with any trading partners— or even possibly unrelated areas of the globe? I consulted Manly P. Hall, the Freemason philosopher, writer, and esteemed historian. It appears that the Druids of northern Europe also held belief in a sacred Ark and its associations with the moon deity: "The Druids also had other symbolic implements, such as the peculiarly shaped golden sickle with which they cut the mistletoe from the oak, and the cornan, or sceptre, in the form of a crescent, symbolic of the sixth day of the increasing moon and also of the Ark of Noah. An early initiate of the Druidic Mysteries related that admission to their midnight ceremony was gained by means of a glass boat, called Cwrwg Gwydrin. This boat symbolised the moon, which, floating upon the waters of eternity, preserved the seeds of living creatures within its boatlike crescent."[14]

One of the things that we find supposedly in the Ark of the Covenant is the golden pot of manna. Folklorists have associated this with mistletoe for decades. Mistletoe is a plant sacred to the druids. Its white, circular shape indicates it as moon dew, and so it may be that *manna* may have been derived from the word *moon*. I also had to note that even the Druids saw this Ark as carrying the creative seed, something that was to become extremely important in relation to meteorites later on. Amazingly, Hall then goes on to relate the Ark to another famous icon from history—the siege horse of Troy:

As a beast of burden the horse was the symbol of the body of man forced to sustain the weight of his spiritual constitution. Conversely, it also typified the spiritual nature of man forced to maintain the burden of the material personality. Chiron, the centaur, mentor of Achilles, represents the primitive creation, which was the progenitor and instructor of mankind, as described by Berossus. The winged horse and the magic carpet both symbolise the secret doctrine and the spiritualised body of man. The wooden horse of Troy, secreting an army for the capture of the city, represents man's body concealing within it those infinite potentialities which will later come forth and conquer his environment. Again, like Noah's Ark, it represents the spiritual nature of man as containing a host of latent potentialities, which subsequently become active. The siege of Troy is a symbolic account of the abduction of the human soul (Helena) by the personality (Paris) and its final redemption, through persevering struggle, by the secret doctrine—the Greek army under the command of Agamemnon.[15]

We are now being told that the Ark is, in fact, a symbol of a secret doctrine, something known only by secret societies. This was to become important to me, as I discovered when I entered the world of the secret society. But for now, with the thought in mind that the Ark may be found in other cultures, I looked towards the subcontinent where so much mystery and myth has been fostered: India.

CHAPTER 5

EXPLORING INDIA

As far as the Ark is concerned, India is a country virtually ignored by modern historians (both alternative and mainstream). The rush to be Indiana Jones and to discover the secrets of the Egyptians or the Temple of Solomon have inadvertently sidelined one of the world's richest cultural resources. Great civilizations, from the Greeks to the Persians, pale in comparison with the history and religion of this unique place. India existed as an empire long before western Europe even organized a feudal society. And India surpassed even the Arabs in its understanding of mathematics: The concept of the number zero was first established on the Asian subcontinent. In the previous chapter, we discovered how the regions of Egypt and Mesopotamia (and the Celtic faiths) developed their Ark concepts, but the Ark in India may have preceded all of these. I decided to explore India's relationship to the Ark because of hints left for me by the Naga serpent cults and the kundalini enlightenment process. According to Paul William Roberts in his book, *Empire of the Soul: Some Journeys in India*, "Recent research and scholarship make it increasingly possible to believe that the Vedic era was the lost civilisation whose legacy the

Egyptians and the Indians inherited. There must have been one. There are too many similarities between the hieroglyphic texts and the Vedic ones, these in turn echoed in somewhat diluted form and a confused fashion by the authors of Babylonian texts and the Old Testament." Similar beliefs are expressed by the Theosophist Colonel Henry Steel Olcott, who wrote in *The Theosophist* that "We have a right to more than suspect that India, eight thousand years ago, sent a colony of emigrants who carried their arts and high civilisation into what is now known as Egypt."

Modern scholarly research (and 19th-century Theosophist belief) clearly shows that the Vedic origins of India and its customs influenced the Egyptians, Babylonians, and Hebrews. These same sources tell us that Abyssinia/Ethiopia itself was colonized by the Indians, and that the Brahmins were similar to the Druids. The *Argha*, or Ark, was represented in India as a vessel of copper by the Brahmins in their sacred rites, and was intended to be a symbol of the Mother Goddess giving birth to enlightenment. The forms of this Ark are as a canoe or elliptic boat similar to the crescent moon. In the center, we normally find the oval shape rising, said to be the solar *linga* or phallus, similar to that of Osiris, and in union with the Mother Goddess or *yoni*—the divine union of opposites. This Argha of the Indians, as well as being mirrored in the boat of the Argonauts, is also seen in the vessel of Eleusis, known as the *Mundus Cereris*. *Mundus* means *world*, and *Ceris* was the goddess of the Otherworld—this was, therefore, the boat to the Otherworld.

There is such wisdom in the religious and ethnic literature of India, that to claim to know it all and to understand half would be a lie. This rich, vibrant, and exciting country has given us so much that my mind is staggered. I just knew that the Ark would be found in the religious texts or rituals of this amazing place, so I scoured books, articles, and contacted experts. Nobody, it seemed, had any idea of anything similar to the Ark in India. How could there possibly be such a thing? The Ark was a Jewish device, whether literal or literary. But then I found it, while going through several old pictures of India. One of them struck me, and I dropped the rest. This one picture led me on a journey into the heart of India and on the trail for the Indian Ark, which is still there today, for all to see.

THE JUGGERNAUT

The picture in my hand was of a festival, and it was the way the people were reacting to a sacred item that caught my eye—they were frantic and mesmerized. It was the festival of the Juggernaut (or *argha-natha*, meaning *Lord of the broad shaped vessel*).

Juggernaut, we are told in various dictionaries, can mean any massive object or inexorable force that advances, crushing whatever may be in its path. Alternatively, it is an idea or custom to which one devotes oneself. Both explanations will turn out to be true.

The word derives from the deity *Jagannath* (meaning *Lord of the World*), which is another form of Vishnu incarnated as Krishna (a solar deity). Vishnu is the source of the universe. According to the cosmic myth, Vishnu sleeps in the primeval ocean on the thousand-headed snake Sesa. He is the creator god, and has a consort (and dual nature) in Laksmi, just as Osiris has Isis and Yahweh has Shekinah or Matronit. The status as universal god is seen in the Bhagava Gita:

Now I will tell the chief of my holy powers

Though there is no end to my fullness.

I am the self in the inmost heart of all that are born...

I am their beginning, their middle and their end...

I am the beginning, the middle, the end, of all creation,

The science of the soul among sciences,

Of speakers I am the speech,

Of letters I am A.

I am unending time,

I am the ordainer who faces all ways,

I am destroying death,

I am the source of all that is to be...

I am the dice-play of the gamester,

I am the glory of the glorious,

I am victory, I am courage,

I am the goodness of the virtuous...

I am the force of those who govern,

I am the statecraft of those who seek to conquer,

I am the silence of what is secret,

I am the knowledge of those who know,

And I am the seed of all that is born...

> There is nothing that can exist without me.
>
> There is no end to my holy powers…
>
> And whatever is mighty or fortunate or strong
>
> Springs from a portion of my glory.[1]

Just as the creator god in Egypt was one god, and all others were elements of him, so too Vishnu was the creator god, with the other deities being secondary expressions of the divine. As Osiris has his counterpart in Set, Vishnu has Siva. Similar to how Osiris is incarnated as Horus and Yahweh as Christ, so is Vishnu incarnated as Krishna (Christna). Krishna is the one who establishes the Sacred Law, just as Christ established the new covenant. The priests of Vishnu were mystically repeating the primeval sacrifice, making the world born anew again and again. They were constantly meditating on the creative point in the cycle of life—neither life, nor death, but the spark of creation. All great and good men are said to have Vishnu within, just as we are all sons of God—He is the innermost being. He is raised up in the Ark in this literal festival for all to comprehend, just as the Egyptians, Mesopotamians, and Celts did.

The festival of Jagganath can still be found at the infamous shrine at Puri in the state of Orissa in the east of India. From the eighth to 13th centuries, the Orissan school of architecture rivaled those of Europe, and the wonderful Lingaraja Temple at Bhubanesar, Orissa, has virtually the same ground plan as the Temple of Solomon (following sacred geometric ratios). Nearby, at Konarak (in the northeastern corner of Puri), we also have a temple to the sun. It is a masterpiece of the medieval architecture, and is now a UNESCO World Heritage site. The construction is said to have taken 12 years' worth of revenue—a symbolic statement of the cycle of the sun. The main tower has the same general form as that of Lingajara and Jagannath. In fact, the entire temple is a manifestation of the chariot of the sun—the *rath* or ark of the sun itself, built to an enormous scale in stone. There are 24 wheels, each about 10 feet in diameter. The spokes are sundials and can give the specific time of day, as well as the days of the week. The seven horses pulling the temple also represent the seven colors of the spectrum, which, all together, make the color white. However, it was more than the fact that this was a massive stone ark that caught my eye. The etymology here made me sit up and wonder.

The sun, as we saw in Egypt, was the orb or Ra, riding on the Solar B'arque. The word *Konarak* actually breaks down into *kon* (*corner*) *arka* (*the sun*), or the *corner of the sun*. The very word for the sun deity, which is the light of the Ark, is *arka*, and Indo-European etymology suggests this may be one of the roots for our words *ark* and *arc*, due to the passage of the sun in an arc or the rays of the sun. There is another clue in the word. If what I say is true, and that the sun is also seen as the divine or life-force, then this may come out in the language. *Arka* also means *essence*. Essence, of course, is the life force or substance of being. It is the very thing that gives life—the sun. In fact, the word was even used for medicinal drugs and alcohol exported from India during the medieval period by Muslim traders and is now known as *arak*—something we also call *spirit*.[2]

But first we must return to the Jagannath festival. During the 19th century, the British rulers had no comprehension of what was actually occurring during this festival, and, when reporting on it, they could not separate the deity from the vehicle, and so named the vehicle (and thereafter every large, unwieldy object) the Juggernaut. It is believed that Jagannath was originally a tribal deity and was mostly crafted from wood, which would become important. Eventually Jaggannath became part of a holy trinity with Balabhadra (his brother) and Subhadra (his sister).

CAR OF JUGGERNAUT.

The Juggernaut vehicle used in the Indian festival of the same name, as depicted in the *Illustrated London Reading Book*.

The concept of a massive object crushing whatever may be in its path comes down to us from the festival or *jatra* of Ashada Shukla Dwadashi, which is for all three deities and involves the car or chariot (*ratha*) of Jagannath being processed through the streets in much the same way that the Egyptian processed their sacred b'arques, or the Jews took out their Ark on various sojourns. This ratha is of enormous and unwieldy size, and people have been actually killed beneath its heavy wheels. In fact, there are three rathas, one for each of the deities. Each year these are made anew from various trees. It is a tradition that is believed to stretch back thousands of years, although some believe that originally the three deities were Buddhist, with Buddha, Dharma, and Sangha as the trinity. There is little or no evidence for this, although there are pre-Aryan origins that have been well documented.

In the same fashion as the Egyptian b'arques, the deity as ashes (*ashti*— reduced by the light of the sun) is placed in a small casket, which itself is placed upon the ratha. This occurs every 12 years, in a vague memory of some astrotheological tradition. In fact, we can also see parallels with Egypt, as this ratha is driven for 2 miles from the temple to the beach, as if it were originally some kind of boat. I then discovered from the Vedas that Jagannath was also known as *Daru of Purrusottam*, which means *sacred log of wood of Puri afloat on the eastern seas*. Daru was the real name of Jagannath, as this latter term was the name for the trinity found at Puri.

These ratha festivals occurred across India quite frequently. As in Egypt and elsewhere, it was the only way the people could see their deities. The *Illustrated London Reading Book* of 1851 states the case thusly:

> Juggernaut is the principal deity worshipped by the Hindoos, and to his temple, which is at Pooree, are attached no less than four thousand priests and servants; of these one set are called Pundahs. In the autumn of the year they start on a journey through India, preaching in every town and village the advantages of a pilgrimage to Juggernaut, after which they conduct to Pooree large bodies of pilgrims for the Rath Justra, or Car Festival, which takes place in May or June. This is the principal festival, and the number of devotees varies from about 80000 to 150000. No European, Mussulman, or low cast Hindoo is admitted to the temple; we can therefore only speak from report of what goes on inside. Mr Acland, in his Manners and Customs of India, gives us the following amusing account of this celebrated deity:

"Juggernaut represents the ninth incarnation of Vishnoo, a Hindoo deity, and consists of a mere block of sacred wood, in the center of which is said to be concealed a fragment of the original idol, which was fashioned by Vishnoo himself. The features and all the external parts are formed of a mixture of mud and cow-dung, painted. Every morning the idol undergoes his ablutions; but, as the paint would not stand the washing, the priests adopt a very ingenious plan—the hold a mirror in front of the image and wash his reflection. Every evening he is put to bed; but, as the idol is very unwieldy, they place the bedstead in front of him, and on that they lay a small image. Offerings are made to him by pilgrims and others of rice, money, jewels, elephants, &c., the Rajah of Khoudah and the priests being his joint treasurers. On the day of the festival, three cars, between them sixty feet in height, are brought to the gate of the temple; the idols are then taken out by the priests, Juggernaut having golden arms and diamond eyes for that one day, and by means of pulleys are hauled up and placed in their respective carriages: to these enormous ropes are attached, and the assembled thousands with loud shouts proceed to drag the idols to Juggernaut's country-house, a small temple about a mile distant. This occupies several days, and the idols are then brought back to their regular stations. The Hindoos believe that every person who aids in dragging the cars receives pardon for all his past sins; but the fact that the people throw themselves under the wheels of the cars, appears to have been a European conjecture, arising from the numerous deaths that occur from accidents at the time the immense cars are in progress."

These cars have an imposing air, from their great size and loftiness: the wheels are six feet in diameter; but every part of the ornament is of the meanest and paltry description, save only the covering of striped and spangled broad-cloth, the splendid and gorgeous effect of which makes up in great measure for other deficiencies.

> During the period the pilgrims remain at Pooree they are not allowed
> to eat anything but what has been offered to the idol, and that they
> have to buy at a high price from the priests.

In essence, what we have here is a priestly, moneymaking Juggernaut that is kept rolling by religious fervor. Nevertheless, it is interesting to see an ancient procession still in practice today that mirrors the procession of the gods from ancient Egypt and Israel. The deity is placed at the very center of the transport, and taking part in the religious act guarantees absolution.

THE TEMPLE AT PURI

The temple at Puri, where our deities reside, is topped by the mystic wheel or chakra of Krishna, giving us some indication of the later kundalini or chakra system of the Hindus. It is even said that to reside within this temple for three days enables escape from the cycles of life, just as Jesus himself remained three days in the tomb.

The whole process of the chariots represents the world's in motion, the trinity of the Sun (Jagannath), Earth (Balabhadra), and Moon (Subhadra), representing also the divine attributes of creation, maintenance, and destruction. These are drawn together as a divine union of perfection. Evidence of this divine union within the temple can be gleaned. Although nobody from the Western world is allowed within the Temple precincts, I managed to track someone down who had actually been within the sacred spaces. He told me that one of the figures, normally veiled, was a *lingam*, or *sacred penis*, indicating the union of opposites to allow for the continuance of the cycles. It also reminded me of the tales of Osiris, itself a retelling of the creation. A close observation of the body of the Lord Jagannath reveals that his face resembles a snake, as worshipped by the Nagas and the body what is known as a *khamba*, as worshipped by the Savaras. In effect, it is a union of the deities of the two tribes.

We also find that the festival involved temple prostitutes, known as the wives of the deity or wives of the shining (*devadasis*). These wives would, in the same ritual found in ancient Egypt, have sex with the king or priest to divulge the land of its fertility. Similar roles can be found in Sumerian rituals.

The Chakra of Vishnu at the topmost point of the temple at Puri. The Red flag denotes that Jagannath is within the building.

THE SONG OF SOLOMON

There is a strong similarity to the Song of Solomon, and I was amazed to find this link. Solomon, I knew from researching *Gnosis: The Secret of Solomon's Temple Revealed,* was (in all likelihood) not a real man, and the Temple of Solomon itself probably never existed. In fact, what I discovered was that the whole story of the Temple, Solomon, and the Queen of Sheba was nothing more than a gnostic or esoteric fable of teaching. But what did it teach? The union of opposites achieves enlightenment, and a connection to the divine. It was within Solomon's Temple that the Ark was to reside, and if this Temple was nothing more than a fable, then what we have is a case for the suggestion that there was no Ark. However, it could be that an Ark did reside in a Temple in Jerusalem, and that the Juggernaut was giving us a clue to one of its real natures (as a carrier for god and a propaganda tool for material gain and power). The Song of Solomon (or Song of Songs) was one of the last books to enter the Jewish canon, as its secular nature caused consternation for the Jewish priesthood. The problem of the obvious sexual nature and tone of the book was overcome by stating that Solomon was in fact speaking of his love for Israel and that the acts were metaphorical. Indeed they were, but not just as a union between king and country. In fact, the rustic maiden that Solomon takes to his bed is the queen of heaven herself, Ishtar.

The book has now been shown by scholars to have derived from songs used in the cult of Ishtar, being transplanted into Palestine as the worship of Astarte.[3] In turn, Astarte and her symbols (of stars, the crescent moon, and the serpent), are still with us in the various images of Mary, who through divine union gives birth to Christ or the Krishtna. The *shulamite* lady spoken of in the Song of Solomon is nothing more than a female version of Solomon. Hence we have the perfect union of Solomon and Solomoness.

With the Jagannath cult rituals we actually have the inner wisdom realized physically and symbolically for all to see. In the book *Missing Link of Lord Jagannath Cult* by Tribikram Mallick, the author tells us that the Jagannath cult is: "the outcome of an endeavour made by Lord Krishna to harmonise all mutually conflicting doctrines of various sects around the time of the Mahabharat war. Srimad Bhagabat Gita taught to Arjuna in Kurukshetra reconciled them and under the authority of Lord Krishna, immensley enlightened Vyasa carried the message to the platform at Naimisharanya where leading savants and seers assembled to fix and finalise the religious doctrines and to follow the right way to Vedantik goal of Satchidanand—Being, Consciousness and Bliss can be realised." These created images "are the replica of divinities realised above physical and mental consciousness."

Mallick continues and tells us that the wood used to create the images was that of Lord Krishna himself, which had travelled across the sea as wood. This is the point between the worlds—between consciousness and unconsciousness, between this world and the next. Here Krishna is the embodiment of this location—he is what can be attained from this journey. His symbol, fashioned from his image of wood, is set up for us to remember. "They are presented for the devotee, to say in the language of the Gita (Ch. XI, Verse 54 (to enter, behold (by the help of evolutes of creation (Tatwen) and know the ultimate truth, the divine." These images are to help us to remember, to meditate on, and to access the divine—which is the truth of our own divinity.

Mallick then tells us that those who speak of Buddhism and Jainism in relationship to the Jagannath cult are wrong, and that the symbolic devices are misunderstood: "The qualification rendered in English runs; 'until vital airs enter sushumna; until the point of consciousness remains fixed and the breath is controlled and until concentration easily assumes the fourth stage to yield the ultimate truth, it is not proper for a person to speak or write on knowledge of God and Scriptures.'" In essence, we are told that, to comprehend Jagannath properly, we must have achieved enlightenment and access to the divine. Mallick then tells us what the truth is, as he sees it:

The first symbol of Vedic doctrine is the "Tapering Flame" in the forehead of Lord Jagannath. This is one of the conditions of fire. Yoga treatise calls it Atmajyoti, sould of man in flame Laxmi Tantra, a treatise of Pancharatra Agama calls it "Chitkala"—mark of consciousness. Iconography says that it is a symbol of Vishnu and Vaishnavas paint this symbol on there foreheads and arms as a mark of respect to Lord Vishnu. It is the symbol of awakened kundalini, a fiery power connected with Lord Vishnu. Shiva Smahita describes the kundalini as "Vishnu Nirvana"—power which serves for the rest of Vishnu, Rig Veda also mentioned it as "Saptardha Garva" which is three and a half coils of later treatises on Sadhana. There is indeed an intimate relation between Lord Vishnu and kundalini—(serpent power coiled) where the pervading Lord rests and sleeps. This is given as flame in a U-shaped jar or vessel (Agni Kunda of Veda); and Agni (a flaming God), which rises in serpentine manner, is manifestation of the "Serpent Fire."

Mallick also tells us that this deity's eyes are always open (like the snake) because it is this act that is the cause of eternal consciousness—that is, being conscious of the unconscious or always aware. This, we are told, is the symbol of true enlightenment and access to the divine, the wide, round eye sockets with the pupil at the center—the dot in the center of the circle. But who is this deity in reality? Mallick again gives us the answer: "He is Innerself in all beings." There is little wonder, when one considers the links between the Brahma of the Hindus and the Abraham of the Jews, that the processes of enlightenment across these cultures are so similar. There is also little wonder that the images of Egyptian b'arques, Semitic arks, and Hindu raths are so alike.

SACRED TREES

Even the sacred collection of the equally sacred wood (Krishna) is similar to the biblical accounts of the Acacia required for the Ark. Just as Osiris floated upon the Nile in ancient Egypt and a tree grew around his coffin, so too Krishna as he floats upon the sea east of India and turns into a tree. The wood is sacred, so we should find this sacred wood used in the construction of the b'arques of

Egypt, the raths of India, and the Ark of the Jews—for all were symbolic of their divinity. In Egypt, the gods themselves were said by the Pyramid Texts to have been born beneath the Acacia tree of Saosis, found north of Heliopolis. Even Horus, the son of Osiris or Osiris reincarnated, was thought to have been born of the Acacia tree. A hymn of praise to Ra reads: "Homage to thee, O Lord of the Acacia Tree, whose Seker Boat is set upon its sledge, who turnest back the Fiend, the Evildoer, and dost cause the Eye of Ra to rest upon its seat."

If the tree gave life to the gods as a creative portal, then it would also take the souls away again to the Otherworld. In India and Syria the Acacia is associated with the moon god and the Otherworld, and there is little wonder when we discover that a drink made from the Acacia includes ingredients similar to those of the Ayahuasca brews of the Amazon. This is the same brew still used today by Amazonian shaman to enable them to enter the trance state and access the Otherworld. In fact, the resin of the tree was seen as the divine blood itself from the Mother Goddess who would allow this access. Even the tree itself was metaphysically and physically the perfect union.

A grove of Acacia trees in the Serengeti region of Africa. Acacia trees are commonly called thorntrees or wattles, and their bark was often used to construct simple boats or b'arques.

The tree, in essence, is the symbolic spine of man, the world tree, or the world mountain. It is the between state that reaches upwards to the heavens and yet has tentacles below in the underworld in the belly of the Mother Goddess. It is the gateway, the ladder, and the connection between the very worlds symbolized by the upper and lower regions. No wonder, therefore, that the tree would come to be symbolic of the deities—the same deities that enabled our access to the Otherworld—such as Osiris and Isis, the gods of the Underworld.

The tree also has its own sacred skin or covering known as *bark*, exactly the same as the *b'arque* of the Egyptians—the astral vehicle of the gods and a progenitor of the Ark of the Covenant. Graham Phillips, in *The Templars and the Ark of the Covenant*, also points to the Egyptian origins of the word. He shows that the word *ark* and *bark* have a common origin in *Ak*, which was an Egyptian sacred container or indeed vessel. In Latin it became *barca*, a royal boat, and eventually fell into common use as an ordinary small boat. The word *Ak*, he points out, not only referred to an inanimate object, but also to an object through which God himself spoke, such as the title of *Akhenaton* or the *vessel of the Aten*.[4]

INDIA AND ISRAEL

Is there really a link between India and Israelite religion and symbols? Let's first take a look at the sacred texts of India, the *Vedas*, meaning *knowledge* (or gnosis), to see if we can ascertain any similarity. These texts of knowledge are split into distinct parts, detailing astrology, astronomy, and ritual practice, and known as the Rigveda, Samaveda, Yajurveda, and Atharvaveda. Each of these is divided into four sections, with the philosophical discussions coming under the title the *Upanishads*.

The Hindu texts of the Vedas are said to be eternal, in that they have existed forever in space. These are similar to the Akashic records, which are said to be part of the greater universe and can only be accessed by adepts, seers, and holy ones, who, it is said, overhear them rather than create them. Those seers who have managed to access the Vedas have passed on their knowledge to others, and so began our process of making the metaphysical into the physical. In fact, this in itself, without any analysis of the texts, reveals a distinct link with the Hebrew *Torah*, which is said to be the word that has existed forever—only to have been written down by the Hebrew scholars in the same fashion and with amazingly similar contents as the Vedas.

Historically, the four sacred Vedas are thought to have been first written down from much more ancient oral traditions in around 1800–800 B.C., placing them before the Hebrew scriptures. In fact, the Vedas are the oldest scriptures still in use as part of a continuing tradition.

The origin of the scriptures is not entirely clear. However it seems to have originated from the Aryan tribes coming into India from Iran. These Aryan tribes brought with them many deities, which became known as the Vedic gods. So who were these gods? Arthur Anthony Macdonnel, in *Vedic Mythology*, states: "The true gods of the Veda are glorified human beings, inspired with human motives, passions, born like men, but are immortal."[5] This is similar to these inwardly mobile Aryan deities, and also resembles them in their actions and duties in other parts of the world, where Aryan influence can be observed. The Scandinavian lighting and storm god *Thor*, for instance, can easily be equated to the Vedic and Aryan *Indra* as one of the popular hammer gods. Donald Mackenzie, in *Indian Myth and Legend*, confirms this: "Indra is the Indian Thor, the angry giant-killer, the god of war and conquest."[6]

The Aryan migration spread deities around the globe and into India especially. These deities were easily combined with pre-existing deities, because of worldwide similarities due to the enlightenment process—which was itself the very catalyst for religions across the globe. But was there then also a link between India, Aryan influence, and the Hebrews? In a scholarly work titled "Is There A Connection Between Ancient Indian And Hebrew Language?" Gene D. Matlock reveals that there is:

> Had you been a cartographer and geographer working for the British East India company in the 17th and 18th centuries, you would have found all over India thousands of Hebrew-like place names with similar meanings in both languages as well.... The similarity of these Indian and Hebrew names certainly traumatised European colonists. Unwilling to admit that the Jews had never sprouted spontaneously in the Arabian desert, or were from outer space as I read recently, but were from the East as the Bible itself tells us, they merely erased these matters from their minds or convinced themselves that they were "coincidences," even though the "coincidences" numbered in the thousands and were peppered over every region of India.[7]

Just how these traumatized people managed to cover up the whole history of India and the Hebrews is still a relatively untold tale. However, Godfrey Higgins released a two-volume work on the very subject titled *Anacalypsis: An Attempt to Draw Aside the Veil of the Saitic Isis; or an Inquiry into the Origins of Languages, Nations and Religions Volume 1*. I wish to quote from this work as some of the earliest evidence of the similarities between the two peoples:

The outlines of the history of the extended empires, which I have here exhibited, would have been more conspicuous had our makers of maps and histories recorded the names of the places as they must have appeared to them. But from their native religious prejudices and necessary ignorance of the nature of history, it seemed to them absurd to believe, that there should be places or persons in the East having exactly the same names as places or persons in the West; and to avoid the feared ridicule of their contemporaries, which in fact in opposition to the plainest evidence, and which they themselves could not entirely resist, that they thought well-founded, they have, as much as possible disguised the names. Thus, that which otherwise they would have called David-pouri, they called Daud-poutr, Solomon, Soleiman; Johnguior, Jahanguior, etc., etc. In the same way, without any wrong intention, they have been induced to secrete the truth, in many cases, from themselves, by hastily adopting the idea that the old Jewish names of places have been given by the modern Saracens or Turks, the erroneousness of which a moment's unprejudiced consideration would have shewn.[8]

So did the Jewish people migrate from the East, via India, as we are told in the Bible? "The Western country [Israel] seems, as much as possible, to have been accommodated by the Eastern." We gain more insight the more we read this fascinating book: "When Mahmud of Gazna, the first Mohammedan conqueror, attacked Lahore, he found it defended by a native Hindoo prince called Daood or David. This single fact is enough to settle the question of the places not being named by Mohamedans."[9]

> ...the natives of Cashmere as well of those of Afghanistan, pretending to be descended from Jews... shew you Temples still standing, built by Solomon, statutes of Noah, and other Jewish Patriarchs.... The traditions of the Afghans tell them, that they are descended from the tribe of Ioudi or Yuda, and in this they are right, for it is the tribe of Joudi [Jew] noticed by Eusebius to have existed before the Son of

Jacob in Western Syria was born, the Joudi of Oude, and from which tribe the Western Jews with Brahmin (Abraham) descended and migrated.[10]

Since the Jews i.e. the Yedu tribes of Lord Krishna left the Dwarka region, the original Sanskrit that they spoke during Lord Krishna's time has undergone considerable change of pronunciation and admixture of words, so what was Sanskrit 5742 years ago is now Hebrew.[11]

Even today, we can still see traces of the truth spoken more than 100 years ago. There is a tribe of Sunni Muslims called Pathans, living today in Pakistan, who number more than 15 million. Their language, according to linguistic scholars, has a remarkable similarity to Hebrew. This is supported by the fact that these Sunnis claim descent from King Saul, and also follow at least 21 specifically Jewish rituals.

Even a language used extensively in the times of Christ, Aramaic, can be traced back to Northern India and Kashmir. In fact, this direct line from the subcontinent of India and Pakistan to the Hebrew nations can be traced further back in time. The Egyptian name for the Hebrew was *Habiru* or *Apiru*, and is a direct descendent of an Indo-Hebrew word meaning *sons of Ophir*. And it was the wood of Ophir that was used to line the Holy of Holies, which was to take to Ark of the Covenant in a direct relationship to the use of wood for the Jagannath festivals we have been discussing. This very name itself gives us an even more profound clue to the origins of the Jews and the creators of our sacred Ark.

Ophir derives from *o-piru*, which means Gate (*o*) of the Sun (*piru*). As *sun* did not always mean the yellow sun in the sky, and with the relationship of *Ophir* also to *Ophite* (*serpent worshippers*), this gives us the meaning that this sun was in fact also the inner sun—the enlightenment, brought about by the Serpent Fire. These people were therefore the people of the gateway to the Sun or the Inner Self. These were the true guardians of the sacred inner wisdom. It was from Ophir that Solomon ordered his cedar Wood for his temple building project. Many scholars claim this to be modern-day Bombay in India. It was a deal struck with the Phoenicians, specifically with the fabled King Hiram (to bring these goods). The Phoenicians not only traded widely between these regions, but were also well-known worshippers of serpents—the inner serpent fire.

Not only did the Indians and their inner serpent fire influence the Phoenicians (and the rest of the world), they also influenced the Hebrews and the Egyptians. It is with these cultures that I was finding the remarkable story of the Ark to be most prominent. It was with these cultures that we could uncover the shining enlightenment. And it was from the culmination of these belief systems that the greatest of all semi-divine deities would emerge, Jesus Christ, born from the womb of one who would be known as the Ark: Mary.

This split tree is located on Glastonbury Tor, and represents the two balanced halves that are required to achieve balance.

CHAPTER 6
ETYMOLOGY OF THE ARK

Now it is time to make a serious study of the word and words surrounding the Ark device to see if there are any additional revelations. I gathered books from across the world, closed the door, and settled down to study. To begin with, I drew on the research of my fellow authors to see what they had discovered. I began with Laurence Gardner and his book on the Freemasons, *The Shadow of Solomon*. As Gardner points out, the term *ark* can be a little confusing, in that it is used for both Noah's Ark and the Ark of the Covenant, as well as the basket in the bulrushes that contained the baby Moses. A hidden secret is *arcane* or an *arcanum*; a place to store records is an *archive*; and something of great age is *archaic*. The word in the Bible for *Ark* is, in Hebrew, *aron*, which is a box or container.[1]

In the Masonic world, *God* is equated to the *Ark* or *Arch*. The *G* we often see in Masonic symbols refers not to God but to the *Grand Architect*. This is also evidenced in the fact that the verb *Acrw* (an origin of *Ark*), meant to *set things in order*, just as God was to bring order from chaos and the architect was to create the ordered temple. In India, the Ark or Argha was depicted as a copper vessel; copper is Cypriot

Brass from *ore*, the root of which is *ord* (*order*). Brass and copper became, in the Bronze Age, a symbol of this order or law.

Next I turned to friend and author Graham Phillips in *The Templars and the Ark of the Covenant*, who points to the Egyptian origins of the word *ark* as a container and vessel.[2] I could not leave out that elegant source of knowledge and late Theosophist, Helena P. Blavatsky, who, in *The Theosophical Glossary*, tells us that the word has Chaldean origins and comes from *Argha*, meaning: "The ark, the womb of Nature; the crescent moon, and a life-saving ship; also a cup for offerings, a vessel used for religious ceremonies."[3]

THE MUNDANE EGG

This ancient term *arg* or *arc* (the *c* and *g* are interchangeable) is often seen to be feminine and creative. It is the container of the created and the creator. From this vessel comes forth goodness, similar to the Grail itself. Because the deity, which resides within this feminine principle, was all things to all men, the Universal Mind, the germ of all living things, then this Ark was also equated with the Mundane Egg. It was a symbol of almost every culture on the earth, and was:

> ...revered both on account of its form and its inner mystery. From the earliest mental conceptions of man, it was known as that which represented most successfully the origin and secret of being. The gradual development of the imperceptible germ within the closed shell; the inward working, without any apparent outward interference of force, which from a latent nothing produced an active something, needing nought save heat; and which, having gradually evolved into a concrete, living creature, broke its shell, appearing to the outward senses of all a self-generated, and self-created being—must have been a standing miracle from the beginning.[4]

The same essence within this magical egg was within or upon the Ark. It was the creative spark, the energy of the very universe itself, or the baraka of the Sufis, as we shall discover.

Presumably, the Mundane Egg became the Mother Goddess, who took on the role of the Ark, bearing the self-created god/king/man or perfect illumination. She would be placed upon the upturned crescent moon (a symbol of the Ark, a boat, and the open shell of an egg). Eventually this image was adopted by the Christians, and Mary became the Goddess on the crescent moon, which itself evolved into the bow of a ship, with Mary clutching the baby Jesus and the upright mast, as if uniting the opposites. She was the mother of the Sun-god, similar to the Egyptian Mother of Ra (*MaRe*). Hence *mare* became a term for water, Mary, and the female horse (believed to have been born on the waves).

THE SHIP OF LIGHT

The Babylonians called the moon good Sin, and the Egyptians called him Thoth. He was the god of wisdom, the god of the Ark who traversed the cosmic sea in the ship of light. The Greeks took this lunar image and gave it to Diana, naming it the *Argha*. Eventually it developed into the wonderful journey of Jason and the Argonauts. This is the journey of life and the planets all magically rolled into one.

The Chaldaeans gave their Ark to a goddess called *Nuah*, and eventually the Hebrews used the name as a replacement for *Utnapishtim*, the original *Noah*, who sailed in the great Ark or womb of the goddess across the rising waters and gave birth to the new civilizations and animals of the globe. In fact, the sails of these arks also contains ymbolic language. To the Egyptians, the hieroglyph for *sail* was the same as the symbol for *spirit* or even *breath*. The wind and the spirit are found to be analogous across the world.

Because these arks were symbolic of new life, and because they were the container or vessel for the creative deity, they also took on the symbol of resurrection. In this way they were utilized by almost every culture on the globe, who included either real or model boats with their burials.

The Ship of Isis, known as the Shining Light, was taken everywhere in Egypt for all to see, and I have often wondered how much the ordinary people of Egypt understood. Even the Celtic version of the great ship was called light. As the navigator of old needed the light of a star, the moon, or the sun to guide his path, so too it seems the light of wisdom was casting a faint glow upon the dark sea before me.

This light was old and widespread. I found in T.W. Rolleston's *Celtic Myths and Legends* incredible drawings of ships from Ireland, Brittany, and Sweden all looking remarkably similar to the Egyptian Solar B'arque with the orb floating above the arc of the bow. This was the sun, seen directly above the ship. These ancient navigators were the originators of our symbols. The people needed to move and follow their herds of animals. They couldn't always do this on the shore. Hunter groups and whole families would have followed the rivers and coastlines in small, but often seaworthy, vessels. In ancient times, the navigator was the magician who could follow the line of the sun and the stars. He was Thoth himself, and hence the mast of the boat would be the masculine upright T within the female crescent moon—the union of the two wise deities that follow or were in union with the sun. This very practical and literal use of the boat, and the concept of the life of the sun, merged with the inner wisdom traditions of the globe, which were all the same, because men are all the same. We are all part of a greater universe that is interconnected in beauty. Mathematically (as well as esoterically), what occurrs in the heavens also occurrs inside our selves at the atomic and sub-atomic levels. These sub-atomic levels gave rise to our own consciousness and so, at all levels, the sun or light energy is the creative spark, but it needs an egg to be fertilized.

This arched portal leads to a better place (the Otherworld).

THE ARK OF THE BULRUSHES

There is also another Ark found in the Bible. This small vessel was created to carry the baby Moses. The story of this basket or boat also reveals hidden wisdom. As written in Exodus:

> And there went a man of the house of Levi, and took to wife a daughter of Levi. And the woman conceived, and bare a son: and when she saw him that he was a goodly child, she hid him three months. And when she could no longer hide him, she took for him an ark of bulrushes, and daubed it with pitch, and put the child therein; and she laid it in the flags by the river's brink. And his sister stood afar off, to wit what would be done to him. And the daughter of Pharaoh came down to wash herself at the river; and her maidens walked along by the river's side; and when she saw the ark among the flags, she sent her maid to fetch it. And when she opened it, she saw the child; and behold, the babe wept. And she had compassion on him, and said, This is one of the Hebrew's children. Then said his sister to Pharaoh's daughter, Shall I go and call to thee a nurse of the Hebrew women, that she may nurse the child for thee? And Pharaoh's daughter said to her, Go. And the maid went and called the child's mother.

Moses was the result of a union between a man and a woman from the house of Levi—which itself was the house of the priests of Israel. This indicates a religious intent; it also reveals something more. It would be the Levites who, in later years, would also be placed in charge of the Ark of the Covenant—and so the Ark comes full circle with the Levites. The Levites also derived their family title from the Leviathan, which could possibly be related to the snake *nome* or tribe of Egypt itself (a very powerful and long-standing pre-Dynastic tribe). It is, of course, with the snake tribes across the globe that the enlightenment process would be found, as I discovered in *The Serpent Grail*, and so it would be no surprise to find similar tales in relation to the Levite clan and Moses. It reveals esoteric depth to the story of Moses:

The true name of the Grand Old Man of Israel who is known to history as Moses will probably never be ascertained. The word Moses, when understood in its esoteric Egyptian sense, means one who has been admitted into the Mystery Schools of Wisdom and— as gone forth to teach the ignorant concerning the will of the gods and the mysteries of life, as these mysteries were explained within the temples of Isis, Osiris, and Serapis. There is much controversy concerning the nationality of Moses. Some assert that he was a Jew, adopted and educated by the ruling house of Egypt; others hold the opinion that he was a full-blooded Egyptian. A few even believe him to be identical with the immortal Hermes, for both these illustrious founders of religious systems received tablets from heaven supposedly written by the finger of God. The stories told concerning Moses, his discovery in the ark of bulrushes by Pharaoh's daughter, his adoption into the royal family of Egypt, and his later revolt against Egyptian autocracy coincide exactly with certain ceremonies through which the candidates of the Egyptian Mysteries passed in their ritualistic wanderings in search of truth and understanding. The analogy can also be traced in the movements of the heavenly bodies.[5]

This is the same Moses who would go on to have the Ark of the Covenant created and who came down from Mount Sinai shining with radiance, and who is often depicted with horns upon his head as an indication of his enlightened state. The Ark that held the baby Moses was daubed with pitch, which is an ingredient used for embalming the dead, and was laid in *suph* or weeds, which in Hebrew means *to perish*. The child was placed within this vessel of death to be drawn out and resurrected, similar to the tales of Osiris, Vishnu, and Lazarus. To explain this concept in a little more depth, I need to just revisit the clues around this biblical character, Lazarus, and closely examine his story.

LAZARUS

It is written in the book of John that "... they took away the stone from the place where the dead was laid. And Jesus lifted up his eyes, and said, Father, I thank thee that thou hast heard me.... And when he had spoken thus, he cried with a loud voice, Lazarus come forth. And he that was dead came forth." Although there are similarities between the resurrection of both Osiris and Lazarus, the names are distinctly different, and appear to not be related. But this assumption is wrong. A closer reading of the words will allow the light to shine.

The ancient Egyptian designation for Osiris was *Asar* or *Azar*. When the Egyptians spoke of their gods, they indicated them with *the*, and so we would have had *the Azar*. This term also meant Lord or God, similar to the Greek word for God, *The-os* or *Theos*. One of the Hebrew terms for *Lord* was *El* and was applied to their many deities, such as *El-Shaddai* or *El-hohim*. When the Hebraic writers included Osiris in their myths, they named him in as *El-Azar*— the Lord Osiris. This, in the later Latin translation, was changed to *El-Azar-us*. This use of the *us* was the way that masculine names ended in the Roman language. In fact, in Arabic, Lazarus is still spelt *El-Azir*, missing the *us*. So we now have *El-Azar-us*, which reduced further into *Lazarus*. In this way the Egyptian myth became the literal truth of the biblical record.

Bethany, where Lazarus was raised, was situated on the summit of a hill overlooking the Dead Sea and the Jordan River. It is also said that the place was known as *Anu*. This struck me as important, as *Anu* or *An* was the Sumerian Shining One who lived on the lofty heights, which was none other than the Otherworld. Lazarus then, was raised from the Otherworld, from within the womb.

The story of Lazarus is connected to the ancient and universal processes of initiation and illumination. Lazarus is Ausar/Azar or Osiris, who is regarded as having the energy of Pluto, which is a planet of immense wealth and sexual symbolism. With Lazarus lying at the gate of the rich man, we have an indication of the pent-up energy lying sick and dying. He is covered in sores, an indication of his need to be risen physically and mentally. Dogs come to lick his sores, which are representatives of Anubis (the dog-headed embalmer of Osiris and guide to the Shaman) and Apuat, the *opener of the way*. Lazarus is both being embalmed and shown the way to the Otherworld. He is being prepared.

In the biblical story, the rich man dies and goes to hell. He is not prepared and does not have the required balance, regardless of how rich he may have been in this world. Lazarus, on the other hand, had been made ready and went to heaven, which is the Otherworld of the superconscious.

That Moses was himself raised from the vessel of death and rebirth is a repetition of this old myth. It is, again, esoteric language of the birth, death, and rebirth ritual. We also have indications of the sacred twin aspect, also found across the globe, with Aaron, a name too close to *Aron* (*Ark* or *ar on, the one or supreme sun*) for comfort. Again, this mirrors Osiris and Set, who sealed Osiris within a magic box, from which Osiris was resurrected. Miriam, the mother, sister, or wife of Moses (in this instance) then becomes Isis, who is responsible for drawing Osiris from the water, just as Miriam is for drawing Moses from the Nile. This device follows through time, and becomes Mary, the wife, mother, and sister of Jesus. We can see this correlation with this extract from *Isis Unveiled* by H.P. Blavatsky:

EGYPTIAN. Litany of our Lady Isis: Virgin.

1. Holy Isis, universal mother - Muth.

2. Mother of Gods - Athyr.

3. Mother of Horus.

4. Virgo generatrix - Neith.

5. Mother-soul of the universe - Anouke.

6. Virgin sacred earth - Isis.

7. Mother of all the virtues - Thmei, with the same qualities.

8. Illustrious Isis, most powerful, merciful, just. (Book of the Dead.)

9. Mirror of Justice and Truth - Thmei.

10. Mysterious mother of the world - Buto (secret wisdom).

11. Sacred Lotus.

12. Sistrum of Gold.

13. Astarte (Syrian), Astaroth (Jewish).

14. Argua of the Moon.

15. Queen of Heaven, and of the universe - Sati.

16. Model of all mothers - Athor.

17. Isis is a Virgin Mother.

ROMAN CATHOLIC. Litany of our Lady of Loretto: Virgin.

1. Holy Isis, universal mother - Muth.
1. Holy Mary, mother of divine grace.
2. Mother of God.
3. Mother of Christ.
4. Virgin of Virgins.
5. Mother of Divine Grace.
6. Virgin most chaste.
7. Mother most pure.
   Mother undefiled.
   Mother inviolate.
   Mother most amiable.
   Mother most admirable.
8. Virgin most powerful.
   Virgin most merciful.
   Virgin most faithful.
9. Mirror of Justice.
10. Seat of Wisdom.
11. Mystical Rose.
12. House of Gold.
13. Morning Star.
14. Ark of the Covenant.
15. Queen of Heaven.
16. Mater Dolorosa.
17. Mary conceived without sin.

Miriam is the Hebrew term for the Greek *Mary* or Latin *Maria*. The term means *beloved*, just as any good Isis ought to be. In fact, Isis is often called the *beloved of Osiris*, where the term *beloved* is *Mery* (*Isis-Meri*).

The resurrection or creation machine we now know to be the Ark must therefore have parallels in other ancient and sacred texts, rituals, fables, and structures. The dimensions of the sarcophagus found within the Great Pyramid mirror those of the Ark of the Covenant and the Ark of Noah in sacred geometrical terms. It was a resurrection machine, it was the womb of the Mother Goddess, and it was the world mountain (or axis mundi). This is why so many links between the Great Pyramid and the Ark have been found by researchers across the globe, because the dimensions and meaning behind the symbolic representations are the same. They represent enlightenment, and therefore connection, through the gateway to the divine mind of God, just as God's presence is also found above the Ark. It could also be pointed out that, through Miriam, the Ark of the Bulrushes linked those of Egypt to those of the Hebrews, and thereby created a thread running from Egypt to the Jews. Israel was supposed to be the new Egypt, the new land of God, the promised land, and the scribes of Israel were going to make absolutely sure everybody knew that.

Once this new land had been formed and the people ensconced, there arose the esoteric wisdom in the Hebrew tongue, written down for mankind. There is hidden wisdom within the pages of these ancient Hebrew texts similar to the wisdom found within the hieroglyphs and rituals of ancient Egypt.

Roman tombs carved into the hillside in Cyprus. Note the sun rising between the pyramid on the horizon. This is the gateway to the Otherword.

KING SOLOMON

The boat, ark, or ship was still being utilized as a vessel for knowledge and wisdom, just as it was in other parts of the world. King Solomon, the wise King of Israel (who may or may not have existed in reality), is said to have wanted to build a great navy, and so Hiram of Tyre aided him: "And king Solomon made a navy of ships in Eziongeber, which is beside Eloth, on the shore of the Red Sea, in the land of Edom. And Hiram sent in the navy his servants, shipmen that had knowledge of the sea, with the servants of Solomon. And they came to Ophir, and fetched from thence gold, four hundred and twenty talents, and brought it to king Solomon."

As historians and biblical scholars have been unable to find King Solomon, Ophir, Tarshish (another place the ships supposedly went to), or any number of other people and locations mentioned in these texts, and as these texts are interspersed with wisdom literature, it is only therefore right and proper that we may actually be receiving a message of esoteric knowledge. The wise king Solomon is requiring a navy of ships, which we know to also represent carriers of the divine wisdom itself. He is not looking for one ship, he is looking for a whole navy, to be the wisest and most powerful king of all. Hiram is another Brahman, similar to Abraham, a holy adept (*Abhiram*), and so can provide the knowledge of the divine for these ships, which must have a *knowledge of the sea*, which is, of course, the Otherworld. These ships of knowledge are sent to Ophir to collect gold, which is a symbol of the true and one light—both the sun in the sky and the sun in the mind—of illumination. This is why gold has such a value across the world, as the metal of the sun. This illumination, knowledge, and wisdom was brought to King Solomon, just as the Lord had promised. These were true riches indeed, and the vessel used to bring them was nothing more than the ship, or ark. Using this wisdom, knowledge, and illumination (and with the aid of the adept, Hiram), King Solomon proceeded to erect the great Temple—which is the body or mind of man, wherein lies the sacred space for the Ark to reside. Only in the mind can this connection to God be truly found. This wisdom literature is seen throughout the texts of the Bible, interspersed between and within prosaic, poetical, and some historical sections. It comes through into the New Testament, in the book of Luke, where the references to ships is also present:

> And it came to pass, that, as the people pressed upon him to hear the
>
> word of God, he stood by the lake of Gennesaret. And saw two ships
>
> standing by the lake: but the fishermen were gone out of them, and
>
> were washing their nets. And he entered into one of the ships, which
>
> was Simon's, and prayed him that he would thrust out a little from the

land. And he sat down, and he taught the people out of the ship.
Now when he had left speaking, he said unto Simon, Launch out into
the deep, and let down your nets for a draught. And Simon answering
said unto him, Master, we have toiled all the night, and have taken
nothing: nevertheless at thy word I will let down the net. And when
they had this done, they inclosed a great multitude of fishes and
their net brake....

In this tale we are given many clues as to the true contents of the Ark.
First, the people are pressing upon Jesus to hear the word of God. It was from
the Ark of the Covenant that the Lord spoke, and now the New Covenant,
Jesus, was to answer the call. He took the old ways (Simon's ship) and went
out. He sat down, as if upon the Mercy Seat of the Ark, and spoke the word of
God, as if it were he between the wings of the Cherubim on the Ark itself.
Once the word (breath) of the Lord had been heard from the ship/Ark, the
adepts (the fishermen) were ready to go into the Otherworld and to bring back
all that was good, whereas during the night (the darkness), they had been unable
to find anything. Only with the light of God, the light of the divine, can we truly
be rewarded with good things. The role of the fisherman was not to collect real
fish from the sea, it was to be like the shaman and to enter the abyss, the
watery underworld where no man could go, and to return with gifts from the
Otherworld. Jesus is as the space between the Cherubim was the voice piece
of God, because we are all Christ and can all access this space. In fact, there
is further evidence of this correlation, when we consider that the four Apostles
of Jesus would later on become the Cherubim themselves, protecting the new
Covenant, as the Cherubim of old protected the Ark. According to Ezekiel 1:27:
"...and there was the likeness of a throne as the appearance of a sapphire
stone...and I saw as the colour of amber (gold) as the appearance of fire around
about...from his loins even upward, and from the appearance of his loins even
downward, I saw as it were the appearance of fire." In Revelations: "And his
feet like unto fine brass, as if they burned in a furnace." And in Ezekiel once
more: "As for their faces...one had the face of a cherub, and the face of a
lion...they also had the face of an ox and the face of an eagle."

In these appearances we find in the Cherubim on either side of the Ark.
Later these four faces are adopted for the Apostles. They were the protectors
of the new faith or the new covenant: Jesus, who would then be symbolically
represented within the Shroud. It is no wonder that I would find the Shroud of
Turin to be of immense importance. It is no wonder that the Ark, either the ship
or the word itself, as *baraka*, would be a thread running through the many
great religions of the globe.

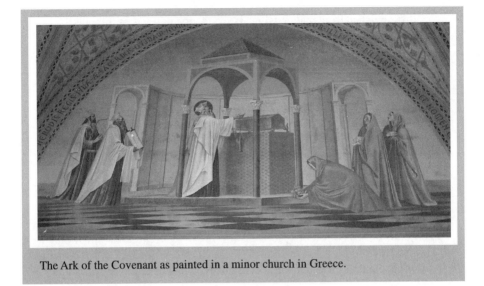

The Ark of the Covenant as painted in a minor church in Greece.

The term *ark*, may, according to some, give us a clue to a more ancient and secret tradition, which is much more widespread than previously thought. It also reveals the creative element. The following is an extract from a book by Anna Kingsford, who was an extraordinary 19th-century medical doctor, editor, and president of the Theosophical Society:

> Ache—A Greek term, signifying beginning, first cause, origin, and said to have been first used by Anaximander (580 B.C.) in the sense of principle (principium) to denote the eternal and infinite basis or substance (sub-stans) of things, and which is therefore not itself a thing, but that from which all things proceed, and of which they all consist, and to which they all return. It is thus the containing, and therefore the feminine, element or mode of Deity, as distinguished from the energising and masculine element or mode; or God the Mother as distinguished from God the Father. It is termed also the fourth dimension, or the within of space, from which the other dimensions proceed; and the noumenon, reality, being, or "thing in itself," which underlies or sub-stands the phenomenon, appearance, existence, or thing perceived. As original, divine, and self-subsistent, and therein

distinguished from matter, which is secondary, derived, and created, Arche denotes the substance alike of divinity and of the soul, the nucleus of the nucleolus in both God and man. The word Ark is derived from it, and like the word Ark, the Hebrew for which is tebah, means any kind of containing vessel. In one of the ancient versions of the Bible-the Coptic—thebi is used instead of tebah, a form which relates it still more closely to Tibet, Thebes, and other places similarly so named apparently as being homes of the Mysteries, and as representing, therefore, the Soul as the dwelling-place of the Spirit, and source of all Divine knowledges. Thus, in its highest application, the ark of Noah denotes the original Divine substance containing in its bosom the "eight persons," God (the Nous) and His seven spirits, of whom all the universe is overspread.

Herein is suggested yet another application of the parable of the Deluge. Thibet, like Thebes, signifies Ark; and if, as long supposed, it was once the sole home of spiritual knowledge in the world and centre whence it was diffused, it may be said of the ancient Thibetan mysteries as of the dwellers in the Ark, "Of them was the whole earth overspread." The facts are noteworthy that Thibet is the highest table-land on the globe, and that the word Ararat is identical with the word Arhat, the Hindu term for the summit of spiritual attainment.[6]

The Ark is the creative principle, the divine spark of God. It is the point of fusion, which makes all things possible. This concept (according to Kingsford) was known across the world and was the highest of principles. This union of opposites, which brings about the neutral point—the in-between, the opposites, neither good nor bad, male nor female, but balance of both, is seen in this extract from *The Secret Doctrine* by H.P. Blavatsky:

...his mysteries can at best be only hinted at in polite ears, never described. Turn to King's Gnostics, "Description of the Plates" (Plate H), and see for yourself what was the primitive Ark of the Covenant, according to the author, who says: "There is a Rabbinical tradition that the cherubim placed over it were represented as male and female, in the act of copulation, in order to express the grand doctrine of the Essence of Form and Matter, the two principles of all things. When the Chaldeans broke into the sanctuary and beheld this most astounding emblem, they naturally enough exclaimed, 'Is this your God, of whom you boast that He is such a lover of purity?'"[7]

The union is given by the Cherubim, as male and female, joining at (and making) the creative point above the Mercy Seat, which is the location or void that God may now speak through. This is all nonsense on the physical level, of course, although it may very well have been manifested as physical or magical items, but it speaks of a much deeper, inner process that we must ourselves go through to reach the divine.

CHAPTER 7

ETYMOLOGY OF BARAKA

Inner wisdom is at the heart of the world's religions, but due to the oppression by organized religion, this mystical element of our psyche has been forced underground. This underground stream has occasionally surfaced throughout time, and we can see from these trickles that the elements of truth were once widespread.

This water of wisdom has given life to the plants that have grown on the surface, becoming great trees that have refused to be chopped down by intolerance or bigotry. These trees are the great mysteries we know today, such as the Holy Grail, Great Pyramid, and Ark of the Covenant. If we grasp these growths firmly and pull hard enough, we can uproot the hidden secrets that first gave life to them. When I did this, I found that the root had a name: *baraka*.

The term *baraka* is a Sufi word, and is the root from which the French *barque* and Italian *barca* derive. In contemporary France, the term *baraka* (of Algerian origin) still has connotations of good luck or blessings, which will come into play as well. It was now time to turn our attention to one of the oldest civilizations, the Egyptians, to try and follow the underground and discover where it's knowledge flourishes.

145

THE EGYPTIAN MYSTICS

The ancient Egyptians believed that everybody was a unique individual. People were said to have two distinct parts: the *ba* and the *ka*. These are not simple concepts. In fact, they have baffled Egyptologists for more than 200 years. But we need to break the words down, for within the names of these two human domains lies the truth of the term *baraka*.

The *ba* is similar to what we would call the personality, or the traits and acts of the man or woman as developed over the course of life. The *ka* is the life-force or soul. It is the first, or number one. This is found to be true in the Indian concept of the word as well. In India, *ka* means *supreme*, and together with *ar* means the *supreme light* or *one light* (*arka*) and *essence*. The Egyptian *ka* came into being when a person was born, and was often depicted as the person's twin or double. This is ancient Egyptian alchemy at play, whereby both the *ka* and *ba* must be united to become one. The twin element has come down to us through the centuries in our Tarot cards, fables, and the twin riders of the Templar symbol.

Because the *ba* was the personality of the unique individual, it was unique. The *ka*, as the life-force (which is the same for everybody) is the creative force running through us. The ka was made by the god Khnum on a potters wheel—therefore it was an energy vortex exactly like the vortices found within the atom. This energy is required for life, and is raised by the efforts of the processes in the mind (similar to the kundalini chakra). The kings or pharaohs had many *kas* due to their immortality. In fact, the goal of every individual was to remain united, or fused, with the energy of the life-force (*ka*) and the personality (*ba*) after death, and to join Ra (the sun) on his journey of re-creation. The individual wanted to return to the creative point, the Alpha and Omega, at the same time and same place. In essence, he wanted to reside in that perfect state. This perfect union comes down to us in the uniting of the three principles require: ba, Ra, and ka—*baraka*.

This is most likely the reason for mummification after death—to keep the body and the symbolic representations of the personality in place for the ka to unite with Ra and reinvigorate life. Should the body rot away, the coffin and *shrouds*, or bands of cloth, would act as the spare body. Now we are beginning to see the value of the Shroud, as the body of Jesus joined his father (Ra), leaving behind his personality infused with the energy of his ka. It is itself a *baraka* or *Ark*.

Ra is the personification of the sun, and his goal is to reunite with his body. This is described as the greatest of mysteries by the ancient Egyptians, because it occurs precisely at midnight. Ra must reunite with his body by midnight to be resurrected as the morning light of the sun. This is personified as the body of Osiris, who is the Underworld personification of the Egyptian one-god. I tend to agree with the writer, Egyptologist, and researcher, Alan Alford, that Egypt was a monotheistic culture, but that different personalities, and aspects of the one god were given different names. In the Underworld state, the ka and ba of Ra was Osiris, and Osiris, once reborn, is Horus, who became Jesus in the Christian mysteries. These great acts of the deities are not just reenactments of the sun, moon, and stellar cycles, they are also deeply held esoteric truths: "The mystical character of these 'books,' in the sense of a codification of an esoteric and secret knowledge...."[1] It is a secret knowledge that has remained hidden for generations.

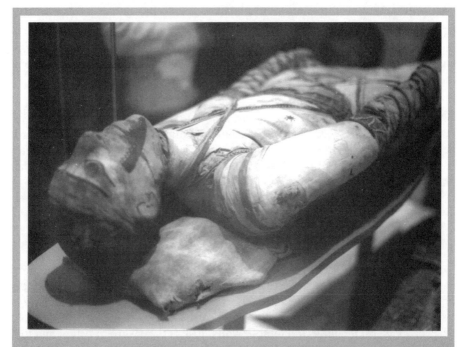

A mummified Egyptian body, as displayed in the British Museum in London. The mummification process preserved the body so that the ba and ka could return and ressurect the person.

Osiris personified the old self or the old creation, and Ra was the new birth, the new man. As with medieval alchemy, creation was made from a mixture of elements and through the process of transformation: "The Egyptians did not believe in creation ex nihilo. On the contrary, the religious texts state clearly that the cosmos was created from pre-existent materials, namely primeval water, matter, and air. Creation involved the transformation of the materials from the state of chaos into a state of order. It involved the construction of a new cosmos from the remains of an old cosmos."[2] This mixture required the reduction of the self (ba and ka) and the reformation in the midnight hour of the parts to create the true trinity of the *ba Ra ka*.

The ancient Egyptians believed that, when the ka left and the body died, it returned to the divine, but remained close to the body. False doors were created in many tombs for the ka (and called ka doors), so that the ka could access the earth at will. The ba could roam the earth, but only when Ra, the sun-god, was in ascendance in the sky. When Ra returned to the underworld, so did the ba. This is the Egyptian explanation for ghosts.

In symbolism, the ka is represented by two upturned arms and the ba by a human-headed bird. Offerings of food were given to the ka, though it was believed that the ka did not eat the food, but instead drew the life-force from the offering.

The union of the *ba Ra ka* is indeed a true blessing, which is where the Arabic *Barakah* and the Hebrew *Barach* take the word: Both are different versions of the Sufi word *baraka*. *Blessing*, of course, is now an English word derived from Old English *bleodsian* or *bletsian*, meaning *to sprinkle with blood*, being derived from the blood rites called *Blots*. This is where we get the phrase, *to blot out ones sins*.

THE BLOOD RITUALS

The Blot rite is Old English or Old Norse, and is followed by some modern pagans. The origins of the rites are supposedly lost, but the term means *sacrifice* or *feast*. The term *Blota* means *to worship* or *to sacrifice*. In the *Hakanor Saga gooa* from *Heimskringla*, Snorri describes how, at these Blots, blood was sprinkled on the altar and temple walls, just as they were in Egypt and the Jewish Temple. In fact, there also appears to be an extrovert use of the term for fusion: "The meaning of the sacrificial feast, as Snorri saw it, is fairy plain. When blood was sprinkled over altars and men and the toasts were drunk, men were symbolically joined with the gods of war and fertility, and with their dead ancestors, sharing their mystical powers. This is a form of communion."[3] This union is found with each other in society and not just with the gods: "When an article of value is passed across the boundary of frith and grasped by alien hands, a fusion of life takes place, which binds men one to another with an obligation of the same character as that of frith himself."[4]

I had a wonderful moment of excitement when I realized that the Ark of the Covenant had to be sprinkled with blood to work properly. It had to have a ka offering. This was the same as the Shroud, which was to be sprinkled with the blood of the Christ, who was seen as an offering by the pagans who converted to Christianity, and who had previously practised the Blot rituals.

The act of the blessing is related to the term *barach* or *baraka*, and means to infuse something with holiness or the divine will (which is also another word for ka). The blessing has always officially been given by the priest of the Catholic Church, and so is the same as the *baraka* of the Sufi's: a blessing or word of will passed from the master to pupil.

In this carving, animals are going to be slaughtered in the Blot ritual.

I could not miss the fact that to the Sufi, the term *baraka* was symbolized by a boat, which became fused with the symbol of the dove. The dove is the Christian and Gnostic symbol of the word or spirit of the Lord, and hence it truly is the baraka. The Cathars took this symbol and, with their own links within Islam, fused the two devices together:

> One important Cathar symbol was the dove. It represented for them then, as it does for us today, the idea of "peace" or, more accurately the more subtle concept of "grace," that state of being in God's love. After the first crusades, when the European Cathars in the entourage of Godfroi de Bouillon established some contact with the Sufi mystics of Islam, the symbolism of the dove sometimes became linked iconographically with the Islamic mystical idea of baraka, which also means "grace" and with the idea that a person can be a "vessel of grace." In some instance, the Cathar dove flying with its wings outstretched was rendered in an artistic motif very similar to the stylised ship meaning baraka in Sufi calligraphy, with the feathers of the dove and the oars of the vessel alike representing the flight and freedom of the soul.[5]

Orthodox Christianity could not allow these ancient esoteric truths to be spread abroad, as the church had built its power based on the literality of the Bible. So they persecuted the Cathars and ultimately burned them *en masse* at their castle in the French town of Montsegur. It appears that these Cathars understood the secret of the Temple of Solomon. They called themselves "the perfect" and they protected the esoteric wisdom of the Ark, for they were the Western version of the Sufi, who protected the ba-ra-ka. Some legends suggest that the Cathars had a great treasure (such as the Holy Grail of Ark of the Covenant), originating from the Temple of Solomon and hidden at Montsegur. I believe that the only vessel that the Cathars were in possession of was the vessel of grace: knowledge.

The triple nature of this incredible name, *baraka*, made me wonder about the various other triple names of God and State. Israel, for instance could be broken into Is (Isis), Ra (the sun god), and El (Lord). Akhenaten worshipped one god, but this one god, Aten, was also called Ra Amun Horus. Even the modern Freemasons worship the triple deity of Jabulon, which is Jah (Jehovah), Bul (Bel or Baal), and On (the sun god). And then there is also the famed

Solomon, which could easily be reduced to Sol Om On—all of which are indicative of the sun and the word (breath). And, of course, I could not forget the Juggernaut: "...the festival or jatra of Ashada ShuklaDwadashi, which is for all three deities and involves the car or chariot (ratha) of Jagannath being processed through the streets."

The term *baraka* is an original term for *Ark*, and is thought by many to be derived from the ancient Egyptian *b'arque*. The Sufis have often been said to have origins in Egypt, and so, having some knowledge of Sufism, I embarked on a journey to explore the term, knowing full well that what lay before me was an often contradictory and argumentative subject matter. I spent many hours listening to a Sufi master, and I often recall his methods, which to many would seem offensive, but to me were esoteric teachings. I once asked him where my path lay, and he replied that the only path I had no longer existed. This path was the one behind me, for the path in front had not yet been made. He told me that if I concentrated on my only path I would stumble and fall. I quickly worked out that this was because I would always be looking behind me, while trying to walk forward. There is only the now, which is between yesterday and tomorrow.

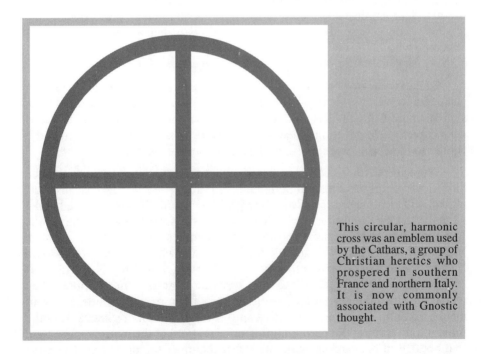

This circular, harmonic cross was an emblem used by the Cathars, a group of Christian heretics who prospered in southern France and northern Italy. It is now commonly associated with Gnostic thought.

SUFISM

Sufism is called the way to the heart, which, of course, means the center. It is the way of the pure, as *Sufi* may derive also from the word *Sata* or *saaf*, meaning *cleanliness* or *pure*. Another view has the word being derived from the Arabic word for wool—*suf*—thus implying the cloak worn by the Sufi. It may also come from the *Ashab al-Suffa* or *Ahl al-Suffa*, meaning *companions of the veranda* or *people of the veranda*. The veranda is the one on the Prophet Muhammad's mosque. These people of the veranda were said to spend their days in prayer and meditation there, near the Prophet. These special adherents were from many lands, including Persia, Ethiopia, Egypt, and even Rome, bringing diverse beliefs and interests with them. There is, however, a more telling term from which the word Sufi may be derived: *Sophia*. This is the concept of wisdom spoken of again and again in esoteric literature, and which has come down to us today through many faiths, even by secret societies such as the Freemasons. This origin of the name was espoused by Abu Raihan Niruni, a Persian mathematician, astronomer, scholar, philosopher, and historian, who lived in the late 10th and early 11th centuries. The fact that a Persian stated this belief relates to something Springett said in his book *Secret Sects of Syria*: "[T]he Sufees are a secret society of Persian mystic philosophers and ascetics, whose original religion may have been that of the Chaldeans or Sabeans, who believed in the unity of God, but adored the hosts of heaven (Tsaba), especially the seven planets, as representing Him."[6]

Whatever the true origin of the word *Sufi*, it cannot easily be summed up in just a few words, due to its mystical mix. Sufism is a mystic tradition of Islam, similar to the Albigensians or Cathars of the Christians, who were known as the *pure ones*. However, no one is sure of the origins of the movement, and it could (and probably does) pre-date Islam in many respects.

Sufism is the mystical side of Islam, and this is why it is so important to the Sufi's to keep this baraka, this continuance, so strong, because the base instincts of man will steal the truth and turn it to profit and gain. This is why the baraka seems so strange to outsiders, because it is the mystical world that is unknowable. To be a true mystic, one must know oneself and one's own unconscious world. Not everybody has the will and the time to do this, whereas others seem to do it by accident. The Sufis see themselves as moving through this world as if they are part of it, and yet all the time knowing there is so much more. They feel at all times the divine presence, and look upon mankind with an eye of mercy. To them, each one of us has a spirit or *Ruh*, which originates from the *Alam*—a creation of the divine light itself. The food of the spirit is more light (but not that of the external sun, rather it is the inner sun of Allah). To mirror and reflect this wisdom of the light is all that can be asked. We should be like the crescent moon, which is a symbol of Islam. The one who truly reflects this light of Allah does not take the light away from Allah, but instead glorifies His name. The one who does this can give divine blessings via the baraka—the baraka is therefore not himself, but the light and wisdom and power of God. One becomes the crescent moon or the Ark.

The Sufi Order is, and has been for centuries, quite widespread. From Africa to India, the order has grown mainly in rural areas. The baraka became known as the chain of transmission, and is often symbolized with a tree known as the *shajara*. We can also find the Sufi doing a meditative and mind-altering dance, which is one of their secrets to the mystical truth, called the *dervish*. This is a beautiful and hypnotic swirling dance to music that can be tremendously fulfilling. The Halveti dervishes do a version known as the Bedevi Topu. In this, the sheikh breaks the turning circle of the dancers and holds hands crossed at the wrists and as they slowly turn they repeat the name of Allah. Eventually the other dervishes form concentric circles around this pair. In this way, it is said that the baraka of the inner reaches the outermost circle. A more beautiful esoteric symbolism is hard to imagine.

Whirling Dervishes perform near Mevlana in Konya, Turkey. The ascentics whirl in circles to an established rhythm to put themselves in a trance, during which they can see and speak directly to God.

SHIP BUILDING

One of the literal reasons that *baraka* has become *barge, b'arque, barca, ark,* and *bark,* is because it is involved in the art of ship building. This kind of ship building, though, involves no floating upon real water; it is more to do with the water of the mind.

To gain enlightenment, one must know one's own mind. To truly do this, one has to understand more than the conscious thoughts that we have. Beneath our gaze is a world of unconscious thoughts that we simply do not know. This world of the unconscious works at incredibly fast speeds—speeds that our conscious mind would have difficulty with. It can also comprehend more input than our conscious mind, and react accordingly. Our unconscious mind can comprehend messages sent to the neural network throughout the body. What if we could somehow become conscious of this unconscious world? We would know so much more, understand the world around us, and appear to be great magicians. We would be as gods, shining.

The process towards this enlightenment involves many energy phenomena, which culminate inside the mind as great blinding lights, similar to those seen during near-death experiences. Near death is the point of access to this altered state, is and can only be gained between cycles—thereby neither being up nor down, nor on or off. In what is known as the hypnagogic state, we are between awake and sleep. One becomes conscious of the unconscious world if one can hold on to this moment. This has been symbolized in beautiful ways by our ancestors. One of these was through water. Water is seen as the portal into the Otherworld because we cannot survive in it; it mirrors our world, and yet is very different. Below the waves we placed our ancient wise ones, such as the Naga serpent race from India, and the Atlanteans. Those who could access this world were fish deities. Jesus is often symbolized as such.

Unless you are the supreme avatar and can walk on water, you need a boat to be able to exist between the worlds, which is the surface of the water. The term for this boat became *baraka,* which evolved into *boat* and *barge.* Although the term *hypnagogic* was not used in ancient times, the act was well known. Here we find the hypnagogic state in relation to the actual Ark of the Covenant:

> 3:1 And the child Samuel ministered unto the LORD before Eli. And
>
> the word of the LORD was precious in those days; there was no
>
> open vision.

3:2 And it came to pass at that time, when Eli was laid down in his place, and his eyes began to wax dim, that he could not see;

3:3 And ere the lamp of God went out in the temple of the LORD, where the ark of God was, and Samuel was laid down to sleep;

3:4 That the LORD called Samuel: and he answered, Here am I.

Notice that "there was no open vision" in those days, because the connection to the divine had been lost. Vision, as also used in Luke 1:22: "And when he came out, he could not speak unto them: and they perceived that he had seen a vision in the temple...." This vision is a vivid apparition, not a dream, and is similar to the terms used in our modern era for effects caused by the hypnagogic. Samuel laid down "where the ark of God was" and was "laid down to sleep" and then the Lord spoke to him. This is the gateway to the divine—between awake and sleep.

Today we see images of Mary the Mother of Jesus standing erect within the upturned crescent moon, boat, or ship. The crescent moon itself becomes a symbol of this state due to its twilight effect, being neither full or invisible, but all the time with the light of the sun. With Noah, we find this semi-divine patriarch saving mankind using this boat—for only those who can exist between worlds can truly know god. This is a very real physical term for *boat* being used in the most profound of esoteric ways: as a symbol for the ability to know the unconscious self. In this way, the term has now come down to us through Sufism almost unchanged, and yet is still being misinterpreted extensively.

In effect, the Sufi use of the word *baraka* means *breath of life* or *essence of life*. It is the spiritual energy infused from and to the universe, through us. Sufis consider themselves to be conduits of this universal energy. However, this is more than mere energy; it is also information and spiritual teaching from the universe itself. This is very similar to the Jewish mystical kabbalistic version of the Torah—the law—just as it is the law that was placed in the Ark of the Covenant by Moses. "The principal root of Kabbalistic tradition is the Torah (the Law), which was created prior to the formation of mankind. When Moses first received the written law he also received certain laws orally. These were not written down but only ever transmitted down through the generations by word of mouth, and then only to the initiated."[7] The Torah is both the word and the law, and it is held to be a verbal messiah. It is the secret held within the Ark.

In some Muslim traditions, if the baraka (or *b'ark-at*) is strong, then when the wise Sufi dies, it will remain with his non-decaying body and may even transmit wisdom to his successors. This is the reason that shrines are so important to the Muslim traditions, because the shrines are seen to be infused with this divine essence from the Almighty Allah, via the Sufi master who is, to all intents and purposes, the Ark. In this way, we can now see why the Kaaba at Mecca is so important. It is a location of the universal baraka energy.

In a way that equals the union of opposites and the coming together of all strengths, so too the family unit entered the religious domain as the family was allowed to own a number of sacred relics. These sacred relics were only thus sacred due to the fact that they were seen to contain the baraka, just as Christian relics held a similar power or latent energy following the crusader invasions of the Muslim lands. It became spiritually important and esoterically aligned for the father to pass down these baraka-filled items—thus continuing the process of baraka—through the ages, both physically and esoterically. To my utter astonishment, these objects are known as *tabarrukat*—a word too close to the *tabot* of Ethiopia.

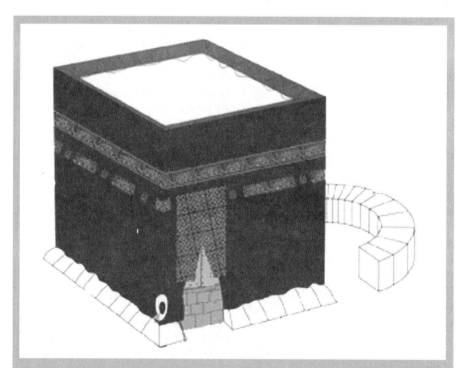

A rendering of the Kaaba, the sacred stone in Mecca that represents the center of the universe. All Muslims pray facing towards the Kaaba, which is believed to be a meteorite (or two) that fell to Earth.

It was not within the sole remit of Christianity to have sacred relics and bits and pieces of dead Saints. The Barkatiyya Sayyids, in fact, had one of the largest collections, among them some hairs from the head of the Prophet Muhammad, and most interestingly a *robe* belonging to the Master Sayyidina Ali—bringing to mind the Shroud, which carries still the essence of Jesus to the devout followers. This robe of Sayyidina Ali is also said to have been worn by a religious progenitor, Shaikh Abdul Qadir Jilani—the founder of the Qudiri Sufi Order. From this man the robe passed as though a family heirloom through the various mystics, in much the same way that the Shroud passed down through the ages.

CHAPTER 8

SECRET SOCIETIES

Thus far in my investigation, I had searched out the truths of the current beliefs in the Ark; I had investigated the roots of the words surrounding it; and I had come to the working hypothesis that the Ark, in all its guises (whether physical or metaphysical), was a symbolic representation of the mind, which carries the inner light. I had seen that there was the tradition of baraka, where the secret knowledge of this inner wisdom was passed on from generation to generation. It was now time to see if this information had used a secret organization to protect the knowledge, as I was being led to believe. My first port of call, simply due to my current knowledge, had to be the Freemasons. Exodus illustrates several elements that are prominent in Freemasonry: "And the Lord spake unto Moses, saying, see I have called by name Bezaleel the son of Uri, the son of Hur, of the tribe of Judah. And I have filled him with the spirit of God in wisdom and in understanding, to devise cunning works, to work in gold, and in silver, and in brass. And in the cutting of stones, to set them, and in carving of timber, to work all manner of workmanship." According to some authors, this element of the craft and wisdom can be found in the esoteric guild of the Freemasons.[1]

The Oxford Word Library says that *worship* is derived from *work-ship*, or namely that *worship* itself is related to the craft of forming a vessel. This craft used an esoteric process called kynning.[2] This *kynning* is, of course, the origin of *cunning*, and originates from words etymologically associated with the wise serpent (*can* is serpent). Jesus and his father, Joseph, were both craft*s*men, as of course were Bezaleel (who built the Ark) and Hiram (who built the Temple). *Craftsman* in Aramaic is *naggar*, and is linked etymologically to *naga*, the serpent deities and wise sages of Kashmir and India, who were also builders, said to have gone abroad to spread their skills. In fact, if we search into the past, what we find is a world of religion and a world of stone built by the ancient masons.

Today, in Royal Arch Freemasonry, there is a distinct reminder of the ancient times. It is a word, or rather a group of words, that has confused many people over the course of time, and one I touched on previously. The phrase or word is said to have been discovered in a vault in the first Temple, when Zerubbabel was preparing the foundations for the second Temple. The phrase is *Jah-Bul-On* and, according to scholars of Masonry, means *I am the Lord, Father of all* or *I am, shall be; Lord in Heaven; Father of all*. None of these is correct. The truth is that this one amalgamated word is no different from Ra-Amen-Horus, the amalgamated god that gave us Akhenaten's Aten. It is *Jah*, which is Jahweh, *Bul*, which is Baal or Bel (the Canaanite solar deity), and *On*, the Egyptian solar deity. All the words refer to light, and are indicative of the truth we seek. They also point to three major cultures: the Hebrews, the Babylonians, and the Egyptians—all great Temple builders. But there is one group that has taken hold of the imagination of mankind and shaken it for more than 700 years after its demise. This group has been implicated in the protection of the Grail, the Ark, and even the secrets of the royal lineage of Jesus and Mary.

THE KNIGHTS TEMPLAR

It is now becoming part of orthodox history that the infamous Knights Templar were somehow linked with (or were the originators of) the modern Freemasons. In fact, the truth is much broader than this, but there certainly are strong connections between the Masons and the Templars.

A group of nine knights, taken from the ruling nobility in the region of France known as Champagne, collected in Jerusalem around A.D. 1118 and formed the Knights Templar. They were pledged to commit their lives and work to a strict code of rules. On the face of it, they were simply ordained to ensure the safe passage of pilgrims to the Holy Land. The knights requested this task of the first King Baldwin of Jerusalem, who refused. But Baldwin soon died, under mysterious circumstances. He was quickly replaced by Baldwin II, who almost immediately granted the Knights this privilege. For the next nine years, the knights excavated beneath the Temple of Solomon in complete secrecy. The Grand Master eventually returned to Europe, supposedly with secrets that were hidden for hundreds of years. Very quickly the Knights achieved a special dispensation from the Pope to allow them to charge interest on loans, resulting in a rapid accumulation of wealth. Soon the great Cathedral building period arrived across Europe, prompted by the architectural secrets discovered by the Crusaders. This knowledge may have come from some of the discoveries made by the Templars, especially when we consider that the man responsible for energizing the building program was none other than Saint Bernard, the same Bernard who gave the Order of the Knights Templar their rules, and who was related by blood to various members. The same Bernard was indicated in the propaganda of the Arthurian and Grail literature.

The Templars grew in wealth and power. Their land holding and banking systems made them one of the most powerful and feared groups in Europe. Nobody could match their international strength. According to George F. Tull in *Traces of the Templars*, they were also "well placed to obtain relics," as they held the respect of nobility and had many strategically placed premises across the Holy Land.

Near Loughton-on-Sea in England there are several Templar connected sites. The Temple here was: "well provided with liturgical books, plate and vessels of silver, silver gilt, ivory and crystal, vestments, frontals and altar cloths. Among the relics kept there were two crosses containing fragments of the True Cross and a relic of the Holy Blood."[3] Tull also tells us of how some of these relics entered Britain: "Sometimes the ships returned with more specialised cargo, as when in 1247 Br. William de Sonnac, Master of the Temple in Jerusalem, sent a distinguished Knight Templar to bring to England and present to King Henry III 'a portion of the Blood of our Lord, which He shed on the Cross for the salvation of the world, enclosed in a handsome crystalline vessel.' The relic was authenticated under seal by the Patriarch of Jerusalem, the bishops, abbots and nobles of the Holy Land."[4]

In Surrey, the Templars held land known as Temple Elfold, with 192 acres of arable land. In 1308 there was mention of a grail and a chalice located there. It is obvious that part of the wealth of the Templars came from the propaganda tools of the medieval reliquary business, proving the Templar's astute business acumen. But in the early 14th century, King Philip of France arranged their downfall, and the supposed secrets and wealth of the Templars disappeared.

At their trials, the Templars were not only accused of worshipping the sacred head, but also the veneration of the serpent. As Andrew Sinclair points out in *The Secret Scroll*, a popular Templar emblem was the foliated staff of Moses, the same staff that turned into a serpent and was emblematic of the serpent religious cult and healing. *The Rosslyn Missal*, written by Irish monks in the 12th century, shows Templar Crosses with great dragons and sun discs. Upon the Secret Scroll itself is the symbol of the 12 tribes of Israel, the breastplate of Aaron (whose serpent staff is said to be in the Ark), with 12 squares (signifying the 12 tribes) surmounted by a serpent. This breastplate was known as the Essene or Shining Light, and was used to control the power of the Ark. As for the serpent, it, as a "...symbol obtained a prominent place in all the ancient initiations and religions. Among the Egyptians, it was s symbol of Divine Wisdom."[5]

On October 13, 1307, King Philip the Fair of France had all the Templar Knights simultaneously arrested. Many were tried as heretics, tortured, and eventually burned at the stake. Some theories suggest that Philip did this to remove his obligation to repay large sums of money he had borrowed from the Templars.

Many people believe that quite a few of the Templars and their secrets escaped from France to Scotland. The dawning of a new age of Freemasonry that emerged in later years is thought to be directly related to the Templars. In the year 1314, King Edward of England invaded Scotland, hoping to bring an end to the border battles. Meeting the Scottish army at Bannockburn, he was surprised by a force of well-trained men fighting for the Scots. The tide of battle turned, and Scotland achieved independence (though only for three years). The standard history has it that these well-trained men who turned the tide against the English army were nothing more than camp followers and servants. Many, though, now believe that these were the famous Knights Templar, who had taken root in Scotland and hidden themselves away from Catholic tyranny. Strangely, immediately after the battle, Robert the Bruce (the new Scottish king) rewarded the Sinclair family with lands near Edinburgh and Pentland. These are the very same lands now associated with hundreds of Templar graves, sites, and symbols (such as Balantrodoch, now called Temple).

An indication of the popular liking for the Templars is shown in the *Peasant's Revolt* of Wylam Tyler in 1381, when a mob marched in protest of oppressive taxes. Strangely, they did not harm the old Templar buildings, but instead turned their attentions on those of the Catholic Church. In one instance, they actually carried things out of a Templar church in London to burn the items in the street, rather than damage the building. It may be that this uprising was a natural incident, or it may be that it was inspired by the actions of a hidden society of the Templars. If it is the case that the Templars inspired this revolt, even though they were not successful, they tried again a hundred years later and forced the Reformation. It was around this period (in the 15th century) that the first records of Scottish and York Masonic meetings appear, and as London was slowly rebuilt by the modern Freemasons, the Templar properties remained unchanged, whereas others were destroyed completely.

LINKS TO SUMERIA

There are several strange links between Sumerian iconography and Templar symbolism. The most obvious Templar image is that of two poor knights seated upon a horse, which is very similar to the idea and concept of the two riders, as seen in ancient Sumeria. This was purely a tactical device in warfare—although there may be some truth in believing that it has origin in the balance hypothesis of the twins, or ba and ka. The famous Templar cross is equally seen in many Sumerian images, normally associated with an upturned crescent moon.

The Templar Seal is an image of two poor knights riding horseback. It is also a popular image in Sumeria.

Another symbol seen in various forms from Sumeria to France is the abraxus, a figure with snakes for legs, a symbol used for gods such as Oannes (Jonah). Not surprisingly, this became the symbol of the Grand Master of the Templar Order. What could this mean? Did the head of the Order of the Templars see himself as the chief of the serpents or chief of serpent wisdom? In conjunction with the fact that the Templars also used the serpent symbol of eternity and immortality (the snake eating its own tail), we also have a serpent secret being held by the very highest of Christian guardians.

The Cross of Lorraine (a symbol used by the Templars before their usual Maltese Cross was adopted) was seen in Sumeria as a symbol for kingship. These influences must have been picked up while the Templars were in the Middle East, and then utilized later on. During the French trials in the early 1300s, the Templar prisoners etched the symbol onto their cell walls.

The Cross of Lorraine was the emblem of heraldry for Rene d'Anjou, said by Charles Peguy to represent the arms of both Christ and Satan and the blood of both.[6] It is also said to incorporate the symbol *phi* or the Golden Ratio of Sacred Geometry. Rene d'Anjou was keenly aware of and interested in many things occult; he once led a search for hermetic texts. The Cross of Lorraine was taken on by Rene, and subsequently by Marie de Guise, the wife of James Stuart V (and mother of Mary Queen of Scots), for its occult symbolism. The Cross of Lorraine is thought to be a sign of secrets; a sign of the Angelic Race, which came down and posited wisdom and the secrets of immortality upon the Royal Bloodline. According to Boyd Rice, it is "a sigil of that Royal Secret, the doctrine of the Forgotten Ones." For this reason, it seems peculiar that in the 1940s Charles de Gaulle made it the official symbol of the French Resistance.

One day I was playing with the Templar Cross, wondering why and how it had evolved. I knew that it had eight points, and all that this entailed (immortality and wisdom), but I wondered about what Fulcanelli believed (that Gothic architecture was a three-dimensional esoteric message). Due to the fact that the Templar mysteries emerged from many places, including Arabic and Muslim influences, Judaic kaballistic beliefs, and Egyptian sacred rites, I was sure that there had to be another message enclosed within this simple shape. Basing my assumption on the three-dimensional aspect, I suddenly realized that if you cut out the cross from a piece of paper and lay it flat, you have a two-dimensional image. If you then take hold of the cross in the very center and lift it, you end up with a perfect pyramid—a symbol of Egyptian and Masonic wisdom, an image considered to be central to immortality. But on some Templar Crosses the edges are angled inwards, to accentuate the eight points. I originally thought that the Great Pyramid of Giza had straight walls, until I looked more closely. The Great Pyramid of Giza holds a secret architecture: its walls bow inwards! Could it be, I wondered, that the Templar Cross also has this hidden symbolism? Was it was fashioned to incorporate the three-dimensional geometry spoken of by Fulcanelli and said to have been spawned into Europe by the Templars and Cistercians? These mysterious brothers in Gnosticism actually understood the meaning behind the symbolism of the pyramids—that it was symbolic in all aspects of the immortality of the serpent.

The Templar Cross is a a three-dimensional representation of the pyramid.

It seems more than possible that the remnants of the Knights Templar developed into the other orders of knights and brotherhoods of western Europe, such as the Knights of Malta or the Knights of Christ. It seems that the Templars had some kind of secret knowledge based on the esoteric wisdom traditions of the ancient Jews, Arabs, and Egyptians. It also seems more than likely that these traditions passed on to the Freemasons.

THE FREEMASONS

The entire history of the Freemasons is based on the building of the Temple. In the end, they have kept the secrets of the Temple within their initiated few, and kept alive for us the truth of the crossover between a literal stone building and the building of our selves. They have kept the spirit of the truth behind this ancient wisdom literature alive within their degrees, and, if what I claim in this book is true, then this is one place that I should find it.

"Of all the objects which constitute the Masonic science of symbolism, the most important, the most cherished, by the Mason, and by far the most significant, is the Temple of Jerusalem. The spiritualising of the Temple is the first, the most prominent and most pervading, of all the symbols of Freemasonry."[7] These are the words of 19th-century Masons. What do we learn from this? In the first place, we learn that Masonry is the science of symbolism. Second, we learn how this symbolism applies to the Temple: we learn that the most important symbol in Masonry is the spiritualizing of the Temple. This does not mean the making real of the physical building of the Temple. No, this means that the Temple is, and was, and will always be seen by Freemasons as a symbolic spiritual device. There is no physical Temple of Solomon, and there never was.

The degrees and statements of the Freemasons seem to back this up. However, the Masons physically manifest their belief (symbolic) systems in the architecture of the Lodge: "Every Masonic lodge is a temple."[8] They build and decorate their Lodges in the form of the Temple, and are therefore both physical and spiritual builders in that they follow the ancient wisdom literature. They encompass the very nature of teaching literature. How do we know this? How do we know that the Masons—or at least those adepts within their ranks—understand the deeper secrets and teachings surrounding the true nature of the Temple of Solomon? Statements such as this prove it: "The traditions and romance of King Solomon's Temple are of great interest to everyone who reads the Bible. They are of transcendent importance to Masons. The Temple is the outstanding symbol of Masonry, and the legendary building of the Temple is the fundamental basis of the Masonic rule and guide for conduct in life."[9]

This statement leads us to believe that to the Masons it is transcendent. This word means *to excel above normal human capabilities*. That is, the Temple hides a deeper meaning for Freemasons than for everybody else, and that meaning is greater than ordinary human reasoning. The truth is that the Temple of Solomon, once built, enables the individual to talk to the divinity. This is the language and terminology utilized to discover yourself and your place in the universe. The Temple is the structure containing the Ark, and the Ark is the vessel of the divine.

"[T]oday the Temple of Solomon is the spiritual home of every Mason."[10] This is as it should be, if you were to follow the teaching centered around the Temple. The home of the spirit should truly be in the building, the temple of the *solo man*. We are left in no doubt about this fact when the infamous Mason Albert Pike states: "To the Master Mason, the Temple of Solomon is truly the symbol of human life." [11] Pike states quite clearly that the Temple is a symbol of human life, nothing more: "...[I]t becomes a fit symbol of human life occupied in the search after Divine Truth, which is nowhere to be found..."[12] Pike reiterates the point that the Temple is about the search for Truth and states quite clearly that as such we shall not find Truth anywhere but in the Temple, which is truly our selves:

> The Freemasons have, at all events, seized with avidity the idea of representing in their symbolic language the interior and spiritual man by a material temple.[13]

> The lodge as a room or hall is an oblong square, which is a half of a perfect square, and which is inside or outside the lower half of a circle. Each lodge meets in the same room, alike furnished, but the lodge working in the Apprentice degree is styled the Ground Floor, the lodge working the Fellow Craft degree is called the Middle Chamber, and the lodge working the Master degree is called the Sanctum Sanctorum, all in King Solomon's Temple.[14]

All of this hidden wisdom came from the Christian incursions into the Holy Land and the nine knights who supposedly created this great brotherhood of warrior monks in union with the pure ones, also known as the Cistercians.

NINE SAINTS

There are tales from Ethiopia of nine saints, emerging from around the 14th century, but accepted by many to have been existent before that period. According to Stuart Munro-Hay in *The Quest for the Ark of the Covenant*, in "The Life of Garima," a 15th-century homily, we are told that following the death of the serpent king Arwe, the nine saints begged for a king in the line of David and were given King Kaleb. This is too close for comfort to another tale, one that has no basis in truth, but rather is symbolic in nature: the tale of the nine Templar Knights who started the order, resulting in their discovery of the ultimate secret beneath the Temple of Solomon. Both the nine saints of Ethiopia and the nine Templars were symbolic guardians of the Ark, which was held within the sanctum sanctorum of the Temple: the mind.

The headquarters of the Knights Templar was in Tomar in Portugal, in this castle, known as the Concento de Cristo.

A SECRET MEETING

Portugal is a beautiful country, with a lot of history and many hidden delights, such as the ruined monastery at Monchique. The Knights of Christ, following centuries of Islamic rule, made this area their own, and were intimately linked with Gnostic influences and the Knights Templar. In fact, after the French trials of 1314, many Templars swelled the ranks of the Knights of Christ. With this in mind, I traveled to Portugal to research the Knights Templar.

I had received a message from my Sufi friend, indicating that if I wanted to learn about the underground stream and the Templars, I should meet Brother Juan at a certain location and at a certain time, and that I need not worry; he knew what I looked like and would make himself known. Now, although all of this sounds like a fiction novel, it is what truly happened to me.

I arrived at the prescribed location and settled down to wait. I took out some reading, as a table lamp lit up the words sufficiently to be able to read. I was no further than the first paragraph when something made me look up. Before me stood an elderly gentleman with a pile of papers under his arm. I had not heard him walk up to me. It was as if he magically manifested before my eyes.

"Mr. Gardiner," he said in a surprising English accent. He held out his hand to greet me. I stood to shake his hand. We chatted for a while about my travels and the wonderful Portuguese countryside, and then I asked his name. He replied that he should be known as Brother Juan, which is John in English, and a very common name, and so I assumed this to be an alias. This is what he told me.

Juan's group, he claimed, was very ancient and had been in operation for many centuries. They were similar in beliefs to what we would know as Gnostics, and they wanted to inform me of something that might help with my researches. They had read one of my previous books (*Gnosis: The Secret of Solomon's Temple Revealed*) and had chatted at some length with friends in a hidden Sufi order. To update those who have not read *Gnosis*, in this book I pointed out that the Knights Templar supposedly visited the Temple of Solomon.

GNOSTIC KNOWLEDGE

The Temple of Solomon is intricately linked with the now infamous Knights Templar. Indeed, it is the reason for their name. The question has always been, why? What was it that the Templars saw in the Temple of Jerusalem that so inspired them? In the years following the return of certain Templars from the Middle East, we have a surge in what is known today as Gothic architecture.

Before this period, churches were mainly small and often made of wood. Suddenly, with the inspiration gathered from the Middle East, the various monastic orders (and generally led by the Templar-linked Cistercians) and Europe were awash with building fever, with more than 80 cathedrals being built between 1128 and 1228 (in France alone). All of these buildings have or had a Gnostic and mystical influence, with hidden symbolism rife within the stonework and giving rise to the great Freemasons. It is an accepted fact that the Templars were instigators in the rise of these Masons, and it is the Masons who hid the profound wisdom in the stones. Another amazing coincidence is that suddenly at this time Europe sees a rise in alchemical, astronomical, medical, and philosophical texts and interests.

The question remains. What did the Templars find in Jerusalem, and were they looking for it? According to John Michell in *The Temple at Jerusalem: A Revelation*: "Legends of the Temple describe it as the instrument of a mystical, priestly science, a form of alchemy by which oppositely charged elements in the earth and atmosphere were brought together and ritually married. The product of their union was a spirit that blessed and sanctified the people of Israel. In the Holy of Holies dwelt the Shekinah, the native goddess of the land of Israel. It was her marriage chamber, entered at certain seasons by the bridegroom." Michell is defining something that can be proven from the mythology and tradition of the Jews and before. He tells us of the traditions revealing the Goddess in the Temple (or Shekinah) and the unity of the ritual marriage. It is a profound statement that gives us insight into the amazing truth of what the Templars were looking for: a link to the enlightenment experience of the Shining Ones. As I have pointed out, the Temple initially was not made for the one God, but for numerous Gods, and anybody who wished to worship their own God was in the right place, regardless. This place was a place of union, a joining of the opposites seen in the enlightenment experience, where the male and female, positive and negative, are joined to bring about the true illumination. It was this mystical experience that was at the heart of the Templar attempted revival. This is what the upsurge in alchemical texts speaks of; this is what the hidden symbolism of the European churches and Cathedrals speak of—especially those similar to the Scottish chapel at Rosslyn.

NUMERICAL SYMBOLISM

This same mystical and hidden symbolism is seen in the numerology implied by the Templars and the Temple of Jerusalem. The Templars were initially nine in number, and were later divided into 72 (72 = 7 + 2 = 9) heads or chapters. Why would this be? To answer this question we have to look at the symbolism of the number nine. It is probably the most important number in mystical numerology, as the mathematical structure of it implies it as the perfect number. For instance, the fact is that nine always reverts back to nine: $9 + 9 = 18$, $1 + 8 = 9$; $9 \times 9 = 81$, $8 + 1 = 9$; $99 + 99 = 198$, $1 + 9 + 8 = 18$, and $1 + 8 = 9$. This scenario carries on again and again. It is also composed of the all-powerful 3×3, or the Triple Triad. It is the end number, the fulfillment, and the completion of all prophecy: the perfect number. It is the number of the angels or watchers, also known as the Shining Ones. It is also linked geometrically, as the number of the circumference of a circle: 360 degrees $= 3 + 6 + 0 = 9$. The four quarters or elements or seasons are also 90 degrees. Symbolically it is seen as a triangle inverted within an upright triangle, and hence also as the infamous eye of god within the pyramid. The Templar Cross is a hidden symbol of the number, with eight points plus the center point, making nine total. The Celts saw this number as significant of their own trinity: the triple goddess who was three time great (similar to the Thrice Great Hermes or Hermes Trismegistus.)

In China, it was the most auspicious of numbers, and is seen remarkably in Feng Shui with the eight exterior squares for the cultivation of the land, and a central or ninth square, which is called God's Acre. This concept of the number nine being paramount to Feng Shui links it to architecture as Feng Shui is about the best place to put a building. This building is, of course, the lower body or nature of man, the place on Earth. The number nine or God's Acre is the other dimension or spiritual side of man. In Feng Shui, nine implies a heavenly power or higher human consciousness in the place that is built.

Now we have some further background on the Templars, the Temple, Gnosis, and the number nine. We know that the Temple of Solomon (in all likelihood) did not exist, and, if it did, then it was used as a basis for esoteric teaching. This knowledge was carried away by the Templars and others into Europe, just as they carried their newfound architectural, medical, and mathematical discoveries. Unfortunately, the Catholic Church could not allow this kind of self-empowerment to continue.

THE ORIGINS OF THE TEMPLARS

Brother Juan told me that one of the secrets of the Templars (and the other orders into which the Templars dissolved) was that they had been in existence for a much longer time than I previously suspected. The real influence on Christianity was from this ancient group via the new name. It turns out that, according to Juan, the Templars were created (or reformed) 2,000 years ago, at the time when the Temple of Solomon was being fabricated. The specific group responsible were the Essene—the very same people who were responsible for writing many of the biblical texts and who left us the Dead Sea Scrolls. Out of this group arose the Kassideans (or Assideans), who were to become known as the Knights of the Temple of Jerusalem. The influence of this group was so profound that even Pythagoras knew of them, and developed his own esoteric school due to their influence.

I pushed Juan for textual evidence, and he showed me a parchment that he claimed was medieval in origin, which had been in the possession of the Templars. He claimed that the Latin scribbles, which included images of serpents and faint Templars crosses, outlined their true origin. Alas, I was neither allowed to take the parchment or photograph it, for fear of profaning the sacred relic. I was told, however, that Brother Juan's sect were warriors (or knights), and that there were always two branches: fighters and priests. These two strands cut across religion and culture, and were in place to protect the secret of the Ark from the profane. As I was deemed to not be profane, and as I would write my knowledge in such a fashion that all might know the truth, I was allowed to know their secrets. These secrets are esoteric, hidden truths, hidden only because people cannot see. We have travelled through these Gnostic beliefs together, and they are here laid out in this book. My strength, I was told, is my independence.

That was the last I heard of Brother Juan, and I have been unable to track down this group, if they exist at all, although my Sufi friend insists they do. I also do not know whether this information was intended to help or hinder, but it made perfect sense to me. Some of this information was new to me, and probably to many others. I spoke to several Templar experts who had not heard of the link either, so I decided to take a look to see if I could uncover the truth. What I discovered was that this information was not new, but had been out in the public domain some time ago, only to be forgotten.

Albert G. Mackay was the secretary-general of the supreme council of the 33 degree for the Southern Jurisdiction Freemasons. He wrote extensively on the origins of the Freemasons, and had attempted to prove their lineage backwards in time to the dawn of man. In one book, *Lexicon of Freemasonry*, he wrote: "The Kassideans or Assideans arose either during the Captivity or soon after the restoration. The Essenians were, however, undoubtedly connected with the Temple (of Solomon) as their origin is derived by the learned Scaliger, with every appearance of truth, from the Kassideans, a fraternity of Jewish devotees, who, in the language of Laurie, had associated together as 'Knights of the Temple of Jerusalem.'"[16] It appears obvious that Mackay was speaking from the same knowledge as Brother Juan, or that Brother Juan had read or knew of *Lexicon of Freemasonry*.

Further investigation into the knowledge of the Freemasonry links revealed that the Kassideans and the Essene supposedly perpetuated the knowledge of Hiram, the builder of the Temple, following the completion of the Temple. As

Hiram is a construct himself of a more subtle Gnostic language, then it appears that the Kassideans continued this hidden language of Gnosticism—such as the Sufi baraka. It was, by tradition, the role of these Knights of the Temple to repair damage and protect the Temple itself. This, when read esoterically, means to preserve the knowledge and Order, which is precisely what many are pointing to in our modern age with the Templars.

But who were these Kassideans, according to orthodox historians? The Hebrew version of the name is *Chasidim/Hasidim*, and Psalm 39:5 uses the term for *men endowed with grace*. I wondered about this, because the concept of grace had cropped up before, as those who were vessels of grace, such as the Ark itself. *Hasidim* (*hasidut*) means *pious*, and so this group were the pious ones (also reminding me of the Cathars, who were pure ones). The origin of the Kassideans can only be traced to roughly 300 B.C. They were maintainers of the Mosaic Law, opposing the Greek ways that were invading the Hebrew nation via the Syrian King Antiochus IV. In this they were similar to the Essene. They were also warring knights in their own right, as 2 Maccabees 14:6, states quite clearly: "They among the Jews that are called Assideans, of whom Judas Maccabeus is captain, nourish wars, and raise seditions, and will not suffer the realm to be in peace."[17]

Amazingly, the revolt led by the Hasmonean family under the leadership of Judas Maccabee succeeded and removed the control of the Greeks. It seems peculiar for these pious ones to involve themselves in war, but it relates to the warrior monks we know as the Templars, who were the first of their kind. However, even from the times of the Temple, the Kassideans saw fit to fight for their beliefs and to protect the buildings, rituals, and doctrines of their Lord. As the Holy Land was later lost to Islam, it makes complete sense that the new Templars would repeat history yet again and attempt a Holy Crusade to regain the land and Temple back from the Muslims. It also makes sense that if there was an Ark or Shroud kept in the Holy Land, then it would have been the responsibility of the Knights of the Temple to spirit it (or them) to safety. When we consider that the Templars were actually the first Knights to enter Constantinople and collect the Shroud of Turin, then we are dealing with a clear focus and knowledge of the location of the Shroud.

The Templars, the warrior monks, were connected in various ways to the Cistercians. This peaceful brotherhood wore the white habit and were called pure, which has led me to consider their similarity to the Essene. Now, with the knowledge that the Kassideans were also a warrior brotherhood, linked with the Essene (who wore white and were known as pure ones), the correlation becomes strong and confirms Brother Juan's story. Both sets of groups revolved around the Temple, and both had similar roles and attire. The only thing that separated them was time.

But then I found a group in Germany, directly relating this link into the orders of knights in medieval Europe. During the 11th to 13th centuries, there arose in Germany a group known as the *Hasidei Ashkenaz*, having been influenced by the mystic Jewish philosopher Saadia ben Joseph, and that died out (as if by pure coincidence) at the same time as the Knights Templar. The group was pious, hardheaded, and determined to see the role of the one God central to life. This period is exactly that of the rise to power of the Templars and the Cistercians, based upon the spread of mystical influence being brought back as a direct result of the incursions into the Holy Land by the Western knights and the spread of Judaism around Europe. When Rabbi Eleazar Rokeah was asked where he had learned such things as the mystical elements of God from, he replied that it had come down to him from an unbroken oral tradition going right back to Moses at Sinai.

Upon discovering this, I was amused, as it was from an Ark that Moses had come, and was an Ark that Moses was to make following his ascent and descent of Mount Sinai. It appeared, on this level at least, that a constant line of protectors of the Ark had emerged from as far back as Moses. They were the pious ones, the ones who fought for God, and they were the pure ones, the ones who worshipped God. Two direct lines: the warriors and the priests. If they had lasted so long in our history, hidden and yet in sight, was it not therefore possible that they still remained?

Occasionally, this group (if it is a continual line), has raised its head above the surface to regain those things for which it has fought, only to then slip away again beneath the surface. It brings to mind that other group found within the Sufis. I already covered the word *baraka*, which is so important to the Sufi ways, and the links between the Kaaba and the Ark, but here, the Sufi also related because it was the priestly mystical element within the greater faith, as the Cistercians were to the Christian faith and the Hasidei to the Jews. The Sufis had already been equated with star and meteorite worship through their origins in the Sabeans, who adored the host of heaven (which were, of course, the stars and planets). Could the Sufis have also been part of a line that stretched right back to Moses and beyond? They certainly claim it privately for themselves. In "The Trail of the Serpent" we have the following statement: "The Sufee doctrine...involves the idea of one universal creed which could be secretly held under any profession of an outward faith."[18] In short, no matter what faith you appeared on the outside, whether Jewish, Muslim, or Christian, beneath, you followed the mystical creeds of this way of the Ark.

Of course, I am now reminded of the tale I began with, the tale of the nine saints of Ethiopia. These same tales, which I had found to have spread across Europe and to have influenced our very way of life through Christianity, Crusades, and the Inquisition, had also spread their ideas into Ethiopia. We now have another reason why it is believed that the Ark resides in Ethiopia: it is the continual line of the baraka.

I then stumbled on the Hasidei Ashkenaz version of the vampire myth (the *estrie*) in their Holy book the *Sefer Hasidim*, by Rabbi Judah. I already knew that *bakka* (related to *baraka* and *ark*) meant *bat*, and was related to the concept of the vampire—the human who was neither alive nor dead. But what I didn't know until I discovered it in the *Sefer Hasidim* was that the Hasidei Ashkenaz had beliefs in them as far back as the 13th century, and said that they were born at twilight, between the worlds. In fact, almost all of the original Jewish traditions of vampires are to be found from within the Hasidei Ashkenaz.

One thing we do know about these mystics is that, to access their deity, they needed to be extremely ascetic. This involved bringing on an altered state of consciousness. The methods of doing this were matched by the Essene, who had similar ascetic practices. The truth is that these efforts would take the mind and place it in a position closer to the hallucinatory realms, and enable the adherent to believe he or she were seeing or conversing with God. There is little wonder that they were mystics and had such strong faith. They were hypnotizing themselves with ritual and other psychological techniques.

The Masonic Lodge in Llanfairfechan, Wales.

In the late 18th century, a mystic by the name of Martines de Pasqually entered the stage, and gave us a new breed of adepts, known as Martinists. Pasqually was a Portugese Jew. He created what many call the most interesting group of the time, and which constituted (under the cover of Freemasonry) one of the last links of the long chain of secret mystical organizations. Their goal was self-proclaimed illuminism—nothing short of connection with the divine. Pasqually named his members *Coen*, an adaptation of the Hebrew name *Cohanim*, which designated the highest sacerdotal caste constituted at Jerusalem *under Solomon*. This would assure the same for Pasqually as it had done for Solomon—strict adherence to the doctrine and defence of the Temple. These Coens (and Cohanim), were said to be direct descendants from Aaron, the brother of Moses, who strangely has a similar name (phonetically) to the Ark (*aron*), and of which the etymology is unknown (but assumed to be of Egyptian origin).

A stained glass image of the Masons of Lichfield Cathedral erecting the superstructure of a gateway to the Otherworld.

The Coens claimed to be heirs and depositories of the secret Jewish tradition of the Ark. Pasqually built up a curious metaphysical and mystic system, borrowed from secret traditions. The system represented a weak but very clear echo of the diverse esoteric doctrines originating from the East.

In essence, Pasqually rose up within the Freemasons as a mystical Jew, and brought together the teachings of what many call diverse beliefs. This was, yet again, the rearing up of the teachings of self-empowerment and enlightenment—in these cases with the kabballah, the Jewish accumulation of ancient mystery rites, including the kundalini. These were the Coens, the descendants of Aaron. But were they therefore protectors of the Ark?

There was something else that Brother Juan had said to me that now rang true. According to Juan's group, the Ark of the Temple disappeared before the second Temple was built, because (quite simply) it had only ever existed in writing. But copies had been made and kept by the various secret societies, who all shared their common heritage. One of these copies, he said, was still held by the Freemasons today, who call it the Substitute Ark. It was written about in the Select Degree of Royal Arch Freemasonry. I found this to be true, and several Freemasons I asked confirmed that copies were still at large within various Lodges. These copies, said Brother Juan, were physical and symbolic representations of that connection to the divine that they were supposed to protect and that the profane simply did not have the eyes to see. I remembered at this point that there had been so many tales of the Ark hidden or taken away to this place or that, and that none of them had never been proven. The Talmud explained that Solomon had caused caves to be dug beneath the Temple to allow the Ark and the Temple treasures to be hidden. These have never been found, and scholars say that this story is a fable. This reveals that the whole story of the Ark is just a fable, and to search for the physical remains is something we do in vain. Or is it?

CHAPTER 9

THE STONE

As Graham Hancock points out in *The Sign and the Seal* (and others do elsewhere), the original arks of Egypt carried gods or solar deities. These deities were made of stone, and were similar to the tablets of testimony that were supposedly placed inside the Ark of the Covenant, and that the Israelites believed embodied their God.[1]

This has led some scholars to conclude that the Ark itself contained a sacred stone. For once, I was to completely agree. But I also see this stone as the Philosopher's Stone. This is the stone or seed that is the source of everything—it is the seed stone that can only be accessed in the very center of our unconscious world. This stone has to become representative of Jesus, who was called *the cornerstone*. The cornerstone, of course, is the stone which unites two walls, binding them together so that they may stand. It is the most important stone in the entire building, and it is used extensively in Freemasonic literature. It is an essence of ourselves that we must have if we are to stand upright.

And so, as ever, I was being led back yet again to the inner experience, the illumination or shining of ages past, the combination of all elements of the divine. One of the earliest references to the Stone is found in the German epic poem *Parzifal*, composed by the Bavarian poet Wolfram von Eschenbach sometime between 1200 and 1216. The story (made more famous by the Cistercians and purposefully written to include the Knights Templar as great heroic knights) includes what is known as the *lapsit exillis*. This name has been translated in many ways; one of these is as a corruption of *lapsit ex caelis*, or the *stone from heaven* (similar to a meteor). The most common interpretation, however, is *lapis elixir*, or the *Philosopher's Stone*. This concept belongs to the alchemists as the *ars totum requirit himnem* or *the art requires the whole man*. This truth of alchemy reveals to us that the art was the work upon the man, and the Stone is the center of the man—the creative seed, which begins and continues the cycles of our existence.

However, one thing I have learned is that there are many layers to religious devices and faith systems. As man manifested (or made real) the inner light in his texts, art, and structures, so too did he adapt and make inward the outward nature of the universe. Things he saw around him, or things he was in awe of, were all parts of the greater one—the same one-god who was also within. In this way, real trees were venerated; real rivers, lakes, and seas were access points to the Otherworld; and real stones became seeds or eggs of the divine work.

Further evidence of this, in an actual literal object and in a real location, can be found with the Kaaba of Islam. In *The Ark of the Covenant*, by Roderick Grierson and Stuart Munro-Hay, we find the description of the worship at the Kaaba. Dressed in white robes, thousands of worshippers kneel in great circles around the immense black cube at the center of the circle. It produces one of the most profound symbolic representations in man's history: the heaven and earth united in this space or void. The proportions match those of the sanctuary in the Temple of Solomon, which contained the Ark, which contained the sacred stones. The Kaaba, as the cube, is the very heart of the universe to Islam, and Muslims must turn towards the center to pray—towards the very heart of the universe itself. They walk around it as stars around the pole, for the Kaaba is the point on which the pole of the seven worlds and the seven heavens are planted—the sacred spot closest to the Divine.[2]

All of this reveals a number of things. First, the Kaaba is the very center of the universe—it is the stone at the center—similar to the rock beneath the Temple in Jerusalem, whereupon stood the Ark (both of Noah and of the Covenant). It is exactly the same as the Philosopher's Stone, which is the source of creation at the center—the same as the dot in the middle of the circle. Second, the proportions of the black cube and the sanctuary of the Ark are the same, indicating the same sacred geometrical meaning. Third, the Kaaba is a real meteorite. Fourth, the circumnavigation around the Kaaba emulates the movement of the stars and heavens around the pole, which is symbolic of the center of existence. The pole is one of the constants in life, and is the macrocosmic dot in the center of the circle. Everything else, from our perspective, revolves around it. We can see this pattern played out with the circumnavigation of the Kaaba creating the outer ring on Earth as it is in the sky. The pole is therefore the heavenly representation of the center stone of creation, as the Kaaba and the Rock on the Mount are on earth. This makes Mecca—the location of the Kaaba—a veritable heaven on Earth. It is a new Jerusalem. Muslims say that the Kaaba and Mecca are as exalted at Jerusalem and the Temple. The wife of the Prophet, Aisha, said that in no place had she seen heaven "closer to earth than Mecca.... While Jewish tradition maintained that the Temple Mount had not been covered by the Flood, and Samaritans believed that their own holy mountain Gerizim had remained above the waves, Muslims in turn asserted that the Flood had not threatened the Kaaba. Although the waters surrounded it, the Kaaba stood above them, reaching to heaven."[3]

One thing I noted immediately was that the stones or locations were above water, just as in the Ark of Noah and the b'arques of Egypt. They were the center of everything, surrounded by the waters that wash away the old and give birth to the new. They were at the pinnacle; they were in the heavens.

This idea of the heaven (or heavens) being at the center of the universe is borne out by the Koran, which explains that there are seven heavens and seven earth's—all of which have a navel represented by a sanctuary, similar to Plato's Atlantis. Reading this as part of the esoteric process, what we have are central points on each level, and heavenly ascent/descent through which we must pass to reach the divine. We are also told in both Jewish and Muslim texts that the throne of God is above the seventh heaven, which is the pole of the universe. The pole or top of the pole is the spine, and the orb or throne at the top is the head—our head. God therefore sits within the head—the true Holy of Holies.

There is also, arguably, another sacred stone or *bayt* (*betyl*) associated with the Kaaba, which was transferred there by the tribe of the Quraysh (Muhammad's tribe) and which relates entirely to our spine concept. The stone is known as *maqam Ibrahim* or the *Station of Abraham*. Abraham was supposed to have stood on this stone, known variously as *Bakka, Bacca,* or even *Makkah* (*Mecca*), as he built the Kaaba at Mecca. This of course also gives us the term *back*, as in backbone or the spine. It appears that Bakka (similar to the bat, vampire, or Station of Abraham) was also Mecca, which is the backbone or ladder up which we must raise ourselves to heaven. It is the point on earth between the worlds. It is also, according to the Bahai faith, the Ark itself: "He is the Almighty, the All-Knowing, the All-Wise! The winds of hatred have encompassed the Ark of Batha (Mecca/Bakka), by reason of that which the hands of the oppressors have wrought."[4]

It has been postulated that Mohammed actually went on his night journey (inward vision) while falling asleep in the empty space around the Kaaba.[5] This is an interesting concept, that the actual space was symbolically important to the early writers. According to the Koran, Mecca was also known as the "first House appointed for men...full of blessings and of guidance for all kinds of beings: In it are signs manifest; the Stations of Abraham; whoever enters it attains security." It was also named in the Psalm 84 in the Bible: "Blessed is the man whose strength is in thee; in whose heart are the ways of them. Who passing through the valley of Baca make it a well; the rain also filleth the pools." We also find reference to it in the Indian Vedas: "Brahma (Abraham) stayed in this abode which is illumined by heavenly light and covered with Divine blessings. It is the place that gives life to the people and is unconquerable."[6]

Although this text does not specifically name Bakka, it does, according to Indian scholars, infer it. Brahma is Abraham, a statement that could sound on the surface quite ridiculous. Let's take a moment to examine this, and in so doing we may also find more Masonic links.

The tablets of stone and the Grail are depicted here as infused with the spirit of God.

ABRAHAM

We discover that Abraham (the Israelite father of mankind) and Hiram (of the Freemasons), are one and the same, and both are based upon serpent worshippers with Indian Naga or serpent deity backgrounds. A grand statement, but one that I am not alone in making. Flavious Josephus said in his *History of the Jews*: "These Jews are derived from the Indian philosophers; they are named by the Indians Calani." Megasthenes, sent to India by Seleucus Nicator, also said that the Jews were called Kalani, and that they were an Indian tribe. Clearchus of Soli said: "The Jews descend from the philosophers of India. The philosophers are called in India Calanians and in Syria Jews. The name of their capital is very difficult to pronounce. It is called Jerusalem." If Abraham, as the father of the Jewish race, is also a legendary figure of India, then who is he? And did he exist at all?

The obvious person for an Indian Abraham is Brahma (*A-Brahma*), who has a consort and sister named Saraisvati. Brahma is the subtle life-force or the spirit, and Saraisvati is the River of Life.[7] Brahma is the essence carried upon the waters as the Ark. This relationship is amazingly similar to the name of the biblical Abraham's wife, Sarai. Abraham is said to have learned his trade in Ur, which is very close to the Persian border, and is also en route to India. The name of Brahma spread throughout this entire area—so much so that the Persians adopted him as one of their deities. So the area where Abraham is said to have learned his priestly trade is the area where the Indian Brahma was being spread and worshipped.

The Chaldeans (residents of Ur) were called Kaul-Deva, and they were a priestly caste living in (among other places) Afghanistan, Kashmir, and Pakistan (*Kaul-Deva* meaning the *Shining Calani*, hence these were enlightened *Shining Ones*, a group going back to ancient Sumeria and outlined in my book *The Shining Ones*).[8]

So Abraham/Brahma learned his trade among the Chaldees, who were a priestly caste related to the Indian subcontinent and were the Shining priesthood or enlightened souls. In this respect, Abraham was simply a title given to the high priest or Lord of the sect of Brahma. But if, as in ancient Egypt, he needed to duplicate the life of the gods, then he would have needed a wife/sister. The fact that Saraisvati was both Brahma's consort and sister also relates to the Biblical account of Abraham. In Genesis, Abraham discusses the relationship: "But indeed she is truly my sister. She is the daughter of my father, but not the daughter of my mother; and she became my wife."

This same pattern of hidden Gnosis would later become part of the Mary/Jesus myth. The complex twists and turns that modern writers seem to have to create to explain the seemingly peculiar nature of Jesus' relationship with Mary the Mother and Mary Magdalene are really quite remarkable. In fact, the truth is simple.

Sarai is Saraisvati, but she is also Isis, the greatest of Egyptian goddesses. Mary is a duplicate of Isis, who was the consort of Osiris (hence the wife element). She was therefore the mother of Horus the Savior (hence the mother of god). But Horus was Osiris reincarnated, so Isis was also his sister. Mary (the Mother), Mary Magdalene (the lover/consort), and Mary of Bethany (the sister) are really and truly the hidden aspects of a much older Gnostic tradition. The three Marys, are, in reality, three aspects of the one feminine principle—the feminine trinity—something that is also found in ancient Celtic traditions.

Of course, we could find ourselves in trouble, as nowhere does it state that Mary of Bethany was the sister of Jesus. However, it does state that Mary of Bethany was the sister of Lazarus, whom Jesus raised from the dead, or more pertinently, *was* Jesus, raised from the dead. In Egyptian mythology, it was the role of the Son of God and savior, Horus, to raise his father (himself), Osiris, from the dead, and, in a sense, resurrect himself, as Horus was Osiris resurrected. It is a statement for us all—that we all need to be reborn afresh from the chains or this world. But this can only be done by ourselves.

This story is an allegory of the sun god Osiris being reborn. It also gives us the remarkable fact that Mary of Bethany, as the sister of Lazarus, was (in literal and esoteric reality) the sister of Jesus.

As we find that Jesus and Mary were based on a much older Egyptian mythology, which itself stretches back even further in time to ancient Sumeria (and probably Vedic India), we also find that the story of Abraham and Sarai are no different. In the Koran we find that Abraham's father was called Azar (Osiris), and so Abraham was Horus, just as Jesus was Horus. We also discover in the Bible that Lazarus rested in the bosom of Abraham, just as Osiris (as the crippled god) rested in his resurrecting son's arms. It is a continual pattern similar to the baraka.

ABRAHAM'S SONS

It was this Abraham, Brahma, or Osiris who is said to have spawned the Children of Israel. Let's take a look at Abraham's sons and see if we can reveal the hidden serpent lineage or serpent secrets. Abraham's son Ishmael, by Hagar (his maidservant), also had children who lived in India, or Havilah (land of serpents), as it is in Genesis. Both famous sons of Abraham, Ishmael and Isaac, have names that revert back to the worship of the serpent Hindu deity Siva.

Ishmael is *Ish-Maal* in Hebrew, and in Sanskrit *Ish-Mahal* means *Great Siva*. *Isaac* is *Ishaak* in Hebrew, and *Ishakhu* in Sanskrit means *Friend of Siva*. Most startling of all is the very name of Abraham himself, which could mean that Abraham was nothing other than a Naga King or deity—*Ab Ram*—and actually means exalted snake.

HIRAM AND THE TEMPLE

Hiram of Tyre, the son of a Jewish mother and a Phoenician father, is credited with the decoration of the fabled Temple of Solomon. This temple, the Bible informs us, would one day hold the Ark of the Covenant.

In 1 Kings, he was said to have been the "son of a widow of the tribe of Naphtali.... He cast two bronze pillars."

The standard of the Tribe of Naphtali, according to Jewish tradition, is a serpent or basilisk. This could have come from the Jewish sojourn into Egypt, as Jewish tradition states that Naphtali was the brother of Joseph chosen to represent the family to Pharaoh. Hiram is also said to be a son of the Tribe of Dan, and even the Tribe of Dan had an emblem, which was the serpent and the horse. Barbara Walker, in *The Woman's Encyclopaedia of Myths and Secrets*, points out that "Writers of the Old Testament disliked the Danites, whom they called serpents (Genesis 49:17). Nevertheless, they adopted Dani-El or Daniel, a Phoenician god of divination, and transformed him into a Hebrew prophet. His magic powers were like those of the Danites emanating from the Goddess Dana and her sacred serpents.... Daniel was not a personal name but a title, like the Celtic one."[9]

Here we have a distinct conclusion: that Daniel of the Bible is related to the very same Danu or Dana goddess of Celtic Europe and that this goddess is conclusively related to serpents. We also have confirmation that the Jewish people collected their belief systems from those around them. Thus far, as we have gathered, they have melded the beliefs of India, Egypt, and Phoenicia into their own growing system.

According to the book of Chronicles, this son of Dan (Hiram) was a cunning man, imbued with understanding and skilful in the work of gold, silver, brass, stone, and timber. He was also credited with certain tools that could pierce stone. According to 1 Kings, the Temple was prepared in stone before it was brought to the site. It was similar to a ready-made or prefabricated building. It was said that neither hammer nor ax, nor any tool of iron was used in the building. So how was it built?

Moses receives the tablets from God. Note the triangular shape of God where the tablets are contained.

THE SHAMIR

In *Exodus*, Moses is told to build an altar to the Lord without tools, lest he should pollute it, and it seems the same symbolism was utilized here in the building of the Temple. According to Rabbinical teaching, the prefabrication was performed by the *Shamir*, a giant worm or serpent that could cut stones (not dissimilar to Norse and Celtic beliefs where Valhalla and Camelot were built with the fire of the dragon). According to the Islamic accounts of Rashi and Maimonides, the Shamir was a living creature. This is hardly likely, unless we understand this creature to be ourselves. What is more likely is that the idea of the wisdom of the worm (which evolved from the word *orm* for *serpent*) or snake, *Shamir*, was used in the construction of the symbolic Temple of man (a Gnostic belief).

It was fabled that the serpent-linked Nagas escaped their country and took this deep (and seemingly architectural) wisdom abroad. This linking of the esoteric and underlying principles of self-illumination manifested in architectural symbolism eventually gave rise to modern Freemasonry.

Returning to Hiram, we find that the name *Hir-Am* actually means *exalted head of the people* (*Hir = Head* or *exalted*; *Am = people*) and is closely related to *Abraham* (*Ab Hir Am*). However, it also has another and more telling meaning. *Ahi-Ram* actually means *exalted snake*. In either meaning, Hiram was the exalted head or snake, both meanings being paramount to the discovery of the thread of the snake cult and religious underlying beliefs—the mixture or union of the opposites within one's own head.

Hiram was also believed by some (according to David Wood in his book, *Genisis*) to be descended from Cain via Tubal-Cain, who was said to be the only survivor of the superior race after the flood. The race is supposed to be called *Elohim* (*people of the fiery snake*) or the *Shining Ones*, also known as the *serpent people*. This tale is derived from a text known as E or Elohim, from around 750 B.C. and gives rise to the stories of the Dionysiac Architects, themselves also linked with the Freemasons. But let's just take a quick sideline look at these Dionysiac/Dionysian Artificers.

THE DIONYSIAC ARTIFICERS

The Artificers are said by Masonic historians to be the prime originators of their guilds. They were a secretive group or secret society with doctrines (said by Manly P. Hall in *Masonic, Hermetic, Quabbalistic & Rosicrucian Symbolical Philosophy* to be) similar to the Freemasons. They are thought to have been great builders, reminiscent of the idea of the great builders who escaped India.

It was believed this secret society, under Hiram Abiff, built the Temple of Solomon and erected the great brass pillars now known as Boaz and Joachim in Masonry. They were also known as the Roman Collegia, and were said to have wandered around similar to the medieval Masons, building fantastic places, such as the Temple of Diana at Ephesus.

The Collegia influenced Islamic building efforts, which were later to become a turning point in European architecture after the Crusades, possibly through the Collegia's influence over the Templars.

The Collegia are thought to have been known before the Romans in Greece, and were said to have worshipped Bacchus. Some even believe that Jesus, when he mentions that he will rebuild the Temple, is pointing out that he too is of the Collegia. Considering the Masonic fascination with the Druids, there is little wonder that William Stukely believed them to have been the builders of Stonehenge and other ancient monuments. Many Masonic writers love to associate themselves with the Druids and (according to George Oliver in *Signs and Symbols*) claim that they "had a high veneration for the Serpent. Their great god Hu, was typified by that reptile."

If it is true that the Dionysiac Architects and the Bacchus/Dionysius-worshipping Greek and Roman Collegia were among the originators of the Freemasons, then it is highly likely that they were linked also with the serpent-worshipping Druids also known as Adders (from the original *nadder*, similar to *naga*). They were all a later showing of the worldwide serpent cult—the same as those in India, Egypt, and elsewhere who all had fantastic building skills. We can still see a remnant of this great architectural and secretive cult in the Masons. As George Oliver points out, "The Serpent is universally esteemed a legitimate symbol of Freemasonry." Freemasonry and its origin are linked to the wisdom of the serpent. This serpent wisdom can be traced into India, the home of Brahma. Abraham and Brahma, not to mention the infamous Hiram of the Freemasons, are all being interwoven like a fine tapestry into the tales and origins of our great world religions. They all have links as deities and are all involved in the special places associated with enlightenment.

The Veda claims that the abode of Brahma "is illumined by heavenly light." But how does this relate? Apart from the obvious fact that this light is, in reality, the illuminated self. I wanted to find other connections to the word *Bakka*. Maureen Wesley suggested that Bakhet was a place to which the fleeing Akhenaten was thought to have fled. She directed me to the Al-Ahram Weekly Website (*www.weekly.ahram.org.eg*), an online Egyptian newspaper containing an article by Mursi Saad El-Din. The article explains the contents of a new Arabic book by Saad Abdel-Mottaleb El-Adl, titled *Aknaton: Father of the Prophets*. According to El-Din, in this book, the author "takes on the monumental task—through reading of primary sources and secondary historical sources—of trying to prove that the Egyptian monotheist pharaoh was none other than Abraham." Whatever we may think of the link between Akhenaten and Abraham, El-Din highlights something that is of interest to Bakka. He claims that Akhenaten, having been banished from his newly built city of Akhetaten, headed for Bakhet, "which in the ancient Egyptian language means the land of light. Bakhet, in El-Adl's opinion is Bakka, the form which he argues, the word Mecca is derived."

Whether Akhenaten is Abraham or Moses remains a mystery, but the fact remains that the progenitor of stories of the Israelite escape from the clutches of the Egyptians is seen to have been one that lead them to Bakka—the land of light. In this respect, the Hindu link of Brahma to Abraham makes sense, but so too does the fact that Brahma (Abraham) was said by the Vedas to have stayed in "this abode which is illumined by heavenly light." Mecca (or Bakka) is not only Holy to the Jews, who spoke of it before the Muslims, but it is also Holy to the Brahmins of India. These Brahmin were fully conversant with the inner serpent energy systems.

THE VAMPIRES

What struck me most, however, was the etymological similarity of *bakka* to *baraka* of the Sufis, so I had to take this thread and pull on it a little harder. Amazingly, the term *bakka* in Old Swedish (Old Danish *bakke*) turns out to mean *bat*. This is the animal the Swedes had associated with night (*nattbakke* = *night bat*) and it was the animal that seemed to take to flight at the point of twilight, between the worlds. The bat was then associated with the vampire— the peculiar being that is neither alive nor dead and must drink of the blood of the living, or life-essence, to be full—to take the Blot offering. There is also the etymology of vampire to consider, and of which there is a lot of debate. To many, the word derives from the Slavic *upir*, meaning *witch*, but it also could just as easily have another meaning. In Sir Walter W. Skeat's *English Etymology*, we find that vampire is spelled *vampyre*; and, of course, a *pyre* is spelled *fire*. In this respect, I needed to discover what *vam* meant, and soon found that as *van* or *vam* simply meant *before* (from *avant*). *Vampire*, then could mean *before the fire* or *the fire before*—and *before* means *in front of* or *in preference to*. In fact, it is no different from certain biblical references to the Ark. See this section from Joshua 3:11: "Behold, the ark of the covenant of the Lord of all the earth passeth over before you into Jordan." This, as with many other references to the Ark, has it placed before us. In this instance, it is where the Ark itself manages to divide the waters into two, causing or revealing a duality. The vampires walked the very road that ran between the worlds of this life and the next.

The fire, as we see above the head of Buddha or the Apostles in Acts 2, is nothing more than the symbol of the bindu point of enlightenment—the seventh chakra. This seventh chakra is the place where God is said to converse with us. These vampires were named after their enlightenment symbolism, and as bakke, they were also the bat—the animal of the twilight period.

None of this differs from the Ark, which is between the Cherubim—in the mid-point. We can see evidence that this mid-point between the Cherubim is between the opposites, such as male and female, when we take a look at an extract from the Talmud: "When the Jewish people would go up to Jerusalem during the Festivals, the Keepers of the Sanctuary would roll back the curtain covering the Holy Ark, and would reveal to the Jews who came up to Jerusalem, the cherubs, which were in the form of a male and female, embracing each other."

We also find the following in Numbers 3:25: "And the charge of the sons of Gershon in the tabernacle of the congregation shall be the tabernacle, and the tent, the covering thereof, and the hanging for the door of the tabernacle of the congregation." These two elements to the tabernacle were known as the inner (*mishkan*) and outer (*'ohel*) or the *tabernacle* and the *tent*. The relationship of these two elements to the tabernacle was known as the *hendiadys*, which means *the union of the one thought*. Here we have in the very portable Temple where man and God meet a union of the duality of the outer and inner minds. This is the reason that the tabernacle was known as the tent of meeting, because it was where the opposites united.

In *Searching for the Ark of the Covenant*, Randall Price has also seen the Ark as the place: "where heaven and earth met... Therefore, at this one site on earth, the two spheres of the temporal and the eternal were joined at the Ark." The Ark is, even in this acutely Christian book, seen as the place between the worlds. The Ark, b'arque, baraka, bakka, and Mecca are all the same. They are all articles or places of contact with the divinity. And if that divinity is truly held to be within ourselves, then this Ark is also ourselvesconsi.

BRILLIANCE OF PLACE

This now leads us back to Mecca or Bakka and a peculiar reference to the pre-Islamic times. A tradition recorded by the Islamic historian Wahb ibn Munabbih (circa A.D. 700) claims that both the Black Stone of the Kaaba and the Station of Abraham, as separate stones, were sapphires that had descended from heaven and were placed at the foothills of Abu Qubays. God later took away the brilliance of their illuminating rays and placed them at Mecca. It was believed at this time that both stones were precious and holy, and both were venerated as such, due to their extraordinary illumination. Later on, when the Quraysh tried to rebuild the Kaaba, the people objected, because the sacred edifice was to be demolished. However, as the builders attempted to remove the stones, there was a great lightning strike and the earth moved, as if they were somehow connected (or were the connection points) between heaven and earth. The stones were left in place and later an inscription was discovered, which read: "I am God the Lord of Bakka [Lord of the Land of Light]. I created it on the day that I created heaven and earth and formed the sun and the moon, and I surrounded it with seven pious angels. It will stand while its two mountains stand, a blessing to its people with milk and water." Of course, what we have here are obvious allusions to the very same tablets of stone that Moses supposedly brought down the mountain and placed in the Ark of the Covenant. It is also, yet again, the merging of Abraham with Moses. But there is more. We are told that the Ark would be hidden at Mount Sinai and Mount Nebo, between them, and here in this Islamic tradition we have two stones standing while the two mountains stand. This is the reason that those searching for the literal and physical Ark always struggle when they come across two mountains—because they neglect to understand that these mountains are symbolic, just as the two stones are symbolic.

If the Ark is hidden anywhere, then it, the Israelite copy, would be hidden within the Temple area on Temple Mount, just as the Jewish *Mishna* tells us: "With regard to Moses the Master said: 'After the First Temple was erected, the Tent of Meeting was stored away, its boards, hooks, bars, pillars, and sockets.' Where Rabbi Hisda said in the name of Abimi: 'Beneath the crypts of the Temple.'" Indeed, not just the Ark, but the Tabernacle, the incense altar, pot of manna, tablets, and Aaron's Rod, were all buried within a secret compartment beneath the wood shed on the western edge of the Temple—near to the Holy of Holies. In fact, this wood shed became a 13th station within the Temple. And this is the real secret of the number 13 made infamous by the Last Supper—the disciples being 12 and the 13th being the Christ. This hidden location is within the mind; it is the true Christ within; it is the sun to the 12 zodiacal signs; it is astrotheology at play. No actual physical evidence of any of this has been discovered. There are no artifacts, no remnants, of this supposed truth. What we do know is that the whole thing speaks of dualities and of uniting in oneness; it tells us of great lights and shining and of a gateway to heaven and access to God. It speaks of an internal experience. When the Ark disappeared, when the connection to our own divinity vanished, so too did all the other blessings or vessels of the Temple. When we stopped speaking to God, we stopped everything else, and the Temple was destroyed. This is why Mecca is so important to Islam; this is why they must keep up the constant vigil in the mind of the people, to remember that it is central to their very lives. They must, as the ancient Egyptians did, keep the cycle running.

In this way, Jerusalem, the Great Pyramid of Egypt, Stonehenge, and innumerable other locations around the globe became manifested realities of an internal reality. The Ark was made as a direct symbol of the inner truth. It therefore has all the symbols and seeming truths of the internal connection with the Universal Mind. Mecca is one of those locations and holds the symbolic device, which has lost all its symbolic resonance and become literally true as the gateway to the divine.

In the 11th century, a pilgrim by the name of Ibn Jubayr from Granada visited the Kaaba and the Station of Abraham. He claimed that it was covered in silver and that he could still see the footprints of Abraham. These footprints are the symbol of the fact that we must base ourselves upon this stone. There is more to these footprints than meets the eye, as T.W. Rolleston points out in his book, *The Religion and the Celts*:

> In Egypt the Feet of Osiris formed one of the portions into which his body was cut up, in the well-known myth. They were a symbol of possession or of visitation. 'I have come upon earth', says the Book of the Dead (ch. Xvii), 'and with my two feet have taken possession.

I am Tmu.' Now this symbol of the feet or footprint is very widespread.
It is found in India, as the print of the foot of Buddha, it is found
sculptured on dolmens in Brittany and it occurs in rock-carvings in
Scandinavia. In Ireland it passes for the footprints of St Patrick or St
Columba. Strangest of all, it is found unmistakably in Mexico.

Researchers at Mount Sinai have found a white semi-circle image of the
moon within black stones. But they also found something else: footprints. These
footprints are engraved in the direction leading up the mountain, as if the feet of
God were directing us towards heaven. They were, in fact, leading people
towards the altar of the moon-god Sin and his sacred stone.

The stone of the Kaaba was placed in a box just as the tablets of the law
were placed in the Ark and then in the Inner Sanctum, or the same as the Tabot
of Ethiopia today. This stone was inscribed with the words of God, placed in a
box, and then held within the inner sanctum of Islam—it is no different from the
fables we read in the Bible regarding the Ark of the Covenant—especially
when you consider the etymological links of the word *Bakka* with *Baraka* and
Ark. Indeed, as I have already stated, even the dimensions of the Kaaba match
those of the inner sanctum of the Temple of Solomon. These same dimensions
have also been found across the world in megalithic monuments, and as T.W.
Rolleston points again out in his book *The Religion and the Celts*:

In connection with this subject I may draw attention to the theory of

Mr W C Borlase that the typical design of an Irish dolmen was intended

to represent a ship. In Minorca there are analogous structures, there

popularly called navetas (ships), so distinct is the resemblance. But

he adds, 'long before the caves and navetas of Minorca were known

to me I had formed the opinion that what I have so frequently spoken

of as wedge shape observable so universally in the ground plans of

dolmens was due to an original conception of a ship. From sepuchral

tumuli in Scandinavia we know actual vessels have on several

occasions been disinterred. In cemeteries of the Iron Age, in the

same country, as well as on the more southern Baltic coasts, the ship

was a recognised form of sepulchral enclosure'. If Mr Borlase's view

is correct, we have here a very strong corroboration of the symbolic intention, which I attribute to the solar ship-carving of the Megalithic People. The ship symbol, it may be remarked, can be traced to about 4000 BC in Babylonia, where every deity had his own special ship (that of the god Sin was called the Ship of Light), his image being carried in procession on a litter formed like a ship. Thus is thought by Jastrow to have originated at a time when the sacred cities of Babylonia were situated on the Persian Gulf, and when the religious processions were often carried out by water.

Stones across the world have been laid out using sacred geometry and in the form of ships. None of this should surprise us, of course, as stones have been revered and worshipped across the world for thousands of years as enabling contact with the divinity, especially in the area surrounding Mecca. Long before Islam, the Nabateans of Petra venerated stones, as did the Arabs of Syria.

These links in language and legend are simply remarkable. Even rock carvings of ships were found at a place known as *Backa* (the etymology of which should not escape us) in Sweden. The ship, boat, or b'arque, carved or made of stone, was the center of ritual life. It was the place where ancient man had connection to the Otherworld.

BUILT BY SHAMIR

I want to return to the Shamir that I touched on earlier, for this will open the way to other discoveries. As we saw, the builders of the fabled Temple of Solomon were not allowed (by the command of God) to cut the stones using tools of iron, so we are left with a peculiar state of affairs. Either the Temple was never built and the tools used are symbolic, or it was built using the miraculous Shamir, which was apparently capable of cutting the toughest materials without either friction or heat. It was the stone that splits rocks, and may not be contained in any iron or metal vessel, but instead kept wrapped in a woollen cloth and then in a leaden basket with barley bran. When the Temple was destroyed, the Shamir disappeared.[10]

Hundreds of authors, researchers, and academics from across the world have struggled with this Shamir for centuries. We have had many explanations regarding its true nature, from white powdered gold to alien technology. Nevertheless, there is a simple symbolic answer to the problem of the Shamir, which can only come about when we accept the evidence that the Temple never existed in the first place. The Shamir is the power of the mind, directly from the inner divine, and it is used to truly build the Temple of the wise: us. In this simple esoteric fashion, the Shamir is no iron tool and touches no rock. Instead, we are told that it was the stone that has split rock. The Shamir is the true source stone, seed, or egg, also called the Philosopher's Stone, which resides within each and every one of us. Only by using this tool, the center point in the circle of our own reality, can we indeed begin to build the Temple that is built with no iron tools.

This Shamir was also said to be the size of a barleycorn, but bright like a fragment of a star. It was said to be an eye or a part of the foundation stone that made the universe. It is part of the creative process. It is like the light and presence of God himself—too terrible and yet wonderful to look at—thus revealing the duality and awe of the Gnosis implied. Only those who have truly undergone this illumination process can comprehend the true meaning of these words.

This image, painted on the ceiling of St. Giovanni in Rome, depicts Moses with his tablets of stone and shining horns.

HOLY OIL

It is interesting to note that in *The Ark of the Covenant*, by Roderick Grierson and Stuart Munro-Hay, we find this same duality implied in the meaning behind the Ark: "From the Bible we learn that the great danger of the Ark was that it could bring death as well as life."[11] We also find that the power ascribed to the object was immense, causing the very walls of cities to collapse and enemies to die of disease. Anyone who touched it without the knowledge of the ritual revealed to Moses would soon find themselves dead.[12] This tells us that the enlightened individual (in this case, Moses with his shining horns) was the only one who could evade the dark side or death of the Ark. We are even told how to evade this dark side of the Ark and avoid death using a technique for containing power by using the application of holy oil on the furniture of the Tabernacle, conferring holiness and protecting them from harm. The same anointing was given to Aaron and the priests, so that they were in the same state as the furniture.[13]

We should note here that this equilibrium is only established with the use of holy oil. This oil is the oil of anointing, and gives us the term *krst*, *Christ*, or *chrism*—the anointed. It is another term for Horus, the son of Osiris and Isis, and the perfect shining one or enlightened son of God. Anointing with oil was not just a Jewish tradition; it was a common practice across the whole area, including Egypt. In essence, to be anointed means that one is illuminated and purified, so that standing before the Ark would not bring that almost certain and terrible death. In this case here we have our clue to this illumination: balance of the duality.

Incredibly, the ingredients of holy oil are set out in Exodus: "Moreover the Lord spoke to Moses, saying: 'Also take for yourself quality spices—five hundred shekels of liquid myrrh, half as much sweet-smelling cinnamon, two hundred and fifty shekels of sweet-smelling cane.'" This cane that the Lord prescribes for the holy oil is *kaneh-bosm*, and is translated as *fragrant cane*. However, the final *m* on *bosm* makes the word plural, whereas in the singular, it is *kaneh-bos*, sounding remarkably similar to *cannabis*. In this respect, the holy anointing oil contained not fragrant cane, but fragrant cannabis. Cannabis is a drug that has been used across the world, for thousands of years, to bring on altered states of consciousness and induce trance states. The Chinese, Egyptians, Scythians, Thracians, Hindus, and even the followers of Dionysus all used cannabis.

Is it possible that this holy oil could actually have been a substance that aided the ancients to hear the voice of God? Indeed, the term *Messiah* is another version of *Christ* or *anointed*, and it was not until the kings of Israel were anointed with oil that they were called *Messiah-kings*. Leviticus 21:10 states: "He who is the high priest among his brethren, on whose head the anointing oil was poured...for the consecration of the anointing oil of his God is upon him." So, according to law and tradition (and beginning with Moses), the one with God's anointing is known as the messiah—such as the messiah King David. However, there was a slight gap in the use of this holy oil until the new anointed, Christ, emerged from within the written pages of the Gospels. It was Jesus, the new symbolic and balanced Horus or *krst*, who would be the symbol of the process of tapping into the unconscious.

Access to the divine or inner self via the holy oil was deemed to be more important than baptism itself. In the apocryphal Gospel of Philip we find that "the anointing is superior to baptism. For from the anointing we were called 'anointed ones,' not because of the baptism. And Christ also was named because of the anointing, for the Father anointed the son, and the son anointed the apostles, and the apostles anointed us.... He who has been anointed has the All. He has resurrection, the light...." We find in the same section that if one "...receives this unction, this person is no longer a Christian but a Christ." And, in the similarly apocryphal Acts of Thomas, we find confirmation that this oil is derived from an actual plant that has properties of divinity: "...you are the unfolder of the hidden parts. You are the humiliator of stubborn deeds. You are the one who shows the hidden treasures. You are the plant of kindess. Let your power come by this." This oil reveals the hidden treasures, which, to the Gnostics who wrote these words down, simply meant the awareness of the unconscious mind and the freedom this process gives, which they termed resurrection and new life. This is revealed in the Armenian Church, where the holy oil or Muron is believed to have begun at the instigation of St. Gregory the Illuminator. This holy Muron has been in constant use for 1,700 years now, and the Catholics of Armenia combine new mixtures in a cauldron every seven years using the remnants of the previous oil—thus continuing the long line and keeping to the seven tradition implied in the kundalini process, which is itself a method of hallucination.

This use of oil seems to have been entirely related to the inanimate objects in the tabernacle or Temple, which had to be anointed to be pure. Through the narcotic effects of the oil and the balancing out of the mixture, the esoteric trip was complete.

Even the Shroud of Christ is of a dual nature as a death shroud and as part of the resurrection. This duality is implicit, because it is in the very nature of the esoteric principles of these ideals and ideas. The Grail, the Ark, the Shroud—all are concepts of the duality merging back together as one. So far we have found that the Grail (with its link to snake venom) and the Ark (with its link to hallucinogenics) were part and parcel of a much wider physical and psychological process than previously perceived. I stored these thoughts for further research. However, one other drug element was current in my mind: the burning bush.

This statue, erected in the Spanish quarter in Rome, shows Moses with his horns and the 10 Commandments.

THE BURNING BUSH

In *The Moses Legacy* by Graham Phillips, the author makes a strong case for the burning bush of Moses to actually have been a mistranslation of the bush that burns. I shall quote from the book, with Graham's kind permission: "For the early Hebrews' priests, however, the eating of the food that had been imbued with the glory of the Lord, allowed them literally to talk as God."[14] Graham doesn't make the connection here because it was not in his remit, but the food being imbued with the "glory of the Lord" that "allowed them literally to talk as God" simply has to also be some kind of narcotic. But, we move on: "When we examine how this practice appears to have originated we discover an intriguing possibility to explain how Moses first discovered God. The ancient Edomites appear to have used a sacred fruit that grew on Jebel Madhbah to induce visions. Writing of the sect who appear to have been the Edomites, the Greek historian Diodorus Siculus refers to this fruit: 'Being eaten, it has the power to effect fantasy. Their priests will sometimes use the fruit to bring on such fantasy, which they say is the voice of their God.'"[15] Amazingly, these Edomites used a fruit which they called the "voice of their God." This is similar to the anointing of oil, which also allows the user to hear or speak the words of the Lord. Philips links this now to the burning bush:

> Having spent many years researching the use of medicinal plants in the classical world, American botanist Dr Karen Varbles of Brigham Young University, Utah, believes that the plant to which Diodorus refers is a hardy desert shrub called Datura stramonium. Commonly known as the thorn apple, it is a thorny shrub with white, lily-like flowers and a spiny black fruit. The fruit is the hallucinogenic. In fact, it might well have been this variety of bush that was the burning bush in the Exodus story.... So what was the bush originally supposed to have burnt? Perhaps the original story had Moses himself being burnt without being consumed. Indeed, this is exactly what the fruit of the thorn apple does. Apart from being an hallucinogenic, it has a fiery, hot taste and causes sweating and burning sensations throughout the body.[16]

BLAZING THROUGH IRON

However, getting back to the Shamir, I found another interesting point: Shamir must be kept in a Shroud and then in a lead basket with barley bran to hide it among others of its kind, because the Shamir would blaze through iron or bronze. This, amazingly, also related to the Ark, because the Levites—the protectors of the Ark—had to cover the Ark in a blue cloth before moving it, lest the shining radiance destroy them. Only in this state of covering could they show the Ark to the people. This reminds us of the Tabot of the Ethiopians, who (to this day) parade their arks covered in shrouds.

According to the Talmud, Solomon captured the Shamir stone from the hoopoe bird, who, it was said, needed it to survive. This same hoopoe bird (in esoteric traditions) is nothing more than the communication within our own mind—the small voice within the otherwise silence of our mind. In this sense, Solomon was simply finding the Shamir with the aid of his internal dialogue, which needed the Shamir—the internal life, creative principle, and power—to survive. Graham Hancock makes a good point when he says in *The Sign and the Seal*: "The first point that became clear to me was that the Jews as a people had only become conscious of the loss of the Ark—and conscious that this loss was a great mystery—at the time of the building of the Second Temple."[17] This makes perfect sense, if you consider that the Second Temple was built not from memory of the first or Solomon's Temple, but from literary works of esoteric fiction—the Temple of Solomon was never there in the first place and neither was the Ark. Only in this light can Hancock's statement make any sense.

In *Lost Secrets of the Sacred Ark*, Laurence Gardner attempts to prove that the tablet of testimony and law brought down from the mountaintop by Moses were called *Schethiya* (and that, with the Shamir, the two stones were similar to the Urim and Thummim, or light and perfection).[18] In truth, there is a remarkable link here, and this is so because of the esoteric element of the stones. Schethiya is known as the stone of perfection, and the Shamir was indeed the great light. Together, light and perfection would be used to build the nation of Israel and the Temple. The Urim and Thummim were stones, thought to have been used by the Temple priests for understanding the will of God.

THE TETRAGRAMMATON

According to the ancient traditions of Judaism, a small parchment (called the Tetragrammaton) with God's unspoken name inscribed on it was slipped into an opening under the Urim (the male stone) and Thummim (the female stone) stones on the priest's breastplate. The power of the spelling of God's name made the stones glow, and messages were transmitted from God to the Israelites. Only by uniting the male and female stones, before the Ark, could the true and perfect light shine.

Whatever you may think of this—whether literal or symbolic—it would have been a remarkable magic trick. One thing is certainly true: all religion emerged from the dark recesses of ancient magic. Incidentally, I have to point out that this very same breastplate gave its name to the group who departed Jerusalem and headed for Damascus, where they dutifully compiled thousands of fables with esoteric and Gnostic light: the Essene. These Essene saw themselves as the followers of the deity or angel of light himself—Lucifer—and, according to what is known as the *Apocrypha*, Lucifer was cast out of heaven and replaced by Michael and Gabriel. There is an astrotheological significance to this, as both angels of light represented the two tail stars of Ursa Major, with Michael being the head and Gabriel being the cup. And so we come back to the white-robed Essene yet again, as if they were the true guardians of the Ark's secrets.

The esoteric significance of the Urim and Thummim can be found when you realize that they would only work if the High Priest stood before the Ark, between the golden Cherubim. The divine wisdom could only be ascertained from the Ark—where God resides—in balance between the Cherubim and with light (Urim) and perfection (Thummim).

An image of the Ark of the Covenant. Note the upstretched wings of the Cherubim, who stand guard over the Ark and provide balance in all things.

THE WHITE POWDER

Now we must address another stone or tablet used by Laurence Gardner as evidence for his white, powdered-gold substance. It is important that such elements are addressed to discover the inner truth. In the *Lost Secrets of the Sacred Ark*, Laurence Gardner tells us that the artists of the past depicted Moses with the tablets resembling great tombstones. He points out that the Mesopotamian-inscribed tablets actually carry much more information than the Ten Commandments in just a few inches. Abraham apparently inherited the Sumerian Table of Destiny, mentioned in the seven tablets of the Enuma Elish, a creation epic of Sumeria, in around 1900 B.C. and it contained all that man had ever known and would know.[19] Gardner points out that there was no mention of any writing, simply that the tablet contained the information. The reason, of course, is simple. Abraham did not exist as we know him in the Bible texts. If he did, then he is closely linked with Brahma of India. The literal elements of this tale need not apply. We are looking for symbolic elements to the tale of these tablets—and to draw Gardner's link—also to the tablets of Moses. Well, as perfection and light, as knowledge of all that is and is to come, we cannot be talking of anything other than what emerged from within the Essene themselves: Gnosis.

GNOSIS

Gnosis is knowledge. All knowledge, from the divine within us to the secret name of God, is simply your own name! It is the point of contact with the quantum world, which is envisaged again and again as a seed, stone, jewel, or egg. Here, the law, that most important of elements to a post-nomadic culture (and the covenant between the people and God) is inscribed on the seed stone, which is at the center of our minds, which is exactly where the New Testament will inform us the new covenant shall be placed. This law, written on the seed stones, also reveals the secret doctrines of the initiates, as we find in *The Secret Teachings of All Ages* by Manly P. Hall:

> Moses Maimonides, the great Jewish Philosopher of the twelfth
> century, in describing the Tables of the Law written by the finger of
> God, divides all productions into two general orders: products of
> Nature and products of art. God works through Nature and man
> through art, he asserts in his Guide for the Perplexed. Thus the Word
> of the Lord is the hand, or active principle, by which the will of the

Creator is traced upon the face of His creation. The Tannaim, or initiates of the Jewish Mystery School, alone possessed a complete understanding of the significance of the Ten Commandments. These laws are esoterically related to the ten degrees of contemplation constituting the Path of Ecstasy, which winds upward through he four worlds and ends in the effulgence of ain soph.[20]

In the same book we are told that these tablets of the law represent the duality, which must be reunited:

The two tables signify respectively the superior and the inferior worlds - the paternal and the maternal formative principles. In their undivided state they represent the Cosmic Androgyne. The breaking of the tables signifies obscurely the separation of the superior and the inferior spheres and also the division of the sexes. In the religious processionals of the Greeks and Egyptians an ark or ship was carried which contained stone tablets, cones, and vessels of various shapes emblematic of the procreative processes. The Ark of the Israelites - which was patterned after the sacred chests of the Isiac Mysteries - contained three holy objects, each having an important phallic interpretation: the pot of manna, the rod that budded, and the Tablets of the Law - the first, second, and third Principles of the Creative Triad. The manna, the blossoming staff, and the stone tables are also appropriate images respectively of the Qabbalah, the Mishna, and the written law - the spirit, soul, and body of Judaism. When placed in King Solomon's Everlasting House, the Ark of the Covenant contained only the Tablets of the Law. Does this indicate that even at that early date the secret tradition had been lost and the letter of the revelation alone remained?[21]

Another statue of Moses with shining horns and the tablets of the law.

There is also a link to the Ark that Graham Hancock insisted resides in Ethiopia. According to Exodus 35:22, we find a list of items of jewelry given to Moses to provide the gold for the Tabernacle furnishings. The original Semitic word for the armlet, signets, or tablets was *tabba'ats*. This tabba'at was, according to Laurence Gardner in *Lost Secrets of the Sacred Ark*, "previously identified as sappir."[22] This sappir or saphire was a jewel, the same jewel likened to the stone or source of all, and found within oneself. The Kabbalistic term *Sefirot* comes from this Hebrew word for *Sappir* (or sapphire) and loosely means the *radiance of god* or the *shining one*, an allusion to the enlightenment one must achieve to gain mastery over the self. *Sappir* is rendered *sapphirus* in many ancient texts, and, in the Talmud, two sappir stones were placed within the Ark by Moses. But these stones may not have been the modern sapphires. Theophrastus and Pliny described the sapphirus as a stone with golden spots, and may have been indicating the lapis-lazuli or physical Philosopher's Stone, which has elements of pyrite with a golden sheen. The lapis-lazuli was called *chesbet* by the Egyptians, and was obtained from some of the oldest mines in the world, dating from as early as 4000 B.C. It was used to make magical amulets and figurines worn by the Egyptian high priests.

To Jewish mysticism, the true element of the Sefirot is Da'ath: "the secret sphere of knowledge on the cosmic tree."[23] This is the very knowledge believed to be obtainable when in the Otherworld. It is "the omniscient or universal consciousness of God which, properly speaking, is not a Sefirah, but a cognitive presence of the One in each of them."[24]

According to esoteric writer Dion Fortune: "When working with the tree either to call down the greater knowledge of the superhuman universe and its infinite organisation, or to bring our self up the tree from the lower sephirah for spiritual upliftment and higher perspective, all energy must pass through Da'ath on its way into matter or disintegration into the hypertext of the universe."[25] This makes the gifts of the Israelites to Moses for the furnishings, including the Ark, of the Tabernacle symbolic. They are the stones of the Philosophers.

As for *tabba'at*, it is simply too close to the language of the Ethiopian *Ark* or *tabot* for comfort. The true hidden Ark in Ethiopia is linked with the Coptic Egyptian Church, which keeps its Sabaen roots alive, and is esoteric gnosis—again, the Philosopher's Stone. Indeed we have some scholarly backing for this assumption. In *Searching for the Ark of the Covenant* by Randall Price, we have the following:

> When Graham Hancock's book *The Sign and the Seal*, was first released, the press sought Ullendorff [Professor Edward Ullendorff, Chair of Ethiopian Studies in Great Britain] as an expert to give his evaluation of Hancock's theory. In an interview with the Los Angeles Times, Ullendorff, after calling Hancock's book "a sad joke," declared that he had personally seen the object in Axum: "They have a wooden box, but it's empty.... Middle to late medieval construction, when these were fabricated ad hoc." Ulledorff went on to say that the priests and the government perpetuate an aura of mystery around

the object "mostly to maintain the idea that it's a venerated object."

Yet Hancock and Cornuke, as well as other Westerners who have

visited the site, have claimed that no one is permitted to enter the

church and view the Ark.[26]

Of course, this is a revelation to the millions around the globe who now believe that the Ethiopians hold the real and true Ark. It is also true to say that many of the Arks were fabricated to either manifest the metaphysical into the physical world, or as blatant propaganda to attract visitors. Relics have been used in this way from the middle to late medieval period across the world as a method of improving the fiscal position of the religious establishment. There is no reason to believe that this practice was not already ancient at that time. In this case, it was also part and parcel of improving the standing of the royalty through the tales of the *Kebra Nagast*.

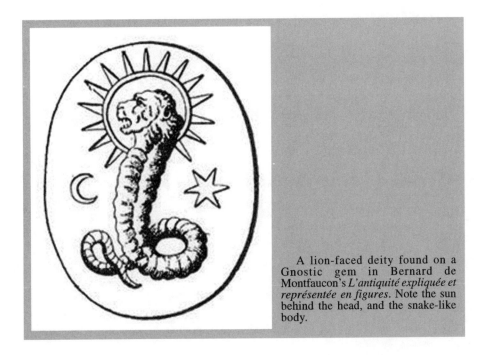

A lion-faced deity found on a Gnostic gem in Bernard de Montfaucon's *L'antiquité expliquée et représentée en figures*. Note the sun behind the head, and the snake-like body.

CHAPTER 10

ETYMOLOGY OF THE SHROUD

As with most things I research, I tend to look sideways to discover what the words of any particular object, person, or location may mean. In this I was to get yet a further shock—for the etymology of the Shroud was to give me many sleepless nights. How much more could this simple tale of the Ark reveal? How many more threads to the seemingly complex nature of the wisdom traditions could I possibly pull on before the whole thing came apart in my hands? I was getting the distinct feeling that I could pull and pull forever. So far I had found the Ark in India, Egypt, Israel, and Mesopotamia.

The relic of the physical Ark was lost to us, with only copies still in existence. But one relic remained: the Shroud. It has been at the heart of controversy, and has been protected by the most powerful people on the planet. It has undergone scientific analysis and it is venerated by at least 1 billion people. But what has it got to do with the Ark of the Covenant? A quick search reveals that the Shroud is referred to as the *Sacred Sendon*, *Sindon*, or *Sidon*, which we are told at the simplest level derives from the Greek and Latin *sindon*, meaning fine sheet, cloth, or winding sheet, specifically of Middle Eastern origin.

Sidony was the name formally used by Roman Catholics for girls born around the date of the Feast of the Winding Sheet. The term is the same as the ancient capital of Phoenicia—*Sidon* or *Saida*—which was pronounced *Zidon* and changed by the Greeks to *Sidon*. In Hebrew, it is *Tsidon*, as the moon God *Sin* is really *Tsin*. In Phoenician, it is *Tzidhon*, meaning *fishing or hunting place*. It is similar to the moon in that it reflects the glory or light of the sun. Of course, this connection to the moon god Sin did not pass me by. Sidon was also the name of Canaan's eldest son in Genesis. But the most interesting form came when I looked into medieval uses of the word *Sindon*. What I discovered was not only astounding, but it matched the very concepts I was developing for my Ark/Shroud/Mary hypothesis.

It was to Moses that the instructions on how to build the Ark of the Covenant were given. As a child, Moses was drawn out of the Ark of the Bulrushes in Egypt. Moses seems to have had a pretty good relationship with God, as we find in Exodus: "And Moses said unto God, Behold, when I come unto the children of Israel, and shall say unto them, The God of your fathers has sent me unto you; and they shall say unto me, What is his name? What shall I say unto them? And God said unto Moses, I am that I am: Thus shalt thou say unto the children of Israel, I am hath sent me unto you." Which is as good as saying, "Mind your own business." However, God is saying to Moses that his name is "I AM." Etymology often reveals secrets, because language holds the beliefs and customs of those who created it firmly within its grasp. And so I looked up the etymology for *AM*, and this is what I found:

Am in Old English was *eom,* in Old Norse *emi,* and in Hittite *esmi,* and meant *to remain.* So God is *he who remains.* In German, *am* becomes *ist,* and in Sanskrit, *as* gave rise to *existence.* However, God in Exodus is still speaking in plural terms, such as "we are," so I wanted to know what the plural version of *am* (*are*) was in Old English, and was amazed to discover that it was *sind/ sindon, sie,* and *earon/aron.* So, the word God used for himself/themselves, *am,* was in fact the same term which came to be used in Old English for the Shroud, and is still with us today in *Sindon/sidon.* However, by the 13th century, *sind/sindon* was dropped as a plural term for *am.* This is the same time that the Shroud was rediscovered by the Knights Templar in Constantinople. Another interesting thing I noted was that *Sin* was the Mesopotamian moon god, as was Thoth of Egypt, and that On was the solar divinity, the sun. It was from atop the Mountain of *Sin*ai that Moses spoke to his *sindon/am* moon/sun God. Also, God was the beginning and the end, the Alpha and Omega, and in these were often written as an A and M—thereby creating the unified point on the page or carving.

There was something else that struck me, something much more interesting, and something that seemed to tie the Shroud and the Ark together in language, regardless of all the other similarities in use, symbolism, and fable. The other word associated with *Am,* and *Sind/Sindon* was *aron*—the word used in the Bible for the Ark of the Covenant. *Aron* twisted and turned throughout time in our language and became *art, archaic, was, to be,* and by the 1800s was almost forgotten. God was not saying *"mind your own business"*; he was revealing that he was the navigator of the Ark.

I decided to look up *Sin* or *Sinite* and found that a Sinite was an inhabitant of Sin near Arka, as found in Genesis 10:17 and Chronicles 1:15. Those who lived in Arka were known as Arkites and were descendants from the Phoenicians or Sidonians. So, even the people—the Sidons or Arkites—were related, just as I was discovering that the word for the Shroud (*Sidon*) was related to the word *Aron* for Ark. The Phoenicians were also the world's greatest navigators, and often visited ports as far away as India, where I had previously found *Arka* to exist.

THE SHROUD

Now it was time to look up the word *shroud*. In Old English, *shroud* came from *scrud*, meaning a *garment* or an *item of clothing*, but this derived from the Old Norse *skrud* or *skruo*, meaning *the sail on a ship*. The word means also *to hide from view*, and so what I seemed to be finding every way I turned was that the Shroud was the Ark that hid God, the navigator from our site, yet also revealed him. It was an enigma, but often these esoteric concepts are. It is however, only by searching deeply into the words and histories that we can begin to see some of the meaning. *To hide from* view, I discovered, could work both ways. It could mean that God wanted to hide himself, or it could also mean *to shelter or protect us*. In this new light the enigma began to clear, and I could see what Exodus may have been really talking about. God was in reality saying, "I am in the Ark with you and I will protect you."

There was yet another level: the element of skin. *Scrud, skrud,* and *skrydda* could all also mean *skin*, and so the Shroud that Jesus left behind was also his skin, just as the snake leaves its skin behind. In the Book of Jasher, we find that a sacred and powerful skin is passed down from Adam to Nimrod. This skin was created by God, and gave the person wearing it great strength. Of course, to take on this skin or Shroud meant taking on the likeness of God—just like the Shroud of Turin.

24 And the garments of skin which God made for Adam and his wife, when they went out of the garden, were given to Cush.

25 For after the death of Adam and his wife, the garments were given to Enoch, the son of Jared, and when Enoch was taken up to God, he gave them to Methuselah, his son.

26 And at the death of Methuselah, Noah took them and brought them to the ark, and they were with him until he went out of the ark.

27 And in their going out, Ham stole those garments from Noah his father, and he took them and hid them from his brothers.

28 And when Ham begat his first born Cush, he gave him the garments in secret, and they were with Cush many days.

29 And Cush also concealed them from his sons and brothers, and when Cush had begotten Nimrod, he gave him those garments through his love for him, and Nimrod grew up, and when he was twenty years old he put on those garments.

30 And Nimrod became strong when he put on the garments, and God gave him might and strength, and he was a mighty hunter in the earth, yea, he was a mighty hunter in the field, and he hunted the animals and he built altars, and he offered upon them the animals before the Lord.

31 And Nimrod strengthened himself, and he rose up from amongst his brethren, and he fought the battles of his brethren against all their enemies round about.

32 And the Lord delivered all the enemies of his brethren in his

hands, and God prospered him from time to time in his battles, and he

reigned upon earth.

The Christ element I already knew, because of *The Serpent Grail*, where I did extensive etymological research into the Jesus/tomb/resurrection ritual hypothesis, and found that it may have been a copy of an ancient serpent-related cult. In Africa, the snake is worshipped for its ability to resurrect itself by sloughing off its own skin and surviving—which it often does in a cave or opening in the earth. It is even pinned or nailed to the tribal tree or a special post as a sacrifice. It is no surprise to find elements of this very ancient serpent worship creeping into Christianity, and finding Jesus also being pinned to a tree and then sloughing off his skin afterwards. It is further supported by the fact that the early Christians were themselves known as serpent worshippers (*Ophites*) and that Christ in the New Testament (Numbers) is said to have been held up like the brazen serpent of Moses in the wilderness: "And the Lord sent fiery serpents among the people, and they bit the people; and much people of Israel died.... And the Lord said unto Moses, Make thee a fiery serpent, and set it upon a pole: and it shall come to pass that every one that is bitten, when he looketh upon it, shall live." In John 3:14, "...Moses lifted up the serpent in the wilderness, even so must the Son of man be lifted up." This links Jesus to Moses, the creator of the Ark and now the progenitor of the crucifixion with his brass snake on a Tau-cross—sealing the final covenant, as Moses had sealed the first. This points to the serpent cult origins. Christ could therefore also be seen as the *sail on the mast*.

THE SHROUD EPHOD USED

In the Old Testament, the garment worn by the High Priest of the Temple was a girdle known as an *ephod*: "It was specifically the badge of the Levite guardians of the Ark of the Covenant, and with its bib folded down over the girdle it formed a small linen apron. In 2 Samuel 6:13-15, King David (the father of King Solomon) is said to have been 'girded with a linen ephod' when he danced before the Ark."[1]

Now, considering for just a moment that Kings David and Solomon

may never have existed, what we have is a symbolic Messianic family,

and a bib or apron being associated with the Levite guardians of the

Ark. But there was also another group, a secretive organiszation called the Essene, who also had a sacred apron, and who we have met on this journey previously. Albert Mackey, the Masonic writer, said in his *History of Freemasonry* that the Essene had a system of degrees and used a symbolic apron, which was the precursor of the ones used by Freemasons and Rosicrucians. This connection between the Essene and the *Ephod* or *apron* is one that carries forward into secret societies, such as the Freemasons.

There is a Masonic tradition that Enoch, inspired by the divine in a vision, built a temple beneath the ground in Jerusalem and dedicated it to God. The temple had seven layers, and each layer held a golden triangle with the secret name of God written upon it. When Enoch died, the location of this Temple was lost. Then, when Solomon decided to build the new Temple according to his father's plans, his workmen uncovered the sealed vaults to Enoch's temple, and so Solomon built his temple upon that very spot. These seven levels of Enoch's temple each contained an arch, and so we have in Freemasonry the Royal Arch Freemasons. It is believed that the seven rooms or layers represent the seven orbits of the planets, but there is little sense in this. In fact, the seven layers represent the veils (or levels) that must be removed (or ascended) to achieve communion with the divinity. Laurence Gardner, in *The Shadow of Solomon*, points out that the seven levels of the Masonic staircase of William Blake (itself a mirror to the Enochian Temple) represented the Great Architect of the Universe, which was consciousness: "The staircase, in its final interpretation, defines seven levels of consciousness, and can be assigned to each of the seven officers of a lodge."[2]

The name of God, secret and written upon the golden triangle on each layer, is the hidden truth about yourself, which must be discovered. Even the golden triangle has hidden meanings, and in reality is the tetractys or triangle of 10 points known by the Pythagoreans. This was simply a triangle with 10 points, and upon being revealed to the initiate as the most sacred of numbers—the 1 and 0—the male and female symbols united within the holy trinity of the triangle—the number of God. These 10 dots are also seen as the 10 laws inscribed by the finger of God on the tablets of stone placed within the Ark by Moses. This triangle reminded me of the painting I spotted in the Louvre in Paris by Nicolas Poussin, titled *Pharaoh's Daughter Finds Baby Moses.*

Poussin's painting, *Pharaoh's Daughter Finds Baby Moses*, is currently located in the Louvre in Paris, France.

POUSSIN'S PAINTING

One day, while visiting the Louvre, I found myself staring at a painting—*Pharaoh's Daughter Finds Baby Moses*—wondering about the pyramid in the background. Then I realized that Poussin had been deeply involved in secret societies, and had Egyptian and Jesuit friends who must have revealed a few secrets to him. I also remembered that Poussin was infamous for hiding things in reverse, so I looked at the pyramid and then followed it down to the water, to the very place that one man dressed in white was pointing—as if the finger of God was inscribing the triangle pyramid itself. There, in mirror image, were the two men who stood upon the shore, but this time encapsulated within the pyramid. The colors (red and white), I already knew from my previous work to be symbolic of the opposites—the male and female, venom and blood, sun and moon. This was Poussin making an esoteric statement not just about the union of opposites, not about the Great Pyramid, but about the golden triangle, the perfection of divinity, the union and balance we must achieve. This was alchemy on canvas, and it was Poussin relating to Moses and the aron-Ark or basket of bulrushes. He was in fact pointing to the truth about the Ark of the Covenant—an internal truth.

It was the goal of the Masons to make physical the metaphysical, just as the Freemason Poussin had done in his art. The Dionysian Artificers, also believed to have been part of the original Freemasons, believed that the use of line and symmetry could affect the psyche of mankind, and thereby lead to the divine. The building, text, or artwork, once complete, would take on oracular qualities, because it enabled connection through raising the spirit and the mind to superconsciousness. It seems the true burial place of the Ark may indeed be within the mind after all, but mirrored by our ancient Freemasons in physical form.

Detail from Poussin's painting in the Louvre illustrating the Gnostic knowledge he learned from the secret societies.

THE EPHOD

In *The Ark of the Covenant* by Roderick Grierson and Stuart Munro-Hay, we find that the ephod was in fact another term for Ark of God, as my suspicions had led me to believe:

> Where the Hebrew speaks of the Ark, the Greek mentions an 'ephod'.
> This is usually understood to be part of the elaborate vestment of
> the high priest. Which of the two words is correct? It seems very
> unlikely that any Hebrew scribe would have written 'Ark of God' in
> place of "ephod", because it creates enormous problems for the
> accepted understanding of the Ark. At the time Saul was speaking
> the Ark had been housed at Kiryath-yearim. If it was also with Saul
> and his troops as they campaigned against the Philistines, there
> must have been more than one of them.[3]

So there was more than one Ark, and the Greeks knew this and replaced the term with ephod—a term also used for Shroud. Just as in modern times, in the first century A.D. there was more than one story of the Shroud, and more than one Ark. The two seem to share several traits. The tradition of more than one Ark seems to have continued in Ethiopia with their many tabots, and it was this aspect that Hancock and others discovered.

The Ark has the same meaning in language and symbolism as the Shroud. They are spoken of in the same breath by the Greeks, and even the tablets of stone were seen symbolically. The only thing that now remained in my investigation was one of the biggest questions of all: Is the Shroud of Turin the real burial shroud of Jesus Christ? The question is massive, and any answer will be extremely controversial.

CHAPTER 11

THE SHROUD

The Shroud of Turin is a very fragile linen cloth. It measures 14.76 feet by 3.28 feet. For centuries this ancient cloth has been venerated and worshipped as an icon and burial shroud of Jesus Christ. The Shroud reveals the faint image of the front and rear of the body of a man, which we have come to recognize as Jesus. There are sepia-colored images that form the body, with reddish marks revealing the locations on the body from where blood appears to have flowed. All this matches perfectly with historical descriptions of a crucifixion.

In 1898, a man by the name of Secondo Pia climbed onto a specially constructed platform near the high altar in the Turin Cathedral. His job was to photograph a length of the Shroud, a job that had previously been thwarted by poor lighting. On that day, however, new electrical lighting was present, and Pia did his best to take a good shot. He returned to his studio with the plates with no expectation other than to see a replication of the faint image. He developed the plates and was shocked to find on the negatives the image come to life. From that day onward the Shroud took on a life of its own, and millions upon millions or people have since believed the Shroud to be an image of Jesus.

By 1902, the images of the Shroud had spread around the world like a raging fire. Professor Yves Delage, an agnostic, was about to fan the flames yet further by telling the French academic circles that the Shroud bore the real image of Christ. Almost at the same time, a biologist by the name of Paul Vignon conducted a scientific analysis on the Shroud, and found that the images did indeed conform with the procedures of an actual crucifixion. Across the world religious fervor broke out, and soon sacred icons and depictions of the face of Christ were being compared to this unique photographic phenomena. There were, however, doubters, most of whom came (amazingly) from within the church. Ulysse Chevalier and Herbet Thurston both condemned the Shroud as a fake, claiming it to have been the work of a medieval forger. The stage was set for the next 100 years, with heated debate between those who had faith in the image and those who did not. By the 1960s and early 1970s, scientists were beginning to take a deeper look at the Shroud, with pollen samples being taken by criminologist Max Frei. These were used to claim that the Shroud had indeed been in the right location and period for it to be the burial Shroud of Christ.

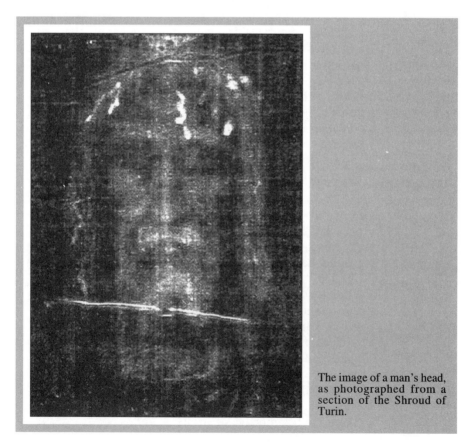

The image of a man's head, as photographed from a section of the Shroud of Turin.

However, in 1977 a conference of scientists was arranged in New Mexico, where it was decided to put the Shroud through more vigorous testing. By 1978 the Shroud was removed from its altar location for the purposes of veneration, and the scientists took this opportunity between the eighth and 12th of October to carry out their intensive study. They formed a group known as STURP (Shroud of Turin Research Project) with 25 scientists and a variety of tests were carried out. The new photography revealed even more accurate images, as now the whole body could be seen. Particles of the red pigment, which appeared to be blood, were also taken and analyzed, revealing that it belonged to the AB blood type. Further testing of this blood in the past few years has revealed the presence of both male and female DNA, which has been put down to contamination of the Shroud, and not an androgynous human. In his book, *Report on the Shroud of Turin*, Dr. John H. Heller had this to say regarding the blood: "Thus far, our positive blood tests had included (1) microspectrophotometric scans of crystals and fibrils, (2) reflectance scans on the shroud, (3) positive hemochromogen tests, (4) positive cyanomethemagoblin tests, (5) positive tests for bile pigments, and (6) characteristic heme porphyri flourescence. Any one of these is proof of the presence of blood, and each is acceptable in a court of law. Taken together, they are irrefutable."[1]

By the end of the 1970s and early 1980s, it seemed to all that this was indeed the image of Christ. However, by 1988 pressure was building to use the new scientific technique of carbon dating. Tiny amounts of the radioactive isotope carbon-14 are absorbed by all living things, and decays at a set rate. By finding out how much carbon-14 any particular object had at the time of its life allows the scientists to know how old it is (by calculating the rate of decay). By the end of the 1980s, carbon-14 dating was believed to be absolute proof of the date of an object.

The Catholic Church finally agreed to the testing, and samples were distributed to the top carbon-14 dating laboratories around the globe. The whole world waited anxiously. If the Shroud was found to be from the first century, then this simply must be Christ's image. If not, then who was this man, how was the image made, and why?

By the autumn of that year the test results were in. The results were announced simultaneously on the 14th of October by the church and the scientists. It appeared that the flax for the linen had been harvested sometime between 1260 and 1390. The world again erupted with the new headlines: forgery! However, within days the carbon-14 testing itself was under scrutiny, as there were found to be too many anomalies. People were involved that should not have been; the laboratories were found to have leaked information; the blind test had not been blind, as it was admitted the weave was easy to recognize and the scientists were a little too overjoyed at their results. Few in the Christian camp took the dating seriously—and it appears now that they had good reason. To add to this, it was then found that all the radiocarbon dating published by the British Museum between 1980 and 1984 had been incorrect— adding to the lack of trust in the scientific establishment. Now the 1988 carbon-14 dating has been proven categorically to be incorrect in most if not all peer-review journals. Not least of these journals was *Thermochimica Acta*, which ran an article by the chemist and fellow of the Los Alamos National Laboratory, stating that the Shroud must in fact be around 2,000 years old, because the samples taken in 1988 were from an area on the Shroud that had been mended in the medieval period.

Further evidence that the Shroud is older than the carbon-14 dating suggests comes from a picture held in the Budapest National Library. The picture is an ancient codex known as the Hungarian Pray Manuscript, or Pray Codex, named after Gyorgy Pray, a Jesuit scholar who made the initial study of the piece. The codex was written between 1192 and 1195, and includes five illustrations, one of which is Jesus being placed in the Shroud. This image has certain distinct marks matching burn holes seen on the Shroud. This means that the Shroud was known well before the dates given by the carbon-14 tests. In fact, the cloth of Edessa was even mentioned at the second council of Nicea in A.D. 787.

ORIGINS OF THE IMAGE

None of this, however, reveals how the Shroud was made in the first place. In *Nature* magazine in January of 2005 Philip Ball, the science writer, said, "It is simply not known how the ghostly image of a serene, bearded man was made." So what is the Shroud of Turin really? There are no signs of decomposition, as attested to by just about every scientist who has ever looked at it. The man in the Shroud is around 5-feet, 8-inches tall, a pretty standard height. He was between 30 and 35 years of age, which match biblical statements. Therefore, either the Bible is right, the Shroud is a copy of the story, or the Bible was written after seeing the image on the Shroud.

The image itself is indelible and heat resistant—unlike paintings. One popular theory is that the image was created by natural amino-carbonyl reaction, which is a chemical process of a decaying body, but this would not have been heat-resistant nor indelible.

In Graham Phillips's *The Templars and the Ark of the Covenant*, we find the statement that God's presence was believed to reside within an image: "In Egypt a god's presence was believed to reside within a specially made image, usually a statue or figurine."[2] But in the Shroud, we are told that we may have the actual image of God's son, which, in the Egyptian view, would be God. Ian

Wilson, in *The Blood and the Shroud*, suggests that the Edessa Cloth was more than a painting. He believes that it was an image. Had it been a mere painting, the Byzantines and others would not have given it such ceremonial pride of place on the Feast of the Annunciation—the day of Mary—who is also related to the Ark and the Shroud. But the Edessa Cloth is said to be a small kerchief, and so could not be the Shroud. As Ian Wilson asks, can we be sure that the Edessa Cloth was really just a handkerchief size? He points out that Gervase of Tilbury and Ordericus Vitalis were from Byznatium, and that they believed the cloth to carry the full image of Christ. If the cloth was the size of a handkerchief, then how could it carry the full imprint of Jesus? The Byzantines themselves copied the cloth, brought to Constantinople around 943–944, and these copies exist in manuscript form. The cloth looks remarkably similar to the Shroud in these images, as Wilson points out. The author of one of these manuscripts said that "it would not be at all surprising if the facts had often been distorted in view of the time that had elapsed."[3]

The first story from the sixth century tells how the image was formed by Jesus as he dried himself upon it. The second tale (of which the antiquity is uncertain) explains how the image was formed in the Garden of Gethsemane:

> And He came out, and went, as he was wont, to the mount of Olives;
> and his disciples also followed him. And when he was at the place, he
> said unto them, Pray that ye enter not into temptation. And he was
> withdrawn from them about a stone's cast, and kneeled down and
> prayed. Saying, Father, if thou be willing remove this cup from me:
> nevertheless not my will, but thine, be done. And there appeared an
> angel unto him from heaven, strengthening him. And being in an
> agony he prayed more earnestly: and his sweat was as it were great
> drops of blood falling down to the ground.

The story goes that Jesus took a cloth and wiped the sweat from him, producing the imprint (albeit a more bloody one than in the first story).

To comprehend what is actually occurring here, we have to try to understand these tales symbolically. The image on the Shroud is real enough, and it is an enigma. Throughout the past 2,000 years, we have heard tales of just how a cloth was made with the image of the Lord. Before that (in Egypt and elsewhere) we have the fact that the divines image would be manifested in an image and often carried upon an ark or b'arque. In essence, we are bringing the metaphysical into the physical—from the Otherworld into this.

But we also have another issue. Just how was this image created? Surely if the image were to have any symbolic reality, then it would have been created through the state of enlightenment. One thing I have found to be true in all my research is that symbolic art is employed at every level, both metaphysical and physical.

Let's look at this extract from the gospel according to Luke. The first thing Jesus does is to go to the Mount of Olives. This is one of the most holy sites to Jews, Christians, and Muslims. It is located on the eastern side of Jerusalem, and is (not surprisingly) named after the copious olive trees that once covered its slopes. During the period of the Old Testament, this was the place used by the Temple high priests to slaughter and burn the Red Cow, whose ashes were used for purification. This Red Cow or Heifer is to be found in Numbers 19 of the Old Testament, and provides some clues of its own:

> And Eleazar the priest shall take of her blood with his finger, and sprinkle of her blood directly before the tabernacle of the congregation seven times. And one shall burn the heifer in his sight; her skin, and her flesh and her blood, with her dung, shall he burn: And the priest shall take cedar wood, and hyssop, and scarlet, and cast it into the midst of the burning of the heifer.... And a man that is clean shall gather up the ashes of the heifer, and lay them up without the camp in a clean place, and it shall be kept for the congregation of the children of Israel for a water for separation: it is a purification for sin.

Here we have a ritual for purification of sin; a ritual that would be destroyed by the new Messiah brought forth from the new Ark (Mary). This ritual begins with the number seven—as the life-blood, the most important aspect of any being—is sprinkled before the Tabernacle. All aspects of the cow—the lower nature—must be destroyed in the fire, including the dung. Only then, once the lower nature has been consumed in the flames of the light, can purification begin.

Next into this alchemical mixture for purification comes cedar wood. A paper by Jeff Johnston, a doctoral candidate in epidemiology at the University of North Carolina, titled "Respiratory Toxicity of Cedar and Pine Wood," explains how cedar wood can cause many respiratory conditions, causing pathological changes in the body. Although no one knows how, this is probably due to the plicatic acid found contained in the bark.[4]

Our next ingredient is hyssop, although this is more likely the caper plant (*Capparis spinosa*), which is known to grow in the Jordan Valley, Egypt, and in the desert. Anybody who has visited the area and seen the ancient temples will probably have spotted this plant without knowing, as it is well-known to grow from temple walls—probably due to the abundance of the plant seeds in the location from ritual use. In fact, hyssop was used extensively in the Bible by David and Solomon. The Greek writer, Dioscorides, called hyssop *azob*, meaning *the holy herb*, due to its widespread use in holy places such as temples. It is a known stimulant.

Whatever the true purpose of the ingredients used in these Temple rituals, the fact remains that Jesus is said to have taken himself alone to the very mount where these Temple rituals themselves began. Could Jesus have been following a purification ritual of his own before he was sacrificed? Could he have taken drugs to induce hallucinations? Were these stimulant drugs or ingredients of any benefit to achieve enlightenment? Without proper scientific testing we shall never know. However, we do know from the evidence of herbalists that these stimulants certainly raise body temperature. It was down this avenue of investigation I found myself venturing.

I knew from my previous research that a rise in body temperature indicates a rise in what is known as bioelectric fields. A crazy thought ran through my mind, one that I had to get to the bottom of. First I contacted the Howard Hughes Medical Institute. The following question (which I posited to them) will explain my thoughts: "I was wondering if the human body could emit certain kinds of radiation at high levels of stress or excitement that would affect fine-woven linen to such a degree that bacteria would be attracted to the areas affected, thus giving rise to the bioplastic elements discovered on the Shroud of Turin by Dr. Leoncio Garza-Valdes?" Before I move on and reveal the various scientific answers, I need to explain what bioplastic fields are, who Dr. Garza-Valdes is, and how I came to this seemingly mad question in the first place.

It was while reading Ian Wilson's extremely interesting book, *The Blood and the Shroud*, that I came across the aforementioned doctor and his discovery. It turns out that the carbon dating of the Shroud that hit the headlines some years ago is wrong. There were just too many problems with it. One of those problems is what may give us the answer to how the Shroud was made in the first place. Wilson learned about this remarkable new evidence from a conference paper titled "Biogenic Varnish and the Shroud of Turin," which said that "it sounded so unpromising that to my own subsequent chagrin I did not attend it." The paper was written by the University of Texas's Dr. Leoncio Garza-Valdes, who discovered a coating on an old Mayan artifact he owned, and which the experts had said was fake. Dr. Garza-Valdes proved that the shiny coating, which had given the artifact the appearance of a fake, was a completely natural-forming bioplastic material caused by the accumulation of millions of bacteria and fungi building up on the surface and giving off a high sheen effect. The doctor also knew that his artifact, an Itzamna carving, would have been involved in blood-letting rituals, and so would have tiny particles of human blood beneath the coating. He scraped a certain amount of material from the artefact and sent it to the lab for testing. The results came in to his favor, as human DNA was discovered to be present. He then proceeded to have the object carbon dated, which resulted in a date of A.D. 400, proving he was in the possession of an authentic historical object. However, this was the wrong date for the Mayans, so he knew that the carbon dating must also be wrong, by almost 600 years. Following additional research, Dr. Garza-Valdes discovered that the bioplastic coating was to blame. The coating builds up over years, with each year a new coating accumulating. This caused the carbon dating to take into account the latest year and to average out all the years of readings that it was getting. In short, bacteria and fungi were fooling the scientists.

Dr. Garza-Valdes found this bioplastic coating on several artifacts, and the thought crossed his mind that this same natural substance could have been the very thing to have messed up the carbon dating of the Shroud of Turin. So he set off for Italy. Once there, he immediately found the same coating present—the same substance that would make the Shroud appear younger than it truly was. So, we are left with the simple truth, that the Shroud must be older than previously thought. Could the Shroud really date from the time of Christ?

Looking at the cloth, we can see that it has the characteristics of a Jewish burial cloth from the first century, when corpses were buried integral, with their eyes and mouths closed. Aloes and myrrh were also used, and are present in the Shroud. The Shroud is also proven to not be of European origin. The sacred dimensions are distinctly Syrian of the first century and were used in ancient Israel. Even the yarn is typical of the Palestine and Syrian periods of the first century with a very specific z twisting opposite to the s twist used in ancient Egypt. The traces of *Gossypium herbaceum* (cotton) were of Middle Eastern origin. Also, the cloth must have been produced in a Jewish environment, because no animal fragments (such as hair) have been found. This follows the Mosaic Law, which prescribes that wool shall be separated from linen. Even the man in the Shroud can be proven to have undergone a special crucifixion, as such deaths normally ended in burial in the ground or as food for scavengers. He has also been proven to have walked barefoot, as the heel area revealed a quantity of earth. These quantities of earth discovered on the heel area reveal that the man walked in Palestine, as the earth recovered contains argonite with strontium and iron—something found in the caves of Jerusalem. Also found were traces of natron, which was used for dewatering corpses in ancient Palestine. Of specific interest is the presence of pollen found in Palestine, but also in Eddessa, which helps me (along with Ian Wilson) suggest that the Shroud was once known as the Mandylion. If this is the case, then the majority of the pollen found would be of Palestinian origin, and this is exactly what is found. Researchers also found traces of the flower *Zygophyllum dumosum* and *Capparis aegyptia*, which live in the Dead Sea area. There was also an image of a coin discovered covering the right eye. This is a *dilepton lituus* (crook or staff held by augurs and precursor of the Cross) and was minted under the procurator Pontius Pilate around A.D. 30—the very period of the crucifixion. On the left eye there is another coin, a *lepton simpulum* (ritual ladle for pouring wine offerings upon a sacrificial animal), also created under Pontius Pilate in A.D. 29. The act of placing coins over the eyes is an ancient Jewish custom, and has been confirmed by archaeology done at Jericho, Jerusalem, and En Boqeq, where skeletons dating from the first century have been found with coins in their eye sockets. This placing of coins reminded me of the death mask of Tutankhamen: "Royal is thy face. Your right eye represents the solar b'arque and thy left eye represents the lunar b'arque." Were these coins representative of the sun and moon, similar to the eyes of Horus?

It matters not who made this Shroud at this point, but only how, and if it is found that the Shroud's creation relates to the enlightenment process, then it too relates that whoever created it was aware of the Otherworld.

HISTORY OF THE SHROUD

In the year A.D. 944, the Byzantine army besieged Edessa (Antioch), now called Urfa in modern-day Turkey, which at that time was occupied by the Muslims. However, it was not for the city that the Christians fought so strongly; it was not the offer of the freeing of 200 Christian captives and a king's ransom that mattered for the capitulation of the city. It was for the capture of the Mandylion, and it was successful. The Muslims gave up their prized possession to the Christians, and the Mandylion has been a great part of Christian lore ever since. It is the image of Jesus. The word *Mandylion* is Arabic in origin and means *kerchief*, as in *handkerchief*, due to the assumed small size. In Greek, it was known as the *Achieropoietos*, meaning *not made by human hands*, which goes well with biblical commandments stating that we should not make images of the Lord by our own hands.

Legend states that King Abgar of Edessa, whose coinage reveals him to wear a crown with an Ark or upturned crescent moon on his head, was a leper. He sent his "trusted aide" Ananias to Galilee with a letter to implore Jesus to come and heal him. But Ananias was an artist, and was under orders to paint a picture of Jesus if he could not get the Messiah to come. One day Jesus was in a crowd, and Ananias tried desperately to paint the image of Jesus, but to no avail. So Jesus, intuitively knowing this, asked for some water, and washed himself. His image was miraculously imparted onto the cloth.

This is the tradition of how the Mandylion arrived and remained at Edessa. It was then supposedly discovered above a gate in A.D. 544. It was discovered in the top arch, which shall not evade those with eyes to see the hidden symbolism. In fact, we don't need to be too deep and esoteric; we have it spelled out to us by the architects of Edessa, as the Shroud was discovered in the West Gate, otherwise known as the Gate of the Arches or Arc.

There is also a tradition that a light or lamp of wisdom was discovered in Edessa during the reign of the Emperor Justinian. It was found in a niche over a city gate or arch, and was elaborately enclosed to protect it from the elements. It was said that it had burned for 500 years—since the time of Christ. This again is Gnostic tradition of the perpetual light—the underlying secret of the ages—being passed down from one generation to the next. It is a concept almost as old as man, for the light is a part or element of the sun itself. This light was the secret esoteric truth of the cloth, itself truly discovered in a niche above a gate or arch.

The cloth was then taken to the Hagia Sophia. It was claimed by the Christians in A.D. 944 following the siege, and taken to Constantinople. It was, for centuries, the most sacred of treasures at Edessa, and is referenced by many historians, including Eusebius and Evagrius. At Constantinople, however, it was kept secret and secluded, and was only (briefly) seen by certain monks, artists, and clergy who were regarded holy enough to look on the face of Jesus. Due to the folding of the cloth, the face was the only aspect of the image revealed. This is how the kerchief aspect became prominent in the minds of men. These early copies were spread far and wide, and eventually formed the standard image of the Christ across much of Orthodox Christianity. Some vague 12th-century accounts speak of the image being full length, and that somebody at some time had undone the trellis work wherein the cloth was kept and had laid it out full. This has given rise to the theory that the Mandylion was the same as the Shroud of Turin.

Ian Wislon (in many books and articles) has stated that the Mandylion was also the Shroud, and that it had been folded in a sacred way to reveal only the head of Christ, and that all other copies were made only from this element. In fact, folding the cloth in this way reveals a numerical device, which has a distinct relationship to the enlightenment process and sacred geometry. It was folded seven times (into eight pieces), mirroring the seven (and sometimes eight) chakras of the Hindu kundalini, one of the so-called path to enlightenment. Wilson also points out that the eighth-century Greek theologian John of Damascus described it as the *himation*, which evokes the outer garment worn by the Greeks in ancient times. Perhaps, as Wilson points out, the Greeks would have found such a tiny handkerchief *himation* a little skimpy. Also, in the 10 century, Leo the Deacon actually spoke of the image as a *peplos*, denoting a full-sized robe.[5] This reveals that the Mandylion was, in all likelihood, the Shroud of

Turin. In fact, Wilson further backs this belief and the folded concept with this: "For myself, however, by far the most illuminating of all the words used for the Edessa cloth has to have been tetradiplon, even though it only occurs twice, once in a sixth-century manuscript and once in the Official History. As a word in Greek, this is extremely rare and completely unknown outside the two above mentioned texts. Yet it is perfectly understandable, since it is a compound of the two ordinary words tetra meaning 'four' and diplon meaning 'doubled' thus 'doubled in four.'"[6]

By the 12th of April in A.D. 1204, the Fourth Crusade had captured Constantinople. It is during this madness that the Shroud/Mandylion disappears. The crusading knights, the Templars, worshiped the image of Christ's head, and may have made three-dimensional representations of it (called the *Baphomet*). This peculiar image is one of the idols that the Templars were accused of worshipping above Christ, and was said to have been either a male or female or both. In essence, *Baphomet* derives from *baphe*, meaning *to submerge*, and *metis*, meaning *wisdom*. It simply means *to be submerged in wisdom*, using the symbolic watery abyss yet again in their images.

It appears that the Templars either took or made copies of the Mandylion, and so may have also known of the whereabouts of the Shroud of Turin. Some even point to the Mandylion in stone at Rosslyn Chapel in Edinburgh as evidence that the Templars knew where the Shroud was, or were in possession of it themselves.

VERONICA'S VEIL

Rosslyn, according to Laurence Gardner, was never about religion in any recognized sense or form. It was, he says, built by Christians as a sacred site dedicated to St. Matthew, and that there is no Madonna, no Jesus, and no Apostles, but there is a Veronica's Veil by the south door, and nearby the image of Moses with horns.[7]

We know that copies of the Mandylion (here called the Veil of Veronica) were made from the earliest of times in Edessa. There was a Sanctum Toellam, possibly one of the Templars own and looted from the Paris Temple during the King Phillip persecutions, preserved in Saint Chapelle in Paris until the French Revolution, when it was sadly destroyed. It seems that all of the icons of the head of Christ still in existence are painted copies of the original Mandylion, which has disappeared, only to be replaced by the Shroud of Turin. They don't seem to have existed at the same time as separate objects. However, there is a third possibility that emerges from the mists of folklore, myth, and tradition: the Veil of Veronica.

Legend states that a pious matron by the name of Veronica showed pity on Jesus as he carried his cross to Golgotha and wiped his brow with her cloth—thus miraculously creating the image of Christ upon the cloth. This miracle gave rise to all kinds of statements about the cloth, such as its amazing powers to heal. Further tradition states that the Veil was in the hands of the Catholic Church from the 12th century onward to around 1608. Pope Paul V then ordered the destruction of the chapel where the Veil was kept. The Veil was moved to the Vatican cellars, from where it disappeared. However, a professor of history at the University of Christian Art in the Vatican's Gregorian University claims to have found the Veil and traced it to the Capuchin monks, who have it behind glass in a monastery near Manoppello. In fact, this image is strikingly similar to the face on the Shroud, and it may be the same man, who was either crucified or was able to photographically impress his image onto linen cloth. Other experts however, such as Dr. Lionel Wickham (on the faculty of divinity in Cambridge), have gone on record as stating that the image may just be a medieval fake.

A Roman head of God displayed between the prows of an arc.

There is no evidence that the Veronica event ever took place, or that a woman by the name of Veronica existed and owned a cloth with the image of Christ's face on it. So we are, again, talking about a story created (possibly in around the fourth century) to explain the existence of an actual object. Often these stories include some esoteric device to reveal certain key secrets hidden from the masses. The name Veronica, for instance, was chosen quite specifically, for it means *true image* in Latin. *Veil*, on the other hand, comes from *voile*, the French version of the Latin *velum*, meaning a cloth, awning, or sail for a ship or barge. Is this the true image on the sail, God between the prows?

THE KNIGHTS TEMPLAR

Regardless of what the terms might mean, it seems that there were several sets of images: the Veil of Veronica, the Shroud of Turin, and the Mandylion (possibly the same cloth as the Shroud). To break all of this down a little, we need to find out what happened to the Mandylion following its disappearance in the early 13th century at Constantinople. The intitial thing to note is that the first knights into Constantinople in 1204 were the Knights Templar. Maybe they were on a mission to recover the Shroud, just as the Byzantines did in 944. This would make a lot of sense, as the Templars were rogues when it came to relics, and they profited extensively from their trade. Extreme holy relics (such as the burial cloth of Christ) would have been of incredible importance. The knights may also have been guardians of the Ark/Shroud, as I discussed earlier. The best we can decipher is that by the 1350s, a French family by the name of de Charney had come into possession of the Shroud, as we know it today.

Many will now be familiar with the downfall of the Knights Templar from 1307 to 1314 and the execution of the last grand master, Jacques de Molay, in 1314, on an island on the Seine in Paris. De Molay was joined on his last day by the master of Normandy, Geoffrey de Charney. It is highly likely that the Templars, and more specifically the de Charney family, were in possession of this cloth, brought from the sacked Constantinople to Europe, and that before his demise the master of Normandy passed on the relic to his children. Then, exactly one generation later, another Geoffrey de Charney was in possession of the Shroud. This second de Charney, a knight of St. Denis, later founded a church at Lirey, near Troyes, which was intended as the shrine for the Shroud. However, he was killed at the battle of Poitiers fighting the English, and so the honor of exhibiting the Shroud for the first time in centuries (if ever) was left to his wife and child, another Geoffrey de Charney. But two bishops took umbrage and told the mother and child to cease their idolatrous show. This, in turn, was overturned by order of the Pope. In the end, the responsibility of the Shroud became too much for the de Charneys, and they placed it into the hands of their distant relatives, the Duke and Duchess of Savoy, who were very influential in

Rome. The Shroud passed down through the centuries until the distant relative of the Savoys—the King of Italy and head of the Royal House of Savoy—came into its possession and placed it in the Cathedral at Turin, where it remains. In 1983, the ex-King Umberto II bequeathed the Shroud to the Pope, so it is now in the ownership of the Vatican.

A statue from the 14th century of the Veil of Veronica at the Eglise D'Eouis. Is this an image of Christ's face on the Shroud?

This is the rough history of what we call the Shroud of Turin. The journey to early Eddessa is the vaguest area of contention, although Ian Wilson has many wonderful snippets of evidence to take the Shroud even further back in time (and to the time of Christ). But now we must return to the questions we began with: How was the Shroud created, and does it have any relationship to the enlightenment process scientifically?

THE IMAGE ITSELF

Ian Wilson points out that endless experiments during the past few decades have consistently shown that distortions arise when anybody attempts to recreate the Shroud image. He states that this is because the Shroud's image is not from direct contact to the body image. If the image was created by a body, then (as Ian Wilson says) it was from some emanation from the body directly transferred onto the cloth when not in direct contact.[8]

The findings of STURP (and Professor Allen in particular) reveal that the body image on the shroud was not composed of any physical substance, such as the pigment of an artist's paint, but was instead the alteration of the surface linen such as by the effect of light or other radiant energy.[9] Of course, there is the element as espoused by Lynn Picknett and Clive Prince in *Turin Shroud: In Whose Image? The Truth Behind the Centuries-Long Conspiracy of Silence*: "Leonardo faked the Shroud in 1492. It was a composite creation: he put the image of his own face on it together with the body of genuinely crucified man. It was not a painting: It was a projected image 'fixed' on the cloth using chemicals and light: in other words it was a photographic technique."[10] With a singular part of this I would agree: Not that Leonardo da Vinci created the image, as we have already shown (and Ian Wilson has also shown admirably), or that this Shroud is of a much older provenance than 1492. No, the element of photographic technique is the part with which I must concur. However, not in the way espoused by Picknett and Prince. Photography is the creation of an image with photons or light radiation, and as we move on it will become clear why this is important.

STURP found, under Professor Allen's guidance, that the image was not made up of any physical substance such as paint or pigment. It was an alteration of the surface of the linen by some effect such as light or radiation. Of course, the first thing any researcher then does is run off and try to replicate technologically the effect using instruments and gadgetry from the period. What we end up with is a series of contrapments that bend rules and include devices that must have been lost to us, or the individuals must have possessed some lost knowledge from alchemy.

We also have another part of the puzzle to consider. If Dr. Garza-Valdes is wrong with his bioplastic bacteria and fungi explanation for how the carbon dating was in error, then what could have caused it? In a letter to the editor of *Nature* magazine on the 16th of February 1989, Doctor Thomas J. Phillips of Harvard University posited the following explanation, that the body of Christ (or whoever it was) "...may have radiated neutrons, which would have irradiated the Shroud and changed some of the nuclei to different isotopes by neutron capture. In particular some carbon 14 would have been generated from carbon 13. If we assume that the Shroud is 1950 years old and that the neutrons were emitted thermally, then an integrated flux of 2×10 to the power of 16 neutrons cm-2 would have converted enough carbon 13 to carbon 14 to give an apparent carbon-dated age of 670 years." This would make the Shroud appear to be somewhere within the 14th century, which is where the incorrect carbon dating originally placed it.

All of this is perfectly in line with my book *Gateway to the Otherworld* (scheduled for publication in 2008) and the quantum energy effects created by the processes within the mind. In simple terms, the adept meditates, prays, dances, fasts, or takes hallucinogens to alter the state of consciousness and thereby raises his or her own body energy levels. This basically excites the atoms within the body, stimulating heat generation, as seen by spontaneous human combustion and in subjects who have undergone scientific analysis following such processes as kundalini awakening sessions. The process also aids the escape of neutrons from atoms—causing neutron radiation, exactly as specified about the Shroud. Any kind of embalming or anointing fluid may have been placed on the body of the live man may have caused a magnification of the radiation in process—thereby imparting the image on to the Shroud's linen without the use of any physical substance. A mixture of olive oil with sweat has been shown by scientist S. Pellicori to work as a catalyst for an image creation when light or radiation is applied. The Shroud is a fragile, yellowing cloth. This yellowing is due to oxidation, dehydration, and conjugation of the cellulose. The fact remains that only radiation (and a few acids) could cause this. In the end, if we remove the impossible, then what we are left with is the probable.

Now I must return to the question I asked of the Howard Hughes Medical Institute: "I was wondering if the human body could emit certain kinds of radiation at high levels of stress or excitement that would affect fine-woven linen to such a degree that bacteria would be attracted to the areas affected, thus giving rise to the bioplastic elements discovered on the Shroud of Turin by Dr Leoncio Garza-Valdes?" Now you will understand that I already knew the answer to this; I just wanted some down-to-earth medical opinion. I instead received an answer about bioelectric fields—the electricity or energy emitted by the body: "Measurements of the electric and magnetic fields from the body, such as electrocardiography (ECG) and magnetoencephalography (MEG), reflect the underlying bioelectrical activity of the tissues and organs. However, without equally advanced modelling and visualisation technologies, much of the potential value of this information is lost."

I could have answered this with, "Have you never heard of Kirlian Photography", or maybe, "Have you ever thought about asking those people who claim to see auras?" But I didn't. I read on:

> To more directly answer your question, we must be sure exactly what we are discussing. Fundamental physics informs us that every movement of charge (electric current) is associated with a magnetic field. Electric fields exert force on charges—if the charges are free to move, a current will result. The relationships are reciprocal—if a conductor containing freely movable charges is passed through a magnetic field, a current is induced in the conductor, thus magnetic fields also induce charge movement.
>
> How does this relate to the human body? Our body is composed mostly of salt water—salts are charged in solution and free to move in the solution. Our nerves and muscles generate currents as part of signalling and contracting—these currents are associated with magnetic fields that cause charge movement all throughout the body. It is due to these that we can measure electrocardiograms, electroencephalograms, etc. This normal set of processes, as well as others, result in electromagnetic fields that originate in the body.

So, in the end, what are we left with? This answer tells us that there are bioelectrical fields, which are electromagnetic signals running throughout the body, which is made up of a substance—salt water—that allows free movement of this current. Quantum physics tells us that photons react in peculiar ways. In my own work I have found that all things are interrelated and interconnected, and (unlike our modern scientists) I do not see all these things separately. They are all related, and if, as has been proven, the body can excite via the control of the mind, then it can emit photons from the atom, thereby electromagnetically discharging radiation, which is what the evidence shows on the Shroud.

The image on the Shroud has been shown to be on both sides on the cloth, in perfect alignment with each other. (It was previously unseen on the reverse.) This, all scholars agree, would have been impossible for a painter to achieve. It would also rule out gaseous explanations (where gases leave the body at death and impart human biomatter upon the linen) because this would not be able to penetrate the cloth in such a way. It also rules out technical photography, but supports my theory of bioelectrical quantum photography.

What is the latest on the dating of the Shroud? According to master textile restorer Mechthild Flury-Lemberg of Hamburg, a seam in the cloth corresponds only to a fabric found at the fortress of Masada near the Dead Sea, which dated to the first century A.D. He said, "The linen cloth of the Shroud of Turin does not display any weaving or sewing techniques which would speak against its origin as a high quality product of the textile workers of the first century." According to the appraisal of the Ghent Institute of Textile Technology in Belgium, the weaving pattern, a 3:1 twill, is consistent with first-century Syrian design. The latest research shows that the cloth is from the right period and region to have been used by the son of God.

The Veil of Veronica sits at the foot of the cross with the serpent, as placed on a statue in Notre Dame Cathedral in Paris, France.

I was now coming to some peculiar conclusions. Could it be, I wondered, that the image on the Shroud was that of an adept who had been in an excited state of ecstasy or enlightenment, which had emitted a distinct radiation? From the dating of the Shroud's linen, it would appear that this could indeed have been the character we now call Jesus. He was, after all, the enlightened one, the Son of God who would illuminate the world. This enlightenment has already been explored by myself and Gary Osborn in *The Serpent Grail*. It is in the in-between state, between cycles of positive and negative energy, between awake and asleep. It is also between life and death. The number of OBEs (out-of-body experiences) and NDEs (near-death experiences) I have researched, where the subjects see bright lights, had increases in body temperature, and were in states of excitement or ecstasy, all related perfectly. These were people who had been either clinically dead or were near death. They all had peculiar bodily affects, such as raised body temperature, and they were all psychologically transformed afterwards, as if resurrected.

The man in the Shroud had been beaten to a pulp, nailed to a cross, and was surely near death. He was (whoever he may have been) in between this world and the next. You just couldn't get any more extreme than that. At the end of the day, I thought, if this were true, then it was just like the supposed statements regarding the Ark emitting light. There is little wonder that Christ is depicted emerging from the glorious rays of the Otherworld via the sacred geometric Vesica Piscis. In almost every way, whether esoteric or physical, the Ark, the Shroud, and Mary carried the light of the divine.

CONCLUSION

I began researching this book without a title, without a goal, and without a clue as to where I would end up. I had no idea that there would be so many links to the Ark. All I honestly had was a hunch that nobody had gotten it right yet. My first foray into the Ark had been like just about everybody else, through the books, and especially the film *Indiana Jones and the Raiders of the Lost Ark*. This marvelous movie has had people racing around the planet on the quest to dig up the weapon, and all have failed, because all of them are looking for the real object. From psychic questing to claims of Israelite government cover-ups, the Ark has been the object of many obsessions, and I too have been thoroughly obsessed with this quest. I have been exhilarated, enthused, scared, and saddened by my search, but I am happy with my results. I have traveled from Rome to Africa, from mystical India to the sands of Egypt, and this is what I have found:

There may well have been a real Ark, kept within the inner sanctum of the Jerusalem Temple, but it would now probably be merely a pile of dust and crumpled gold leaf. I believe the esoteric wisdom we have discovered on our journey is much more exciting than some copy of an Egyptian b'arque (of which there are plenty in museums around the world). The most ancient arks I found in India, from temples laid out as chariots to the great rath of Jaggannath. India was the oldest originator of the Ark concept, and within this remarkable culture we discerned the origins of Gnosticism.

The most amazing Ark of all is the Gnostic concept. The ship of light, the light of the truth, the light of wisdom, the real you that is hidden under the baggage we call our personalities—these are the real contents of the Ark. This light and knowledge is always found in neutrality, in balance. To better explain this and to understand it for our lives today, let me explain a very Buddhist way of looking at it.

The world, as it stands today, is running on desire. Every time you wake up you have a desire, whether it be to take a shower or make a cup of coffee, it is desire led. Our desires are fed by whatever we find around us and whatever influences us. These influences in this modern age are multifaceted, from the television to the Internet, and from books to preachers. All these things influence us, and over the course of our lives they make us what and who we are. As we rebel against our parents (in a perfectly natural desire to leave the nest), we look outwards towards these mental and physical foods. But we are not really conscious that we desire at all; our mind closes this off to us, and we simply know that we are hungry, thirsty, lonely, bored, or any number of other things. Because we are not aware or conscious of these desires, we cannot control them and we cannot balance them. Desires are twofold: there are good desires and there are bad desires, and they are always the opposite sides of the same coin. A good desire is to love our partner. The bad desire effect is to love them to extreme, to be overtly jealous or overbearing. A good desire is to be hungry. The bad desire is to be gluttonous and hoard food. Another good desire is to want to succeed, but the reverse of this is that we desire it too much and step on others on the way up.

We can see in just these few examples that the balance can be tipped and we can veer dangerously off into a world of extreme—losing all sense of balance. The simple way of dealing with these issues is to start by being conscious of them. When you feel hungry, eat, but watch how much you eat and ask yourself whether you really need that second helping. When you see your partner have fun with another person, ask yourself whether your jealousy is warranted. If we keep these thoughts in our minds and ask ourselves whether our desire is for the good, which we should intuitively know, then we are walking the road of ancient wisdom. If we continuously do this, then we get better and better. We become more confident and eventually will no longer need to concentrate so hard on the good and bad desires; we will be enlightened. Once we have mastered this kind of balance, there are further stages—all requiring exactly the same repetitive process—just like alchemy, where we must reduce and grow, reduce and grow. Part of this alchemical process is burning away all the parts of ourselves that are not truly us. As we grow and leave the nest we look around us for help and influence, and unfortunately what most people find today is food that is designed to feed the bad desires. We turn on the television and are fed garbage. Without even knowing it years later we have succumbed to the subtle brainwashing of the media marketing man who pulls on our inner greed—a bad desire. Only by waking up and being resurrected, as the ancient would say, can we look at ourselves in the mirror and see the ugliness of the food we have been eating. Before we can grow, we must burn this off and emerge like the phoenix from the flames.

Often we look around for answers to these issues (once we have become aware of them). Unfortunately, the marketing or propaganda man has beat us to it, and has installed the spiritual cure-all, neatly packaged in the form of religion. We do what we know best and buy ourselves into balance. Today, many in the world are going kundalini crazy, as if this is the true answer to our imbalance. It is not. Of course, kundalini is a magical meditative method of so-called enlightenment, and it can result in rigorous self-analysis and inner visions of light, but it is a system created by man, and all men are different. The kundalini may work for some (and it may have worked in past centuries), but I have found many who claim to have had the experience to be bigoted and arrogant This can be seen as an ego-centered concept of self-improvement and fits well with many, but it most certainly is not balance. Instead, it is an effect of hormones and drugs upon the mind, convincing the one experiencing it that he or she is divine. True enlightenment is much more down to earth.

One thing we also find from religious history is the *avatar*. In simple terms, the avatar is one who has achieved a higher state of enlightenment. Often when we go through these processes we begin to feel superior, and we see the rest of society as if it were some kind of parasite or lice. This, of course, does not ring true, and it is simply a case of lack of compassion, which is one of the things we must learn for our fellow man before we can proceed further— something those who experience without training fail to understand. By learning to be and by being compassionate to others we actually grow our own strength— we feel more confident—because we learn about ourselves. No amount of television or Internet can teach us what we can learn in practice. Of course, there is always bad compassion, whereby we are too humble and get walked all over by others, who would often feel better themselves if they were stopped by somebody more balanced. Those avatars of our religious past are those individuals who, over the course of many years, learned balance, control, and compassion, and knew who they really were. Once they achieved this state, they came back down from their great psychological and philosophical heights and helped others to do the same. If more of us could learn to control our own bad desires and grasp the art of compassion, then we would have a much better world.

These few simple truths, relevant for us all today and for millions of years to come, have been truths ever since we woke up as human beings. They have been discussed, developed, argued over, and finally written down from much more ancient oral traditions in the books of our great religions. These ancient truths are fully on view in the Bible, the Koran, the Mahabharata, the Vedas, the Upanishads, and any number of other ancient texts. Times have changed and language has changed. Dominating empire building religious organizations have stamped out the truths and replaced them with confusing narrow-minded literalisms that they use against us to control us. They tell us hell is literal and we will go there if the Pope excommunicates us. They tell us they will rage a holy war against us if we disagree. But none of this is in balance; none of this is compassionate.

There is wisdom in the original texts. We must ignore the interpretations of institutions with blood on their hands and listen to our own self. These texts were written at different times, yes, but they were written by humans who had good and bad desires, just like you and me. They desired sex, food, and riches in the same way we do today, and they developed ways of dealing with these things and better, more enlightened, ways for us to exist. Read the texts and listen to your own interpretation of them. Ignore the guides and do what our ancient Greek philosophers implored us to do: Listen to your own guide.

It is in this way, and with the knowledge of mystics, that I balance out my own views on ancient texts and truths. The more I learn, the more I know about the world, but best of all, the more I know about myself. I do not see a man walk on water when I read the Gospels, for it is not possible. Instead I see symbolism and wisdom. I see a literary avatar showing us that walking in perfect balance between the worlds is possible. When I see the Temple destroyed, raised, destroyed, and raised, I do not see real wars and destruction that simply evades archaeology. Instead I see the symbol of the whole man—the true temple—which must be reduced and rebuilt before it can truly take possession of the Ark of the Lord. And this is the purpose of the whole thing: that we control the Ark.

Within balance, between the Cherubim, in the neutral state of our mind, resides the inner sun or light of wisdom. When we achieve this perfect state we will realize that there is much more to life than material goods. We will understand that we are at one with the universe around us—that we are part of the greater whole. Our own human mathematical sacred geometrical measurements prove our relationship and ratio to the cosmos; our whole body and mind can truly be part of it—it just has to be tuned in through perfection.

When we achieve this high state of understanding we become energized in spirit. Something occurs inside our consciousness that raises us up to the higher energy state of the quantum world. Our minds become fused with nature, and we are God.

This is the truth our ancestors discovered: Don't allow hatred and intolerance to take it away from us again. Rise up, become enlightened, pass it on.

APPENDIX A

For some reason, many of us seem to know that the answers to our questions about time, the universe, and life after death exist in our own minds. This almost paradoxical situation has been with mankind for thousands of years. Man searched within himself for the answers, and I believe that man has found them. In this appendix I hope to relay some of the amazing symbols of that searching and reveal the hidden meanings behind some of the most enigmatic objects and images of history. I will follow the path of the ancients and search within the skull.

In Sanskrit, skull cups are known as *kapala* (hence *cap* and *cup*), and are generally formed from the oval section of the upper cranium. They served as libation vessels for many deities, most of whom were wrathful. However, they are also associated with gods such as Padmasambhava, who holds the skull cup that is described as containing an ocean of nectar (elixir), which floats in the longevity vase. Almost immediately we have a clue to the contents of this receptacle, and the real purpose: the elixir.

The skull cup is more than its contents (though that was certainly of importance). The selection of the right skull was paramount, and the users were looking for tantric powers or energy. Therefore a violent death would always be better, such as decapitation. The symbolism of the tantric skull cups is very similar to those of the Holy Grail, in that they are symbolic of immortality, and contain the physical essence. Even some Western alchemical writings advise the use of skull cups in the process of the great work, which is the search for the Elixir of Life.

The tantric skull cups are said to parallel the clay pots of the Vedic sacrifices and the begging bowl of Buddha, which, in one myth, contained the serpent.[1] The skulls are said to serve as a constant reminder of death. The contents of the cups is often blood, but also the blood of Rudra—the Lord of wild animals, similar to the Celtic god Cernunnos. Rudra's etymological origins are uncertain. It could mean *the red one* or *the weeper*, or derive from the Syrian *Rhad*, meaning *serpent*. In other areas, it also means *the removal of pain* or *healer*. Rudra is identified with Siva, and he is the divine healer.

Mahadeva, one of Siva's names, is often represented with a snake entwined around his neck, arms, and hair. His consort, Parvati, is likewise represented. Bhairava, the avatar of Siva, sits upon the coils of a serpent, whose head rises above that of the gods. According to Hyde Clarke and C. Staniland Wake in *Serpent and Siva Worship,* Siva is the same as Rudra, the healer, and is called the King of Serpents. He is depicted with a garland of skulls, symbolizing time measured in years, the changing of ages. He is sometimes called *Nagabhushana Vyalakalpa* or *having serpents round his neck*; *Nagaharadhrik* or *wearing serpent-necklaces*; and also *Nagaendra, Nagesha,* or *king of Nagas*. He is also known as *Nakula*, the *mongoose*, which means *one who is immune from the venom of the snake*.

Siva is also seen as a horned god and is connected with the serpent worship in many ways. Both Siva and Siva in the form of Rudra are seen in their dynamic aspect as being entwined with serpents. These are serpent deities of old and are connected here with the cup of the head, bringing several disparate elements together—the skull, the grail, the mind, the snake, and time or immortality. They are regenerative serpent deities offering longevity via their blood within a cup. In essence what we have here is the serpent, which resides within the mind, and therefore within the skull.

Livy in *Historae* mentions a similar Celtic operation from the third century A.D., which simply must be connected to the Indian skull cups. Apparently, the Boii tribe (when they got hold of a victim) "cut off the head, and carried their spoils in triumph to the most hallowed of their temples. There they cleaned out the head, as is their custom, and gilded the skull, which thereafter served them as a holy vessel to pour libations from and as a drinking cup for the priest and the temple attendants."

The sacred water used in the skull cups was often taken from a holy well, which I have established, were places linked intrinsically with the worship of the ancient serpent. The idea here is that this ritual practice goes back beyond even the total memory recall of the Celts to a time when the cups employed the real power of the serpent, not just symbolic water.[2] In essence, the water (whether of wells, lakes, pools, or seas) was seen by man across the globe as an entryway or portal into the Otherworld. Taking this otherworldly water in a sacred cup fuses a special power into the water, similar to the Holy Water taken from the font in most Christian churches.

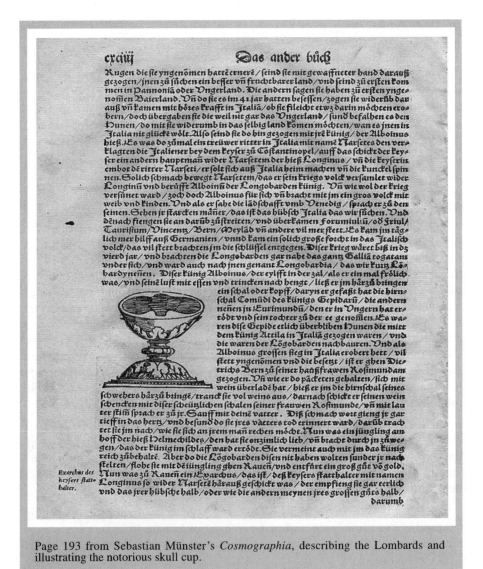

Page 193 from Sebastian Münster's *Cosmographia*, describing the Lombards and illustrating the notorious skull cup.

The etymology of *skull* gives some interesting insights. In Old German, it is *Scala*, which is also a *seashell*; the symbol used by pilgrims on their way to the shrine of St. James in Spain; and a symbol of life and knowledge. In Old Norse it is *Skel*, which means *to have scales* or *to be scale-like*. The word *skoal*, now a fairly common drinking cry, is also closely related and means *to toast from a skull*. This etymology alone shows the deep-seated element of the skull in and its use as a drinking vessel. Remarkably, *skoal* was also used to refer to *chalice*. (The Ukranian word *Cherep* refers both to skull and chalice.)

We must not forget the Christian Messiah was also crucified at the place of the Skull, Golgotha. His sacrificial blood was spilled into the skull. Golgotha is also connected to the sign Capricorn—the half-goat, half-fish or serpent. *Capri* is from Latin, meaning *goat* or *head*, and *corn* is *horn*. This, then, is the *horn of the head or goat*—the *Golgotha*. Jesus spilled his blood into the secret Grail on that fateful day—the secret Grail being the horn or cup of the skull. The essence of the God-man is in the head. And asthe serpent blood is found in the Skull Cups; so too is the blood of Jesus.

Now we can see why the infamous Baphomet head of the Templars was seen as both a skull and a goat; it was a hidden mystery—a mystery that has been misunderstood ever since.[3] The Brazen Serpent, or the healing snake of Moses now seen as Christ in the New Testament, was lifted up at the place of the skull and his offering of blood was collected—the ultimate sacrifice on the tree of life for the ultimate prize of immortality.[4] But truly, if Christ is all and in all (as we are told by the Bible), then we can all obtain this immortality of the one, the shaman deity or Jesus, who visited the Otherworld. Jesus went down into hell for us, we are told; the shaman would enter trance, drink from the skull cup, and visit the Otherworld for us; the priests of Egypt, South America, and the Celtic lands would do the same. This is a universal experience expressed in symbolic form through the skull. The reason is clear, because the mind resides within the skull; the tantric power and the perceived wisdom of the united serpent energies all act within the skull. No wonder it was cut off, turned upside down, and gilded. But is there any more evidence showing this remarkable symbolism?

There is a Naga myth, which relates to the place of the skull.[5] It is about Padmasambhava (Guru Rinpoche) or simply Padma. He is revered in many places and in Tibet held alongside Buddha; indeed, many see him as the second coming of Buddha. He is inseparable from the primordial Buddha. He was in the beginning, similar to how Jesus was the word.

Padma received the wish-fulfilling jewel from the daughter of a Naga king and used it to restore sight and make riches. He is said to have transformed himself into a demon by tying a snake into his hair and practicing a secret language to enable the Nagas to assist him. He spoke to those who had ears to hear; Arjuna (John) taught him astrology, and he learned all about medicine from Jivakakumara.

While Padma was practicing his skills in a cemetery, Garab Dorje was born to a virgin daughter of King Dharmasoka. She had no use for the bastard son, and so tossed him into a burning pit; but the child survived. Then she remembered a dream where she gave birth to a celestial being, so she pulled him from the pit after seven days and, finding him alive, called him Rolang Dewa.[6] During the child's early years he learned many wise things and debated against 500 great pundits who all said he was the Buddha.

Padma then came as a wise man (very much like John the Baptist came to Jesus), and taught Garab Tantras. Padma then went on to seek the secret of longevity and was directed to Kungamo, who dwelt in the palace of skulls. Kungamo turned Padma into a syllable, similar to Jesus as the word, and swallowed him. Inside the stomach he ultimately found the secrets for which he was searching.

Padma is often seen holding a cup filled with the divine liquor, which he offers to his disciples—saying "drink of this to attain liberation." Padma, then, is linked to the Naga serpent cult, to healing, and to the elixir via the palace of skulls; he is the word, the teacher of the Christ, like Garab who was born of a virgin, and he gives the Eucharist cup to his disciples.

In all respects this wonderful, stylized Indian tale has all the elements we could possibly require to show that the Christian and medieval Grail stories are nothing more than a retelling of much more ancient concepts, and that these concepts revolve around a universal and archetypal truth. This truth is that our own immortality and our own salvation lie within our own mind.

APPENDIX B

I have often referred to the number seven and given you a general idea as to its significance. A study of the use of the number, however, is often very enlightening itself. The following is a small collection of sevens from history and religion around the globe.

- ▶ The Biblical Joshua walked around Jericho (the first civilization, according to some, and home of the largest group of shamans) seven times.

- ▶ It took seven stages to bring the sinful world or lower nature crumbling down.

- ▶ Seven heavens are to be found in the Koran and the Bible, and in the traditions of the Shaman and Druids. These seven heavens must simply relate to the levels of enlightenment associated with the Hindu chakra system, which parallel the planets.

- ▶ There are seven steps to heaven, a popular belief and found on many ziggurats and pyramids.

- ▶ There are seven sacraments in the Catholic church.

- There are seven deadly sins and seven virtues. These are methods of balance as we move up the chakra system—negatives and positives—balancing out desires with wisdom. These are the opposite sides of the same coin, or desires that must be checked.

- Life has seven cycles, according to tradition. This emerges from the cycles of enlightenment as we grow older on the path.

- The seventh son of the seventh son is, by Jewish tradition, believed to have great healing powers.

- The myth of magic boots allow the wearer to walk seven leagues in one stride goes back to the mythical magic of the giants or men of renown. These are the Egregores or Watchers, also known as Shining Ones.

- The seven days in a week match the days in creation. The creative principle of man must follow the sevenfold path.

- The Hebraic "to swear on oath" means to come under the influence of the seven, which could possibly infer the seven planets.

- The seven Argive heroes of Greek legend.

- The seven champions of English legend.

- The seven seas.

- The seven wonders of the ancient world.

- The seven gifts of the spirits. These are obviously linked to the seven chakra system, enlightening the spirit within.

- The seven-headed snake in the images from the Naga worship of India, and those of Sumeria atop the sacred tree.

- The seven Japanese gods of Luck.

- The seven joys/sorrows of Mary.

- The seven sages of Greece or Wise Men of Greece.

- The seven sciences.

- The seven senses (according to the ancients). They are under the influence of the seven planets and are in reality the seven planets within us. Fire moves, earth gives the sense of feeling, water gives speech, air taste, mist sight, flowers hearing, and the southwind smell.

- The meanings of seven—scholarly, mystical, withdrawn, dreamy, time, the colors of the rainbow, seven tones of the musical scale, stability, and endurance or duration.

- There are seven elementary hues to the spectrum. When blended together, they form white.

- The atom has up to seven inner orbits called electron shells, and these seven orbits, shells, or levels reflect the levels of the electromagnetic spectrum.

- We see the use of sevens in man, who is believed to stand between the macrocosm (universe) and the microcosm (atomic or subatomic world), for aligning the human spine are the seven chakra (wheel) vortices, which reflect the seven levels of consciousness and existence.

- In the seven system, the bindu is the octave point and could also paradoxically be referred to as level nine—which in occult lore is often symbolized by the *lemniscate* or infinity symbol—a horizontal figure eight. This lemniscate is derived from an intertwined serpent and is often found above the head of the adept in occult symbolism. Similar imagery comes down to us in the halos around the heads of saints or holy men and women. This is revealing the head at the center of the circular enlightenment and today the dot at the center of a circle is still seen as the highest and most important symbol of the Freemasons.

- The seventh chakra level is associated with the pineal and pituitary glands in the brain, which are thought to activate during meditation. This is why these particular chakra centers (and related endocrine glands) were considered important to the ancients. Much of this ideology has been incorporated into great and monumental structures around the globe, including the Great Pyramid at Giza, and other pyramids scattered across the world.

- There is also compelling evidence that the ancients understood that the seven levels are also expressed in the tiny building blocks of matter we know as atoms or subatomic particles.

It's no surprise to find that, intuitively, our ancestors were correct in their belief in the number seven, even if they were not instructed in this knowledge. In this respect, I personally plump for the intuitive aspect as related by the author Jeremy Narby in his *The Cosmic Serpent* book. Having spoken to many subjects over the years who have experienced altered states of consciousness, I have found a remarkable number who saw what they could only describe as atoms, particles, and sometimes even DNA. Research across the globe has now shown this to be a universal experience. Amazingly, the nucleus of an atom has up to seven energy layers or orbits surrounding it, similar to the layers of an onion, or the seven auras seen by mystics around the human being. It would make complete sense for the pattern to be continued from the very elementary to the macrocosmic—from atom to man.

APPENDIX C

'abd

A Sufi term meaning *servant* or *slave*. In Islamic doctrine, this individual is seen as being the servant or slave of God and not necessarily the son, as in the Judeo-Christian father/child relationship.

ablution

An alchemical term for washing a solid with a liquid. However, the real meaning is to purge oneself of those things that cause suffering, such as desire or ego.

Adam and Eve

According to the Ante-Nicene Christian Library, Clemens Alexandrius claimed that *Heviah* (the root of *Eve*) means *female serpent*. "If we pay attention to the strict sense of the Hebrew, the name Evia aspirated signifies a female, serpent." The name is connected to the same Arabic root that means both *life* and *serpent*. The

Persians called the constellation Serpens the little Ava or Eve. In old Akkadian, *Ad* signifies *father*, and according to C. Staniland Wake in *The Origin of Serpent Worship*, the name *Adam* was closely associated in legend with Seth, Saturn, Thoth, or Taautus, who are all associated strongly as serpents. *Abel*, the son of Adam and Eve, means *serpent god*. Cain was thought to be of serpent descent. Adam and Eve are names that spelled out their meaning, and yet over time we have lost that meaning. In essence, the two aspects of the serpent energy must be reunited to attain the perfect man: the Adam Kadmon of the Alchemists.

adder

The word *adder* is derived from *gnadr*, a Druidic term. The Druids traditionally stated, "I am a Druid; I am an architect; I am a prophet; I am a serpent"—linking the Druids to the *Dionysiac Architects* of Freemasonic fable. According to Christianity (and especially St. Augustine) the adder was evil and was one of the four aspects of the devil. The deaf adder depicted sinners who have closed their ears to the truth.

adept

Taken from the Latin *adeptus*, meaning *he who has obtained*. In this instance, it is wisdom that the adept has obtained. The adept is beyond the Initiate stage of enlightenment and is now either a Master Adept or on the road to becoming one.

Adytum

The Greek name for the Holy of Holies in any temple. It is the most secret and sacred of locations known to man, into which nothing profane can enter.

agartha

This Tibetan word means *the underground kingdom placed at the center of the earth, where the king of the world reigns*. It is symbolic and is used extensively to imply the true center. This is a device utilized by the followers of the enlightenment experience to describe the central aspect needed to achieve illumination.

Agathodaemon

Good serpent or *sacred serpent* of the Gnostics and Phoenicians. This good serpent is none other than the Solar Force or Serpent Energy, which aids man along the path of enlightenment. It is also the coiled serpent of the kundalini. In the Bacchanalian rites there was, remarkably, a *Cup of the Agathodaemon*. This serpent-consecrated cup of wine was handed around and received with much shouting and joyousness. The hymn sung through the serpent to the Supreme Father was just the same as the one sung in the memory of the Python at Delphi on the seventh day of the week, mimicking the seventh chakra in the kundalini process to Divinity. Now, thousands of years later, Christians still take the cup of Christ (called *the good serpent* by the Gnostics) and eat the consecrated bread. This modern ritual is similar to the original, but renamed *Cup of the Sacred Serpent*, which gives the body and blood of our oldest god.

Agni

Hindu god meaning *Shining One*. He illuminates the sky. In this, we can see the cross association with the physical sun and the internal sun.

ajna center/chakra

The Eastern Chakra point between the eyebrows that is aligned to the pituitary gland. It is the center of the personality of the individual. It is also known as the *agni chakra* or *fire/shining chakra*.

Akashic records

Records of every person's word and deed that will be found in the spiritual realm. In *Gateway to the Serpent Realm*, I posited the theory that these were to be found in a quasi-quantum vacuum field and that mankind is capable of seeing the records in a superconscious state.

akh

Egyptian term meaning *Shining Soul*. Note the use of the term in the names of certain pharaonic names, such as *Akh-en-Aten*, the Egyptian king who is said to have worshipped only the Outer Sun.

alchemy

Al or *El* means *God* or *Shining*. *Khem* or *Chem* is from the root Greek *kimia* and means *to fuse*. Therefore, *alchemy* means to fuse with God or the Shining—to be enlightened. Basically it was a cover for the Eastern traditions, which were diametrically opposed to the Church of Rome. Alchemy was brought to Europe through the teachings of Geber (Jabir ibn Hayyan, A.D. 721–815) as well as several others. In later years, the psychoanalyst Carl Jung concluded that alchemical images he was finding emanating from his subjects' dreams and thoughts explained the archetypal roots of the modern mind and underscored the process of transformation.

Alexander the Great

Ambassadors of Alexander, after returning from a visit to Kashmir, made mention of the fact that the king had two large serpents, named Ida and Pingala. Obviously these were the two serpents of the kundalini. According to Strabo, the King of Taxila showed him a huge serpent actually being worshipped. Alexander is well known to have made an extensive search for his own spirituality, especially among Indian culture.

alkahest

The alchemical term for *the power that comes from above*, and allows or makes possible alchemical transformation. Sometimes translated as *universal solvent*, it is the concept of transmuting material (or mental) elements into their purest form. It is, in essence, the concept of revealing the hidden and true nature of mankind, which is the real "gold" of arcane philosophers.

Allah

The God of Islam coming from *Ilah* or *El*, meaning *shining much*. It is the inner enlightenment. It is similar to the inner reality of our own divinity, which engulfs us in light.

anahata

The Eastern chakra center related to the heart.

anchor

The *Foul Anchor* symbolizes the boat and mast, which is a symbol of Mary. This is significant, as it symbolizes the union of the male (mast) and the female (boat or crescent moon). In Egyptian symbolism, this union of the opposites was strengthened with the serpent coiling up the mast—similar to the kundalini energy of Hinduism. This union of opposites was also associated with a dolphin, which has speed against the slowness of the boat—thus symbolizing the occult *hasten slowly*, another union device. This dolphin and boat symbol was also used to symbolize Christ on the cross. It is also closely associated with the Ankh.

androgyny

From the Greek *andro-genika*, where *andro* means *man* and *genika* means *woman*. Otherwise known as the *hermaphrodite* (Hermes and Aphrodite joined). This philosophy supposes that once the human is free of his or her innermost darkness, he realizes that he is bisexual in spirit and mind. It is not a literal concept. Once in this state, the alchemist, magician, or Shining One represents the perfect human and is seen as connected entirely to the universe. It is a very ancient idea, and is a stepping-stone to the enlightenment experience.

anima

A term often used by alchemists; Latin for *the soul*.

anima mundi

Latin for the *soul of the world*. It is an esoteric term meaning the modern collective consciousness or the superconscious state.

animism

The belief that inanimate things, such as plants, posses souls.

Ankh

The *Crux Ansata*. A simple *T-cross*, surmounted by an oval, also known as *the ru*, or *Gateway to the Otherworld*. This symbol of Egypt represents *eternal life* and is often found in the names of pharaohs, such as *Tut-ankh-amun*. The anhk has been depicted as being held by a pharaoh, giving his people life. This basically sets aside the immortals from the mortals, for anyone wearing or carrying the ankh gains immortality. It can also be worn as an amulet to sustain life. It is the loop (*the ru*) of the Ankh, which is held by the immortals to the nostrils. (This imagery reflects the biblical God breathing life into the nostrils of Adam.)

Thoth, the Egyptian deity, was said to have symbolized the four elements with a simple cross, which originated from the oldest Phoenician alphabet as the curling serpent. As recorded in *A Discourse of the Worship of Priapus* by Richard Payne Knight, Philo believes that the Phoenician alphabet is "formed by means of serpents…and adored them as the supreme gods, the rulers of the universe." Thoth, who is related to the worship of serpents, created the alphabet. According to C. Staniland Wake in *The Origin of Serpent Worship*, the 19th-century writer Bunsen said that "the forms and movements of serpents were employed in the invention of the oldest letters, which represent gods." This symbol was altered slightly, and became the Egyptian *Taut*, the same as the Greek *Tau*, which is where we get the phrase *Tau Cross*—a simple T.

In shape, the Ankh is very similar to the Egyptian musical instrument, which is shaped like the oval *ru*—the *sistrum*. The sistrum is an Egyptian musical instrument closely associated with female gods—especially Hathor, the serpent/cow goddess, and Isis, the consort of Osiris. In form, they are very similar to the Ankh, with a loop at the top—also representing the egg—and three serpents striking through the loop with small square pieces of metal, which rattle. It's possible these three serpents represent the *pingala*, *ida*, and *sushumna* nerve channels of the Eastern kundalini tradition and that converge and fuse together within the center of the brain (the thalamus)—which, in the individual, was also thought to represent the cosmic egg.

During the ascent of these serpent energies up the spine to the center of the head, the individual will hear sounds similar to the sounds of the sistrum. One will also hear sounds resembling a rattlesnake, and also whistles and flute-like instruments—a white noise now associated with the Otherworld. Underlying these sounds is a very low and strong rumbling sound that fades in at first, and becomes louder and louder as the process proceeds, culminating in the bright, white light explosion in the center of the head. The sistrum then may have been a symbol of this experience.

The sistrum was used in pictures and carvings to show the various gods and pharaohs subduing the power of a particular god.

antahkarana

An Eastern term for the invisible channel, through which meditation bridges the area between the physical brain and the soul.

antimony

An alchemical term that symbolizes the animal nature or wild spirit in man that must be eradicated. There is a metal called antimony that was used by the alchemist Basil Valentine, and that he fed to some Benedictine monks, almost killing them in the process. A tincture of antimony is said to cure some venereal diseases.

anthroposophy

Founded by cult leader Rudolf Steiner, a German mystic. The term means *wisdom of man* and teaches the ancient truth that wisdom, which is truth itself, is to be found within man.

arcanum

Coming from the Latin *arcane*, meaning a secret or mystery. The term is connected to the word *ark*, as in the Ark of the Covenant, or the ark used by Noah. Both are also connected to the barges or b'arques seen in ancient Egypt, which carry the souls of the dead to the otherworld.

ascended masters

On a literal level, these are spiritual teachers of higher consciousness as proposed by Helena Blavatsky, and thought to exist across time and from the East. However, some would see them instead as inner teachers from within us.

ascension

The Ascension of Christ, although taught as a literal event (where Christ ascended to Heaven) is, in reality, the rise of the Christ consciousness within man. It is the kundalini rising up the spine or axis mundi to full enlightenment. It is the realization that man is the Divine.

assiah

A Hebrew term for the fourth world of the Kabbalah. It means *the physical body*. The term was ranslated in the biblical Revelation of Saint John as Asia.

astral body

A projection of the inner self, or the *Haqiqah* of the Sufi. The astral body is thought to exist after death. In *Gateway to the Serpent Realm*, I showed how this can easily be related to quantum physics and the quantum entanglement of the superconscious state with the universe, thus giving rise to the Akashic records. It is related to *astral flight*, which is the travel of the soul during sleep or meditation. The common astral body is also known as the *Kama Rupa* or *Body of Desires*, whereas the true astral body is the Solar Force or Spirit as spoken by Jesus in John 3:5–6: "Except a man be born of water and of the Spirit, he cannot enter into the kingdom of God. That which is born of the flesh is flesh; and that which is born of the Spirit is spirit." Jesus is indicating the two distinct human attributes, one of flesh or body and one of spirit or astral body.

athanor

A term in alchemy for the oven, which itself symbolizes the union of the male and female principles within man—uniting opposites within. It is sometimes symbolized by a mountain or a hollow oak tree.

atman

This is the true inner reality, the Spirit or the Son of God element within each of us. Alchemists say that the atman does not die, it is without end of days, and is absolutely perfect.

aura

The glow, halo, or radiation around living or inanimate objects, thought by many to be the visual element of the soul or spirit. These auras are now photographed using Kirlian photography.

avatar

The manifestation of a higher entity for the benefit of mankind. Christ, Buddha, and Zoroaster are all seen as avatars. These are the inner reality elements of mankind being seen or envisioned by the mystic who has attuned himself to the universal truths held within. The teaching of an avatar expands mankind's understanding of himself, humanity, and the evolution of mankind on a spiritual level. The evolution of the spirit is said to affect the physical evolution of mankind and is thought to be a way back to the divinity.

bain marie

Named after the female Jewish alchemist Maria Prophetissa, this is said to be a warm alchemical bath (a double-boiler container) that is suspended in a cauldron of simmering water. However, as with most alchemical terms, it is also a metaphor for the warm feeling associated with meditation on the road to dissolution or the eradication of the ego.

Baphomet

A mysterious object said to have been venerated by the Templars and thought to be a skull. One possible explanation for the origin of the word could be found in the deserts of Yemen. The people who live there are called the *Al-Mahara*, and they have developed many ways of combating snake poison. The special priests are called *Raaboot* men, and they are said to have learned the secret by transition from father to son. Their legends state that they have immunity from snakebites.

If somebody is bitten, then a Raaboot man is called. He sits by the patient, along with several others, who then chant in a monotone voice "Bahamoot, Bahamoot." The poison is then said to be vomited up or passed out of the body. The Raaboot man then leaves. Is it not possible that "Bahamoot," as a chant for the curing of snakebites, could have made its way through the various cultures and found itself as a word for the head serpent? If nothing else, then the etymology of these two related items is so similar that it again shows in the language of the worldwide spread of serpent worship.

Baqa'

A Sufi term referring to the *Divine Attribute of Everlastingness*. It is opposite to *fana'* or *passing away*. When the Sufi reaches the state of *fana'* he is leaving himself behind and then only the Divine self remains.

Bardo

A Tibetan term meaning simply *between the two*. In essence it is the void. This can be seen in the title of the *Tibetan Book of the Dead*, which is really translated as *The Great Book of Natural Liberation through Understanding in the Between.*

Bel/Baal

A solar god, thought by John Bathurst Deane in his book *Worship of the Serpent Traced Throughout the World* to be an abbreviation of *Ob-El*—the serpent god. Etymologist and historian Jacob Bryant remarks that the Greeks called him *Beliar*, which was interpreted by Hesychius to mean *a dragon or great serpent*. *Bel* is the Assyrio-Babylonian gods *Enlil* and *Marduk*—being the same as *Baal*.

Beltane could be rendered *Bel-Tan*, both words signifying the dragon/ serpent, showing a link across Europe. In fact, *Tan-it* or *Tanit* was the patron goddess of Carthage in Northern Africa, who was also associated with the Tree of Life. Often the Tree is depicted with wavy lines, said to represent serpents. The name *Tanit* means *Serpent Lady*. She is found on many coins from the height of Carthage and is associated with the Caduceus, symbolizing the role of Tanit in life, death, and rebirth. She is basically the same as the Queen of Heaven—Astarte, Isis, and Mary.

birds

The association between birds (or wings) and serpent seems to go back in time many thousands of years. To quote John Bathurst Deane:

The hierogram of the circle, wings, and serpent, is one of the most curious emblems of Ophiolatreia, and is recognised, with some modifications, in almost every country where serpent worship prevailed.... It may be alleged that all these cannot be resolved into the single-winged serpent once coiled. Under their present form, certainly not; but it is possible that these may be corruption's of the original emblem which was only preserved accurately in the neighbourhood of the country where the cause of serpent-worship existed; namely, in Persia, which bordered upon Babylonia and Media, the rival loci of the Garden of Eden.

Deane relates these many thousands of images of the winged serpent to the *Seraphim* of the Bible—the fiery and flying serpents. These could also be the origins for the flying dragons, and why Quetzalcoatl was the feathered or plumed serpent. The reason given by Deane for this symbolism is for proof of deity and consecration of a given temple. If this is the case, then temples across the world were consecrated by the ancient serpent with the serpent energy.

bodhicitta

A Sanskrit term meaning *the enlightened mind.*

bodhisattva

A Sanskrit term meaning *the essence of enlightenment or wisdom*, as both are one and the same. In esoteric terms, this is a soul or being who has earned the right to enter nirvana and escape samsara. He or she has become enlightened or illuminated and is a Shining One, but instead of entering Nirvana, he or she has turned back towards this existence to aid humanity.

Buddha

The enlightened or illuminated one who is a bodhisattva. According to New Age traditions, he was the last avatar of the ages of Aries and was the embodiment of wisdom. The serpent was an emblem of Buddha Gautama, the Messiah. According to Hindu oral tradition and legend, Gautama had a serpent lineage. Not surprisingly, trees are sacred to Buddhists, as Gautama was enlightened beneath the *bo tree*. In the book *Ophiolatreia*, Hargrave

Jennings quotes Captain Chapman, who was one of the first to see the ruins of Anarajapura in India.

> At this time the only remaining traces of the city consist of nine temples...groups of pillars...still held in great reverence by the Buddhists. They consist first of an enclosure, in which are the sacred trees called Bogaha.

The basis of the Tibetan healing arts comes from Bhaisajya-guru, Lapis Lazuli Radiance Buddha, the master of healing. The begging bowl is made of lapis lazuli and contains the Elixir of Life. The definition of the Elixir can be found in a story about the Buddha when he passes the night at the hermitage of Uruvela:

> The leader Kashyapa warned Buddha that there was only one hut available, and that a malevolent Naga (cobra or serpent) occupied it. Buddha was not concerned and went to the hut. However, a terrific struggle ensued, culminating in the hut bursting into flames. The onlookers drenched the flames, but they had to wait until morning to find out whether Buddha had survived. Buddha emerged with his begging bowl in his arms. Inside was a peaceful, coiled snake. The Buddha had slain the dragon of its fiery notions and emerged with a beneficial result.

Cabiri

In Greek mythology, the Cabiri were a group of cthonic deities. The Cabiri were Phrygian fertility gods who protected the local sailors. Legend has it that there were originally two male Cabiri, who were later joined by two female Cabiri.

chakras

The Eastern energy centers in the body (etheric), which run up the spine through the seven endocrine glands. The kundalini (coiled serpent) energy must be raised upward through the centers to achieve enlightenment.

channelling

A fairly modern term for being able to gain insight from the Otherworld through unknown means. The person may not necessarily know how or why he or she can channel, and may not have undergone training. I propose that this is due to being quantum entangled in the superconscious state to the natural world and is a perfectly natural state of evolution, of which we were once more aware.

circumambulation

To walk or go around ritualistically. The walking or traversing around a sacred spot or monument, such as the Buddhist stupas. The effect is to fix the axis of the world in a particular place and time—thus making that place sacred. The idea is to manifest the creative principle within man. It is believed that these sacred places have a scientific bearing, in that they are often places of high electromagnetic energy, which may link with the energy of the human who has governed his own electromagnetic energy through meditation. It is called *the pilgrimage to the self*, and is seen across the world, most famously at the annual festival of the *Ka'aba* in Islam, where the seven circuits are symbolic of the seven attributes of god—the *Ka'aba* is the black (and therefore void) meteorite that fell to earth and is believed by many to be charged with electromagnetism. The *Ka'aba* or *Ca'abir* is a conical stone (although many say square)—resolved itself into *Ca Ab Ir*—the *Temple of the Serpent Sun*, and is the point of connection between heaven and earth. The cone shape is symbolic of luck, and in the Dionysus myths it was the heart of Bacchus. Conical headdresses were worn by the Dioscuri, Egyptian, and Sumerian kings and priests. In J.C. Cooper's book *An Illustrated Encyclopedia of Traditional Symbols*, Bastius said that the cone and the spinning top shared the same symbolism, and are therefore strongly linked to the enlightenment experience and electromagnetism.

cosmic consciousness

The belief that mystics and spiritualists are in touch with a universe that is all and one, and is aware. When we attain this cosmic consciousness we are aware of all things, from all time, from everywhere, all at once. Our external realities of this existence must be cast aside if we are to be able to be conscious of this event of enlightenment. This is the inner reality, the connection to the Divine. In relation to this is cosmic humanity, which sees man as being capable of more than the sum of reality, and of unlimited potential.

daimon

Not the demon of Christianity, but the Inner Teacher, the spirit of the Divine inside each one of us that guides us to perfection. We all have this daimon or daemon, if only we could discover it.

Dead Sea Scrolls

Approximately 850 documents, including texts from the Hebrew Bible, discovered between 1947 and 1956 in 11 caves near the Wadi Qumran (close to the ruins of the ancient settlement of Khirbet Qumran, on the northwest shore of the Dead Sea). The texts are of great religious and historical significance, as they are practically the only known surviving biblical documents written before A.D. 100.

decapitation

Often found in fables and stories, and relates to the killing of the ego, the mystical death, and a process whereby all that is false is eradicated, thus releasing the Inner Divinity.

deva

A Shining One, angel, or celestial being. Devas are said to aid mankind with intellectual and spiritual pursuits from their parallel universe. In truth, these are internal Inner Realities that are probably archetypal and visualized as Shining entities due to the physical and mental affects of the enlightenment process. They have physical manifestations in the literal world as real human guides in ages past.

dharma

An Eastern word, dharma is the innermost nature of every individual and is the true being. It is the meaning of life. Man is not acting to his full ability if he does not know his dharma.

double or twin

Every person has his twin within himself. It is simply the opposites discussed elsewhere, the male and female principles. The *monad* is the whole of this. The Tibetans state that our Buddha or enlightened soul within ourselves has, in opposition, the *Devadatta* (the brother). This is the same as *Set*, who is the twin of *Horus/Osiris*; the reason for the twin pillars (between which we must pass in balance) of the Masons and others; the twin Aker jackal or lions of Egypt (Sphinx), between which resides the Great Pyramid; the Ida and Pingala channels of the East that rise up the spine through the chakras towards enlightenment; of Castor and Pollux; and of Romulus and Remus. It can also be broken down further in that each side has its own opposites. Take for instance the Divine Mother, the Holy Spirit or Ghost: she is good and beneficial, but she has herself an opposite other than the Divine Father. This opposite is known as the *Durga*, and is the ferocious aspect of the Divine Mother.

These examples reflect the dual nature of man, seen as dark and light, evil and good, man and woman. Wherever these opposites are to be found, the writer is representing these internal realities. These are the psychological battles that are enacted within us. When we decide to do good and be good, our alter-ego fights the impulse or desire with opposite desires. In essence, good is all those things that are in their correct place, and bad is all those things out of place.

dragon

Taken from the Greek *draco* meaning *seeing*, from his supposed good sight. This we now know to be related to the good internal sight brought to us through the energy of the serpent.

egg

The *egg*, *Cosmic Egg*, or *Cosmogenic Egg* is universally seen with the serpent—as in the symbol of the *Orphic Egg*, which shows a snake wrapped around an egg. From the serpent mound of Ohio to Mithras and Cneph, the egg is associated with serpent worship. According to most scholars, it is the emblem of the mundane elements coming from the creating God. Therefore it is a symbol of the elements of the universe. But there is another reason that the egg relates to early man.

What is an egg? An egg is simply an entry portal into this world. It is a device to give life. And what animal is seen in relation to this unique device and portal? Again, it is the snake—a symbol of the life force—that creates the device that gives life.

Kneph/Cneph was represented as a serpent thrusting an egg from his mouth, from which proceeded the deity *Ptah*, *Phtha*, or *Ptah*—the creative power and father god who is the same as the Indian Brahma.

ego

Psychologically, the ego is the destructive part of ourselves, causing suffering through desires, which leads to us making decisions about our life that are at odds with the Inner Reality of Divinity. We can only eradicate the ego by realizing its effect on us and our errors because of the force of the ego. Once we realize we have ego, we can set about removing it. Buddhists teach that we need to be free from the suffering caused by this element of our lives. Buddha gave us a clear and distinct Eightfold Path to Enlightenment: (1) creative comprehension; (2) good intentions; (3) good words; (4) total sacrifice; (5) good behavior; (6) absolute chastity; (7) continual fight against the Dark Magicians—the alter ego; and (8) absolute patience in all.

elementals

Believed to be spirits or souls in a lower form of existence than humanity—the spirits of the rocks, animals, plants, and other parts of nature. In ancient times, mystics believe that, as man was closer to nature, he was thereby more capable of perceiving these nature spirits and conversing with them. Names have been given to these elemental spirits, such as *gnomes*, *fairies*, and *elves*. They are spoken of regularly in the texts of Alchemists and Occultists, but are in reality a hidden element. These elementals are the energy signatures of all things as seen through superconsciousness.

It was once believed that mankind could communicate with these elementals and that they aided mankind and even mated with him. However, this is the language of times gone by. In reality, the communication between man and elementals is similar to when animals sense energy signatures, such as before an earthquake, when all the animals disappear, moving upwards towards the hills and mountains. How animals perceive these energy signatures is still a scientific mystery. In this way, the energy signatures, or elementals, communicate with animals. If man, who is nothing more than an evolved animal, could also pick up on these signatures, then he too would be aided by the elementals. The ancient and not so ancient texts that speak of these nature spirits are our only clue as to how mankind can perceive these energy signatures.

epiphany
To experience the revealed God in His Creation. It is spirit manifested in reality. It is the superconscious state seen in ordinary things or through new eyes.

ESP
Extra Sensory Perception, which includes telepathy, clairvoyance, divination, and precognition. Those with this ability may not understand the truth behind their ability, but are (by quirk of fate) able to pick up electromagnetic signature or are quantum-entangled to the earth and the cosmic universal consciousness. They are not necessarily in a state of superconsciousness or enlightenment, but are tuned biologically, chemically, and electromagnetically through particle physics. Those who can use ESP and are superconscious can affect the particle world.

etheric body

The energy counterpart of the physical body and is an idea manifested across the esoteric, occult, alchemical, and mystical world. It is the body of the chakras, connecting them with a body of energy. These may be vortices of subatomic energy, controlled by the mind once the mind is in control of itself, and not confused and sidetracked by the world of external phenomena.

Eye of Dangma

In Sanskrit, *dangma* means *purified soul*. The *Eye of Dangma* is the *Eye of the Purified Soul*. It is the spiritual sight gained by an enlightened or Shining One. This site is that of the superconscious state or altered state of reality, whereby man can perceive the energy signatures of all things, similar to the auras of Kirlian photography.

fall of man

Although believed by millions of Christians, Muslims, and Jews to be a literal event spoken of in Genesis, where Adam and Eve fall from grace, this is a metaphor for the fall of man's higher consciousness to the base nature we know today. The concept of Christ as the Redeemer exists only in the sense that he enabled man to see that there truly was a heaven on earth, achievable now to all mankind, which is the internal dialogue or the inner reality of the self.

fana'

The ego death or the passing away of the self, leaving behind the Divine Self in Sufi tradition. The final element of *fana'* is the *fana' al-fana'*, which simply means *the passing away of the passing away*. This is the stage when the Sufi is no longer even aware of having passed away.

fitrah

This is the pure or prime nature of man in the Sufi tradition. It is the time before man became corrupted by desire, greed, and all manner of evil elements.

Gaia

The goddess of the earth, according to Greek legend. Made famous by the scientist James Lovelock, who claimed that the whole earth, including all living organisms, was a single living entity in unison with itself. The concept is not new. Quantum theory is now proving that this is true and that *all things are one* is a truth. The new term *holism* has been applied to show that all things are interrelated to each other in a series of amazing chemical, biological, electrical, and quantum particle connections.

Gnostic

The term given to an individual who claims gnosis or knowledge of his own divinity. According to gnostic belief, the serpent was virtuous and wise. Satan was seen as the elder brother of Jesus, and the serpent was seen as the sign for the savior. The gnostic *Cainites* revered the snake on the tree, and the Ophites used asps and vipers at their sacred ceremonies. The Templars of Scotland in their Ancient Rite venerate the symbol of the serpent wrapped around the Tau-cross. The famous Templar/Masonic *Kirkwall* Scroll, revealed by Andrew Sinclair in his book *The Secret Scroll* is replete with sacred images of the serpent.

guru

A term given to a teacher in Eastern traditions.

Hallaj

An Islamic mystic who truly understood his own inner divinity. He was condemned to death in A.D. 922 following his statement: "I am God." His writings are outlawed in the Muslim faith.

haqiqah

A Sufi word for inner reality, from the root *al-haqq*, which means *truth*. The inner reality of ourselves is, in fact, truth—and truth is our inner reality, which can only be gained by *fana'* or the passing away of the self.

hermeneutic

A method whereby man can interpret the symbolic in order to better understand.

hidden treasure

In Islamic tradition, the *hadith qudsi* is the declaration of Allah where He says, "I was a Hidden Treasure, so I wanted to be known." Mankind, as reflected images of God, are containers of this hidden treasure, which is the divine self.

hierophant

A Greek term for a teacher of ancient mysteries and esoteric myths.

himma

Muslim term for the power of the heart. This is the heart within mankind—Divine love.

Holy Spirit

Seen as the third person in the Christian Trinity. To modern Christians the Holy Spirit is without gender. However, to other traditions the Holy Spirit was the feminine principle. To Dante it was the husband of the Holy Mother. The Holy Spirit or ghost is the *Fire of Pentecost* seen to inspire the disciples in Acts 2. It is similar to the kundalini, Solar Force, or Serpent Fire. All of these are names for the same principle. It is more likely that the holy spirit is only complete in the form of the kundalini, which is masculine, and when in union with the feminine. In symbolism, the gnostics of Christianity saw the spirit as a fish, a lamb, and a dove—all of which were derived from earlier cults, coming from Egypt, Sumeria, and elsewhere.

Horned God

From Pashupati to Pan, the Horned God is seen throughout history in connection with the secret of the serpent. It is Pan who kicks open the cista of Bacchus, revealing the serpent within. Dionysus (Bacchus) is often depicted with horns, and the Bacchanals of Thrace were said to wear horns in imitation of their god. Even Zeus, who transformed himself into a serpent to bring Dionysus to life, was depicted as having horns. The horns are thought to signify the solar aspect of the god—the life-giving aspect. They are also symbolic of the bull. The goat is also associated with the serpent, as Dionysius is often manifested as a goat. The awakening of Moses is symbolized by horns or shining forth. Moses also wields the Caduceus staff and raises the Brazen Serpent of healing for Yahweh in the wilderness.

hypnagogic state

The state that exists between sleep and awake, when one is most open to the process of enlightenment. Sometimes this state has been encouraged by the use of hallucinogenics, such as drugs, or extreme behavior, such as fasting or whirling.

initiate

A term often misused, but in reality meaning one who undergoes the altering of his own reality to the perception of his own inner self of divinity. There are of course many secret societies and occult groups who claim to have initiates. These initiates undergo various degrees on the road to self-realization. Of course, it can also be said that they undergo manipulation to a distinct way of life and belief system. It is a perfect tool to control the minds of individuals by promising the almost impossible dream of divinity. Few individuals in history can truly claim to have been enlightened, and those who do often live in secrecy.

insan al-kamil

The perfect man, the pure and holy one, or the universal man. This term is used in Sufism for the one who is a fully-realized human being.

jnana

A Sanskrit term meaning *to know* and related to gnosis. Specifically, the term refers to the enlightenment of the consciousness, or wisdom from within. The equivalent Tibetan word *yeshe* means "to know the prime knowledge that has always existed." This reveals the real meaning of the term *gnosis* and jnana as that inherent human and inner wisdom we can find by eradicating the ego.

kabbalah

From the root *KBLH* of the Hebrew language and meaning *to receive*. It is the science of the higher realms, where all superconsciousness is in agreement, as this is the function of our awakened consciousness or superconsciousness. It is the ancient Hebrew system of the internal worlds found within, and can only be understood through the unique symbolic elements of the system and through the eradication of the ego.

karma

The Eastern term for the law of cause and effect. Every action creates or causes another action. Our actions in our current state of existence will cause an effect in our next state of existence.

kundalini

Meaning *coiled one*, and an idea of a coiled serpentine energy that strives to be reunited with the crown chakra on a system of seven basic chakra or *wheels of energy*, which are located on the human body.

lahut

An Islamic term for the Divine. The opposite is the human or *nasut*.

Lucifer

Although nowadays thought to be a name for the Devil or Satan, the ancient gnostics and mystics never saw it this way. In Latin, *luci, lux, luce,* or *lucu* means *light; fer* or *fero* means *to bear or carry*. Lucifer is therefore the Light Bearer. In the fourth century there was a Christian sect called Luciferians. One of the early popes was even called Pope Lucifer. This is the reason why modern-day Christian fundamentalists damn the Masons and others for their deep-rooted belief in the one known as Lucifer. They are not worshipping the Devil, but are instead holding up the Light Bearer as the bringer of wisdom.

manas

The higher spiritual mind of man.

maya

The so-called web of illusion from Eastern traditions. The root is Sanskrit.

Mithraism

The Cult of Mithras originated in Persia and spread throughout the Hellenistic world. The Iranian god Mithras's name means contract or oath, though it is unclear whether this is related to the worship practices of the cult religion.

monad

From the Latin *monas* meaning *unity; a unit, monad.* Man and woman are the physical manifestations of the spiritual monad; the Divine monad resides in each of us as the Father, Son, and Holy Spirit. Mithraism became very popular with Roman soldiers until it was banned by the Theodosian decree of 391. Worship was limited to men only, and seems to have been astrological in nature.

monism

The belief that everything in the universe is made of the same thing, and that metaphysically all things are one and unified.

mukti

A Sanskrit term for *liberation*.

Naaseni

A gnostic sect at the time of Christ called *Naasenians*, or more properly *serpent worshipers*. They considered the constellation of the Dragon as a symbol of their christ.

Nabatheans

A sect from the time of Christ with similar beliefs to the Nazarenes, Sabeans, and Naaseni. They had more reverence for John the Baptist. The Ebionites, those who became the first Christians, were direct disciples of the Nazarene sect.

nadi

A Sanskrit term for the nerve channel of the subtle energies related to the chakra of Eastern tradition.

nafs

A Sufi term for the mind, self, soul, or ego. There are generally seven levels to the *nafs*, similar to the kundalini. These levels are psychological events or elements of our self that we must move through and overcome to achieve truth. These levels are: (1) the imposing self; (2) the reproachful self; (3) the motivated self; (4) the tranquil self; (5) the happy or content self; (6) the harmonious self; and (7) the fulfilled or pure self.

Naga/Naaga

A Sanskrit term meaning *serpent* (especially *cobra*) that also holds the meaning of tree, mountain, sun, the number seven, wisdom, and initiate. All are symbols and emblems familiar with the worship of the serpent and the enlightenment experience. The Naga are said to reside in Patala; however, this has a meaning similar to antipodes, the same name given by the ancients to the Americas. It is a similar term to the Mexican *nagals*, the sorcerers who always kept a god in the shape of a serpent. In Burma they are *Nats*.

Naga is a term for wise men. There is a folk tradition that Nagas washed Buddha at his birth. They are also said to have guarded him and the relics of his body after his death. According to H. P. Blavatsky in *Theosophical Glossary*, the Naga were descended from Rishi Kasyapa, who had 12 wives (therefore, he is the sun), by whom he had numerous Nagas (serpents) and was the father of all animals. Rishi Kasyapa can, therefore, be none other than a progenitor of the Green Man, and this explains the reasons for the appearance of the snake in images of the Green Man and Horned God, such as the Gundestrup Cauldron.

Apollonius of Tyana was said to have been instructed by the Naga of Kashmir. This is the same Kashmir where the serpent tribes became famous for their healing skills. There is a theory that the Nagas descended from the Scythic race. When the Brahmins invaded India, they found a race of wise men that were half gods, half demons. These men were said to be teachers of other nations and instructed the Hindu and Brahmans.

naljor

A Tibetan word meaning *holy man* or *adept*, and is connected with the Naga beliefs.

Nazarenes

Also called *Mendaeans* or *Sabaens*, they were a sect of the Essene around the time of Christ. They left Galilee and settled in Syria near Mount Lebanon. They actually call themselves Galileans, even though they said that Christ was a false Messiah. They followed the life of John the Baptist instead, who they call the *Great Nazar*. In association with the Ebionites and Nabatheans, they called Jesus the *Naboo-Meschiha* or simply *Mercury*, the great healer of serpentine connection.

nirvana

Eastern tradition holds that we must escape from the constant rebirthing in this plane of existence and go to nirvana (paradise). The term is related to *ni-fana*. Nirvana or *ni-fana* is a place we can all attain, free of the desires of this world and realizing our own inner self or divinity within.

Ophites

A general term, used for one branch of early Christian Gnostics, although it is probably too strong to call them Christians in the modern sense. They were also known as the *Brotherhood of the Snake*. According to John Bathurst Deane, the Christian writer Epiphanius said, "[T]he Ophites sprung out of the Nicolatians and Gnostics, and were so called from the serpent which they worshipped." They "taught that the ruler of this world was of a dracontic form" and "the Ophites attribute all wisdom to the serpent of paradise, and say that he was the author of knowledge of men"—linking him to the *Taautus* of the Phoenicians.

> They keep a live serpent in a chest; and at the time of the mysteries entice him out by placing bread before him upon a table. Opening his door he comes out, and having ascended the table, folds himself about the bread. They not only break the bread and distribute this among the votaries, but whosoever will, may kiss the serpent. This, the wretched people call the

Eucharist. They conclude the mysteries by singing a hymn through him to the supreme father.

The Eucharist mediator is the serpent termed the *Krestos*, as Christ was the mediator on the cross, a symbol and act more ancient than Christ and rooted in serpent worship. The serpent was sacrificed on the sacred tree or *Asherah*. The Ophites were also termed *Sethians* (according to Theodoret) after the Biblical Seth and Egyptian Set, both related to the serpent.

Pharaoh

In the Old Testament and the Koran, the adversary of Moses is Pharaoh, who wants dominion over the Israelites in place of God. Pharaoh is the base man who must be overcome in order to be in the land or place given by the Divine. The people of the Lord must deny the authority of the base man to escape and be at peace. Moses is, in Islamic terms, the intellect, which gives one the power of discernment over the ego.

Philo of Alexandria

A Jewish philosopher born in Alexandria, Egypt in 25 B.C. He was sent to represent the Alexandrian Jews regarding the civil strife that had erupted between the Jews and Greeks in Alexandria. Philo sought to fuse Greek philosophy and Judaism by means of allegory.

pralaya

Eastern term for the place between the states of existence or death and rebirth. This place exists to give us peace on our journey, and is the same as the Judaic and Christian concept of paradise. It is, in essence, the void.

pyramids

Used often in Gnostic literature to represent the number 3, or the most perfect of numbers. The Templar Cross, when made three-dimensional, creates a pyramidal shape. Pyramids have been found in many cultures around the world, including Egypt, Mesoamerica, France, Rome, China, and Greece. Some Egyptologists have suggested that the Great Pyramid of

Giza was constructed to symbolically represent an aspect of man's relationship to the sun god Ra.

quintessence

The fifth element of the alchemists. It was their description of the energy signature of an ethereal body of the life-force that they encountered in their dreams or hypnagogic states. They believed that they must discover this quintessence to transform or be transformed by it. It is their explanation for the perception of simple nature within the superconscious state.

samadhi

A Sanskrit term used to denote an ecstatic state of higher consciousness. It is the escape from the essence of all suffering. There are levels attributed to samadhi, which depend greatly on who is teaching it.

samatha

In Sanskrit, *sha* means *peace*, and *mata* is *dwelling*. Therefore, somebody who is named Samatha is *dwelling in peace*.

samsara

A Sanskrit term pertaining to the cyclic existence of pain and suffering in which we find ourselves. We must come to an understanding of this in order to escape to Nirvana.

satori

The ecstasy of the mind that has realized true reality.

semen

Often spoken of in alchemy and mystical texts, but misinterpreted as actual physical semen. In fact, it is the term used for the sexual energy of both males and females, and relates more specifically to the union of the Divine opposites within.

shari'ah

The opposite of *haqiqah* in Sufi tradition. Where *haqiqah* is the inner reality of the self, *shari'ah* is the outer reality.

shaykh

A Sufi master. A *shaykh* or *shaikh* is a holy one who has realized his own self and can, therefore, become a guide for others. The female *shaykh* is known as a *shaykha*.

shushumna

Eastern tradition states that this is the fine thread in the center of the spinal column. In ordinary people this is a dark place, but in those seeking wisdom this becomes light or awakened fire—also referred to as the *kundalini*.

silsilah

The Sufi term for the succession of the *Sufi Order* or *tariqah* (which is also the term used for the path between *shari'ah* and *haqiqah*, or the outer self to the inner self) as it traces its descent from Muhammad. It is a sacred and holy bloodline from shaykh to shaykh, and is protected within the Sufi Order.

sirr or secret

An Islamic term for the individual's center of consciousness, which is the source of being. Only at this center does one come into contact with the Divine Inner Reality. A fleeting glimpse of the sirr is known as an *al-hal*. A permanent self-realization is known as a *maqam*.

snake/serpent

Said to be androgynous and immortal due to the shedding of its skin. It is said to be from the underworld, due to it emerging from below the ground or slithering from water. It is both a female symbol and moon symbol. It is both a phallic symbol and a solar symbol. It is the yin and yang united in the Tao. It is a symbol of the Tao. It is depicted as a spiral, as ivy, and as the vine. In Iceland, it is referred to as a *skar* or *snokr*. In Danish, the snake is the *snog*. In Swedish it is the *snok*. In Sanskrit it is the *Naga*. In Irish it is *snaig* or *snaigh*. In Hebrew the snake is *nahash*.

sod

A Hebrew term used for the arcanum. Most modern and ancient words that begin with or end with *s* can be traced back to the word *snake*. (Words such as *soul*, *spirit*, and *shining* are all related.) Sod specifically relates to such mysteries as those of Baal, Bacchus, Adonis, and Mithras. The Hebrews, not surprisingly, had their sod in the Brazen Serpent of Moses, which in all likelihood was the same serpent as the Persian Mithra. The Sodales, or members of the priestly elite or college, were also "constituted in the Idaean Mysteries of the Mighty Mother," according to Cicero in *De Senectute*.

spagira

An alternative name for alchemy, from the Greek *span*, meaning *to extract*. *Agyris* means *to reunite*.

Sufi Path

Although the Sufi Path can vary in number depending upon the writer, Fariduddin Attar's *Conference of the Birds* shows it to have seven stages, similar to the kundalini.

Taautus (Taut)

Said by Eusebius to be the origin of serpent worship in Phoenicia. Sanchoniathon called him the god who made the first image of Coelus and invented hieroglyphs. This links him with Hermes Trismegistus, also known as Thoth in Egypt. Taautus consecrated the species of dragons and serpents, and the Phoenicians and Egyptians followed him in this superstition. Taautus could be a collective social memory of the first group who worshipped the serpent. The idea of Taautus links with the stories of Thoth, who later became a great sage of gnostic and alchemical beliefs. Thoth was deified after his death and given the title the *god of health*. He was the prototype for Aesculapius, and identified with Hermes and Mercury. All healers, teachers, and saviors are associated with the serpent. Indeed, it was as the *healing god* that Thoth was symbolized as the serpent. He is normally represented with the heads of an ibis and baboon.tabot

The tabot of Ethiopia are copies of the slabs or tablets of stone that are believed to be contained within the Ark of the Covenant. Many scholars believe that the presence of these tabot indicate that the Ark is, or was, in Ethiopia. The tabot are carried ceremonially and wrapped in ornamental cloth.

tanazzulat

The Islamic descent from the One Essence as a manifestation of this world. It is a paradox, as the One Essence cannot be manifested in full form, and so whatever is seen manifested is not fully the One Essence. In this way, the One Essence assumes a manifestation that can be known it is not the true One Essence. This can only be seen properly through *theophanic vision*. The theophanic vision can only be mediated by the *himma* or power of the heart. The theophanic mediator sees things on a sensory level above and beyond those ordinary people can possibly perceive. In the Sufi tradition this theophanic vision is known as an ascent to the spiritualized realm. In scientific terms, this is an individual who has entangled with the quantum world—the collective superconscious world. It is the same as the Universal Intellect.

Tau-cross

The T- or Tau-cross has been a symbol of eternal life in many cultures and gives its name to the Bull in the astrological sign of *Taurus* (which also contains *ru*, the gateway). In fact, the Druids venerated the tree by scrawling the Tau-cross into its bark. In the European Middle Ages, the Tau-cross was used in amulets to protect the wearer against disease.

Among the modern Freemasons, the Tau has many meanings. Some say that it stands for *Templus Hierosolyma*, or the *Temple of Jerusalem*; others believe that it signifies hidden treasure or means *Clavis ad*

Thesaurum—a key to treasure; or *Theca ubi res pretiosa—a place where the precious thing is concealed.*

The Tau is especially important in Royal Arch Masonry, where it becomes the *Companions Jewel,* with a serpent as a circle above the crossbar—forming the Ankh—with the Hebrew word for serpent engraved on the upright, and also including the *Triple Tau*—a symbol for hidden treasure and made up of eight right angles.

The Tau was also the symbol for Saint Anthony—later to become the symbol for the Knights Templar of Saint Anthony of Leith in Scotland. Saint Anthony lived in the fourth century and is credited with establishing monasticism in Egypt. The story goes that he sold all his possessions after hearing from the Lord, and marched off into the wilderness to become a hermit. On his travels he learned much from various sages in Egypt and developed a large following. He was sorely tempted by the Devil in the form of serpents. In one episode, he follows a trail of gold to a temple that is infested with serpents and takes up residence, needing little food for sustenance other than bread and water. He is said to have lived 105 years. Due to this longevity he is credited with protective powers. All of this is a metaphor for the enlightenment process associated with overcoming serpent energy.

The Order of the Hospitalers of Saint Anthony, who would later take much of the Templar wealth, brought many of Anthony's relics to France in the 11th century, although they were said to have been secretly deposited somewhere in Egypt just after his death.

The Taut or Tau symbolizes the four creative elements of the universe. The symbol of the sun or serpent was added, creating a simple circle or the oval *ru*. This loop above the T-cross created the Ankh, the symbol of eternity. The snake in a circle eating its own tale is symbolic of the sun and immortality, not to mention the point in the cyclic process of creation. Together, the T and O are the perfect symbolical mixture of the four elements and the fifth element. The symbol of the moon was added, turning it into the sign for

Hermes/Mercury and showing the Caduceus/Serpent origin. This symbol became the mark or sign that would set the believer aside for saving. In Ezekiel, this is the mark that God will know—the mark on the forehead. As the Victorian historian John Bathurst Deane points out, the Ezekiel passage (9:4) should read "set a Tau upon their foreheads" or "mark with the letter Tau the foreheads." The early Christians baptized with the term *crucis thaumate notare*. They baptized with the symbol of the snake. And Saint Paul himself, in Galatians 6:17 states: "[L]et no-one cause me trouble, for I bear on my body the marks of Jesus."

This idea of wearing the Tau-cross on the shoulder as a sign would later become part of the Templar markings. The Templars instigated in the worship of serpents. The Merovingians (said by some to be descended from Jesus and a sea serpent or fish god—the *Quinotaur* or *Quino-Tau-r*) were supposedly born with a red cross between their shoulder blades. The Tau cross is also strangely used by those practicing sacred geometry as a "marker" for buried treasure, whether physical or spiritual.

ta'wil

This is an Islamic term for the vision within the theophanic world, which turns everything visually perceived into a symbolic representation. It is a way for humanity to understand the unknown superconscious world. In terms of the shaman, this would be symbols devised and taught to the initiates to allow them to better understand the world they are seeing.

tasawwuf

Another term for *Sufism* or *mystical Islam*.

Templars

Friday the 13th of October 1307 was a terrible day for the Knights Templar, as King Philip IV's men descended upon all of the order's French holdings, seizing property and arresting each of its members. Philip owed them huge amounts of money and had no way of paying them back. He secretly hoped that the famous Templar treasure would be his. With the help of his puppet, Pope Clement V, the French king tortured the Knights to discover their secrets. Finally, to justify his actions, the Knights were accused of heresy, homosexual practices, necromancy, and conducting bizarre rituals such as desecrating the cross—as if to show their lack of faith in this Christian icon.

The most unusual and perplexing evidence they came across, however, was the worship of this idol called *Baphomet*. This strange thing—although sometimes referred to as a cat or goat—was generally seen as a severed head. Peter Tompkins in *The Magic of Obelisks* says:

> Public indignation was aroused...the Templar symbol of gnostic rites based on phallic worship and the power of directed will. The androgynous figure with a goat's beard and cloven hooves is linked to the horned god of antiquity, the goat of Mendes.

The list of charges used by the Inquisition in 1308 read:

> Item, that in each province they had idols, namely heads.
>
> Item, that they adored these idols or that idol, and especially in their great chapters and assemblies.
>
> Item, that they venerated (them).
>
> Item, that they venerated them as God.
>
> Item, that they venerated them as their Savior.
>
> Item, that they said that the head could save them.
>
> Item, that it could make riches.
>
> Item, that it could make the trees flower.
>
> Item, that it made the land germinate.
>
> Item, that they surrounded or touched each head of the aforesaid idol with small cords, which they wore around themselves next to the shirt or the flesh.

Some said it was a man's head, but others a woman's head; some said that it was bearded, others non-bearded; some presumed that it was made from glass and that it had two faces. This general mixing of ideas shows where the idea of the head could have come from. That it was a man's head or a woman's indicates its dual nature—and much like the ancient Celtic heads would incline us to the opinion, that it emerged from part of the ancient head cult. The Celts, it is said, believed that the soul resided in the head. They would decapitate their enemies and keep them as talismans. Probably the best-known head in Celtic lore is that of *Bran the Blessed*, which was buried outside London, facing towards France. It was put there to see off the plague and disease and to ensure that the land was fertile— the same powers that were attributed to the Green Man.

It is also said that the name *Baphomet* was derived from *Mahomet*— an Old French corruption of the name of the prophet Muhammad. Others claim that it comes from the Arabic word *abufihamet*, which means *Father of Understanding*. In the end, the worship of the Baphomet tells us one certain thing: that the Templars were initiates and adepts in the ancient Eastern ways and at the higher levels, in all probability, understood the knowledge. This is seen when we understand that *baphe* means immersion, as in baptism, and *metis* means wisdom. Baphomet, therefore, is truly the immersion of oneself into wisdom, the true inner reality and the true and only divinity.

thermuthis

The rearing cobra goddess of Egypt. She is often depicted suckling a child or nursing children, and this was taken literally in that she became the goddess of little children instead of the obvious nurturing element of the serpent energy related to the kundalini. In this respect, the link between the serpent child suckling Mother Goddesses and Mary now reveal the true reality of who, or rather what, Mary was representative of.

Tree of Knowledge

Although literally claimed to have been in the Garden of Eden, it is in fact the *Daath* of the kabbalah, the axis mundi, or spine up which rises the serpent.

Tree of Life

Representing the structure of the soul and the universe—the interconnected nature. It is the *Being*, the *Chesed*, or *Inner Man*.

universal intellect

The Islamic version of the mind free from the manifestations of this world—free from the impure thoughts associated with the banal reality in which we exist. It is called the Intellect of the Intellect, and is where we can see the hidden in everything. It is the process of true enlightenment.

Veronica's Veil

A Christian relic supposedly created when Veronica stopped Jesus on the Via Dolorosa on the way to Calgary. She paused to wipe the sweat of his face with her veil, causing the image of his face to be imprinted into the cloth. Legend suggests that the cloth had magical healing properties, although it has since been lost to history.

V.I.T.R.I.O.L.

An acronym that in Latin means *Visitam Inferorem Terre Rectifactum Invenias Ocultum Lapidum*. This translates to English as *visit the interior of the earth*, which through rectifying you will find the occult stone. Although this can sound completely bewildering to those who do not understand, it does have a simple meaning: The adherent must go inside himself to put right the problems causing suffering, and only then can he obtain the true wisdom of Inner Reality.

Wadjet

Also known as *Wadjyt, Wadjit, Uto, Uatchet, Edjo, and Uraeus*. A predynastic cobra goddess of Lower Egypt who took the title *The Eye of Ra*. She is depicted as a rearing cobra, a winged cobra, a lion-headed woman, or a woman wearing a red crown. She is the protector of Pharaoh. Shown together with *Nekhbet* (who was seen as a woman, a snake, or a vulture), she brings to mind the bird-serpent image of Quetzalcoatl. Wadjet is seen as the fiery Uraeus, anointing the head with flames, similar to the apostles in *Acts* of the Bible. In the Pyramid Texts she is linked strongly with nature. The papyrus plant is said to emerge from her and she is connected to the forces of growth. She is also closely connected to Isis in the form of *Wadjet-Isis in Dep*.

yggdrasil

The cosmic tree of Scandinavia. It is symbolic of the shamanic *world/ cosmic tree* and similar to the Tree of Life and Tree of Knowledge. The roots are constantly attacked by the serpent—a reference to the kundalini serpent said to lie coiled around the base of the human spinal column. The Serpent was known as *nidhogg*, or the *dread biter*. Odin sacrificed himself and hung from the tree for nine nights—showing the resurrective properties of the tree. Odin basically sacrifices his ego with the aid of kundalini.

zahir

An Islamic term for the outward or exoteric meaning of reality.

zen

A Japanese Buddhist sect seeking enlightenment (of the self) through the spontaneous insights gathered by a single-minded devotion to simplicity. Alternatively, it is insights gained through paradoxes generated by verbal interchange, which often fail to be solved with logic. It is thought to come from *zazen*, which has the meaning of *meditation* or *just sitting*.

Zoroaster

Probably born around 1500 B.C. in Iran, his teachings are to be found in the *Avesta* and *Gathas*. Zoroastrianism did not prosper until the sixth century B.C., and lasted until it was taken over by Islam in the seventh century A.D. These are believed to have been the wise men of the Christian Bible, who brought gifts to Jesus at his birth. If the Magi saw their gods as serpents, then there is little wonder that they should see and be associated with this serpent-savior born in human form. According to Eusebius in the ritual of Zoroaster, the great expanse of the heavens and nature were described under the symbol of the serpent in the *Ophiolatreia* by Hargrave Jennings. This was doubly mentioned in the Octateuch of Ostanes. Temples were erected across Persia and the East in veneration of the serpent deity.

NOTES

CHAPTER 1

1. Uleyn, *Reliositeit en Fantasie*.

2. Gyselen, Mommaers, and Martler, *Hoe Menselijk is Mystiek?*, 42.

3. Borchert, *Mysticism: Its History and Challenge*, 18.

4. Borchert, *St. John of the Cross, The Ascent of Mount Carmel*, 20.

5. Simon, *The Essence of Gnosticism*, 44.

6. Ibid., 147.

CHAPTER 2

1. Price, *Searching for the Ark of the Covenant*, 39.

2. Munro-Hay, *The Quest for the Ark of the Covenant*, 6.

3. Ibid., 16.

4. Ibid., 31.

5. Ibid., 43.

6. Grierson and Munro-Hay, *The Ark of the Covenant*, 14.

7. Schonfield, *The Essene Odyssey*, 69.

8. Ibid., 64.

9. Simon, *The Essence of the Gnostics*, 20.

10. Schonfield, *The Essene Odyssey*.

11. Ibid., 163.

12. "The Trail of the Serpent" by *Inquire Within*.

13. Alford, *When the Gods Came Down*.

14. Heindel, *Ancient and Modern Initiation*, 41.

15. Hancock, *The Sign and the Seal*, 382.

16. Gray, *Ark of the Covenant*.

17. Wilson, Ian, *The Blood and the Shroud*, 172.

CHAPTER 3

1. Gardner, *The Shadow of Solomon*, 18.

2. Ibid., 24.

3. Grierson and Munro-Hary, *The Ark of the Covenant*, 2.

4. Munro-Hay, *The Quest for the Ark of the Covenant*, 17.

5. Bombast, *The Book Concerning The Tincture of the philosophers Written Against Those Sophists Born Since the Deluge, In the Age of Our Lord Jesus Christ, The Son of God.*

6. Hancock, *The Sign and the Seal*, 51.

7. Ibid., 55.

8. Phillips, *The Templars and the Ark of the Covenant*, 23.

9. Coulson, *Philo*.

10. Munro-Hay, *The Quest for the Ark of the Covenant*, 47.

11. Grierson and Munro-Hay, *The Ark of the Covenant*, 10.

12. Wilson, Ian, *The Blood and the Shroud*, 197.

13. Tanhuma, *Kedoshin*, 10.

14. Phillips, *The Templars and the Ark of the Covenant*, 22.

15. Munro-Hay, *The Quest for the Ark of the Covenant*, 29.

16. Hancock, *The Sign and the Seal*, 59.

17. *Kitab-i-Iqan* (*Book of Certitude*), Part I.

18. Heindel, *Ancient and Modern Initiation.*

19. Hancock, *The Sign and the Seal*, 333.

20. Ibid., 69.

21. Ibid., 274.

22. Ibid., 288.

23. Budge, *The Kebra Nagast.*

24. Pennick, *Sacred Geometry*, 65.

25. Stirling, *Canon: an Exposition of the Pagan Mystery Perpetuated in the Cabala as the Rule of All the Arts.*

CHAPTER 4

1. Hancock, *The Sign and the Seal*, 313.

2. Gardner, *Lost Secrets of the Sacred Ark*, 100.

3. Phillips, *The Templars and the Ark of the Covenant*, 62.

4. Myer, *The Qabbalah.*

5. Kemp, *Ancient Egypt: Anatomy of a Civilisation*, 185.

6. Miller, *The Golden Thread of Time.*

7. *On the Philadelphian Gold: A Conference betwixt Philochrysus and Philadelphus On the Philadelphian Gold.*

8. Reed, *Rebel in the Soul: An Ancient Egyptian Dialogue between a Man and His Destiny.*

9. Rohl, *A Test of Time: The Bible—From Myth to History*, 23.

10. Osman, *House of the Messiah.*

11. Pritchard, *Ancient Near Eastern Texts Relating to the Old Testament with Supplement.*

12. Myer, *The Qabbalah.*

13. Hall, *Old Testament Wisdom: Keys to Bible Interpretation.*

14. Hall, *The Secret Teachings of All Ages.*

15. Ibid.

CHAPTER 5

1. *Arka*, of course, also gives us the root for *mon-archy*, the one sun ruler, as the king was the power of the sun on Earth, and thereby a human ark. The ancient Armenian word for King was *arka* from their word *aregak* for sun. It is the root *ar* that gives run, and is Ra (the Egyptian sun-god) reversed, the second element Ka is also Egyptian. Armenians are therefore *people of the sun.*

2. Bhagava Gita x:20-41.

3. Meek, *The Song of Songs,* 48-79.

4. Phillips, *The Templars and the Ark of the Covenant*, 62.

5. Macdonnel, *Vedic Mythology*, 2.

6. Mackenzie, *Indian Myth and Legend*, 31.

7. Matlock, "Is There A Connection Between Ancient Indian And Hebrew Language?"

8. Higgins, *Anacalypsis: An Attempt to Draw Aside the Veil of the Saitic Isis; or an Inquiry into the Origins of Languages, Nations and Religions*, 437-438.

9. Ibid., 432.

10. Ibid., 740.

11. Nagesh, *World Vedic Heritage: A History of Histories.*

CHAPTER 6

1. Gardner, *The Shadow of Solomon*, 185-186.

2. Phillips, *The Templars and the Ark of the Covenant*, 62.

3. Blavatsky, *The Theosophical Glossary.*

4. Blavatsky, *The Secret Doctrine.*

5. Myer, *The Qabbalah.*

6. Kingsford, *Clothed With The Sun.*

7. Blavatsky, *The Secret Doctrine.*

CHAPTER 7

1. Assmann, *Death and Salvation in Ancient Egypt.*

2. Alford, *The Midnight Sun*, 95.

3. Turville-Petre, *Myth and Religion of the North*, 251.

4. Gronbech, *The Culture of the Teutons*, 55.

5. Bradley, *Holy Grail Across the Atlantic: The Secret History of Canadian Discovery and Exploration.*

6. Springett, *Secret Sects of Syria and the Lebanon.*

7. Simon, *The Essence of the Gnostics*, 149.

CHAPTER 8

1. Gardner, *Lost Secrets of the Sacred Ark*, 18.

2. Ibid., 132.

3. Tull, *Traces of the Templars.*

4. Ibid.

5. Sinclair, *The Secret Scroll.*

6. Rice, "The Cross of Lorraine: Emblem of the Royal Secret."

7. Mackey, et al., *Encyclopaedia of Freemasonry.*

8. Pike, *Morals and Dogma*, 231.

9. *The Holy Bible: The Great Light In Masonry.*

10. Holman, *Masonic Holy Bible.*

11. Mackay, et. al., *Encyclopaedia of Freemasonry.*

12. Ibid.

13. Ibid.

14. Percival, *Masonry and Its Symbols in the Light of 'Thinking and Destiny'.*

15. Gardiner, *Gnosis: The Secret of Solomon's Temple Revealed.*

16. Mackay, *Lexicon of Freemasonry.*

17. Holman, *Masonic Holy Bible.*

18. "The Trail of the Serpent," *Inquire Within.*

CHAPTER 9

1. Hancock, *The Sign and the Seal*, 293.

2. Grierson and Munro-Hay, *The Ark of the Covenant*, 152.

3. Ibid., 159.

4. "The Epistle to the Son of the Wolf."

5. Hawting, *The Origins of the Muslim Sanctuary at Mecca.*

6. Atharva Veda X, 2, Mantra 33.

7. Basham, *The Wonder that was India.*

8. Gardiner, *The Shining Ones.*

9. Walker, *The Woman's Encyclopaedia of Myths and Secrets.*

10. Hancock, *The Sign and the Seal*, 370.

11. Grierson and Munro-Hay, *The Ark of the Covenant*, 7.

12. Ibid., 17.

13. Ibid., 45.

14. Phillips, *The Moses Legacy.*

15. Ibid.

16. Ibid.

17. Hancock, *The Sign and the Seal*, 378.

18. Gardner, *Lost Secrets of the Sacred Ark*, 29.

19. Ibid., 37.

20. Hall, *The Secret Teachings of All Ages.*

21. Ibid.

22. Gardner, *Lost Secrets of the Sacred Ark*, 40.

23. Epstein, *Kabbalah: The Way of the Jewish Mystic.*

24. Schaya, *The Universal Meaning of the Kabbalah.*

25. Fortune, *The Mystical Qabalah.*

26. Price, *Searching for the Ark of the Covenant*, 177.

CHAPTER 10

1. Gardner, *The Shadow of Solomon*, 124.

2. Ibid., 16.

3. Grierson and Munro-Hay, *The Ark of the Covenant.*

CHAPTER 11

1. Heller, *Report on the Shroud of Turin.*

2. Phillips, *The Templars and the Ark of the Covenant*, 62.

3. Wilson, Ian, *The Blood and the Shroud*, 173.

4. Please see *www.trifl.org* for more information.

5. Wilson, Ian, *The Blood and the Shroud*, 176.

6. Ibid.

7. Gardner, *The Shadow of Solomon*, 164.

8. Wilson, Ian, *The Blood and the Shroud*, 237.

9. Ibid., 245.

10. Picknett and Prince, *Turin Shroud: In Whose Image? The Truth Behind the Centuries-Long Conspiracy of Silence.*

APPENDIX A

1. Kashyapa warned Buddha that there was only one hut available, and that a malevolent Naga occupied it. Buddha was not disturbed by this, and went to the hut regardless. A terrific struggle ensued, culminating in the hut bursting into flames. The onlookers drenched the flames, but they had to wait until morning to find Buddha, alive. The Buddha emerged with his begging bowl in his arms, and inside was a peaceful, coiled snake. The Buddha had slain the dragon of its fiery notions and emerged with a beneficial result.

2. See *The Serpent Grail* by Philip Gardiner with Gary Osborn (Watkins, 2005), or visit the author's Website at *www.philipgardiner.net.*

3. *Baphe* means *to submerge*, *metis* means *wisdom*, and therefore *Baphomet* could simply mean *to be submerged in wisdom.*

4. The blood is seen the world over as the life force, or life energy of the body. It was sacred to the Hebrews especially, but not in isolation. Christ spilling his almost Tantric energy into the place of the skull is therefore invigorating the skull into which it falls, making Golgotha a very sacred place or relic.

5. The Nagas are serpent worshippers from India.

6. The seven days are an allusion to the seven levels of the coiled serpent or kundalini awakening, whereby the serpent energies are visualized and raised in balance into the head and one becomes a Buddha or enlightened one.

BIBLIOGRAPHY

The following bibliography includes all the books that have built my knowledge and given me sufficient insight to be able to lay down the preceding pages. I would recommend most of them, but, as I always say, read in balance.

Abdalqadir as-Sufi, Shaykh. *The Return of the Kalifate*. Cape Town: Madinah Press, 1996.

Ableson, J. *Jewish Mystics*. London: G Bell and Sons Ltd., n.d.

Alford, Alan. *When the Gods Came Down*. London: New English Library, 2000.

Allegro, John. *The Sacred Mushroom and the Cross: A Study of the Nature and Origins of Christianity within the Fertility Cults of the Ancient Near East*. London: Hodder and Stoughton, 1970.

Andrews, R., and P. Schellenberger. *The Tomb of God*. London: Little, Brown and Co., 1996.

Appolodorus, *The Library: Greek Mythology*. Second century B.C.

Ashe, Geoffrey. *The Quest for Arthur's Britain*. London: Paladin Press, 1971.

Bacher, Wilhelm, and Ludwig Blau. *Shamir*. *www.jewishencyclopedia.com*.

Baigent, Leigh. *Ancient Traces*. London: Viking Press, 1998.

———. *The Elixir and the Stone*. London: Viking Press, 1997.

Baigent, Michael, Richard Leigh, and Henry Lincoln. *The Dead Sea Scrolls Deception*. London: Arrow, 2001.

———. *Holy Blood and the Holy Grail*. London: Jonathan Cape, 1982.

———. *The Messianic Legacy*. London: Arrow, 1996.

———. *The Temple and the Lodge*. London: Arrow, 1998.

Balfour, Mark. *The Sign of the Serpent*. London: Prism, 1990.

Balfour, Michael. *Megalithic Mysteries*. London: Parkgate Books, 1992.

Barber, Malcolm. *The Trial of the Templars*. Cambridge, Mass.: Cambridge University Press, 1978.

Barrett, David. *Sects, Cults and Alternative Religions*. London: Blandford, 1996.

Barrow, John. *Theories of Everything*. London: Virgin, 1990.

Basham, A.L. *The Wonder that was India*. London: Collins, 1954.

Bauval, R. *The Orion Mystery*. Oxford: Heinemann, 1996.

Bayley, H. *The Lost Language of Symbolism*. London: Bracken Books, 1996.

Beatty, Longfield. *The Garden of the Golden Flower*. London: Senate, 1996.

Begg, E., and D. Begg. *The Cult of the Black Virgin*. London: Arkana, 1985.

———. *In Search of the Holy Grail and the Precious Blood*. London: Thorsons, 1985.

Blaire, Lawrence. *Rhythms of Vision*. New York: Warner Books, 1975.

Blavatsky, Helene P. *The Theosophical Glossary*. Whitefish, Mont.: Kessinger Publishing Ltd., 1918.

Borchert, Bruno. *Mysticism: Its History and Challenges*. Maine: Samuel Weiser, Inc., 1994.

Bord, Colin, and Janet Bord. *Earth Rites: Fertility Practices in Pre-Industrial Britain*. London: Granada Publishing, 1982.

Bouquet , AC. *Comparative Religion*. London: Pelican, 1942.

Boyle, Veolita Parke. *The Fundamental Principles of Yi-King, Tao: The Cabbalas of Egypt and the Hebrews*. London: W & G Foyle, 1934.

Bradley, Michael. *Holy Grail Across the Atlantic: The Secret History of Canadian Discovery and Exploration*. Toronto: Houslow Press, 1998.

Brine, Lindsey. *The Ancient Earthworks and Temples of the American Indians*. London: Oracle, 1996.

Broadhurst, Paul, and Hamish Miller. *The Dance of the Dragon*. Cornwall: Mythos Press, 2000.

Bryant, N. *The High Book of the Grail*. Cambridge: D.S. Brewer, 1985.

Bryden, R. *Rosslyn—a History of the Guilds, the Masons and the Rosy Cross*. Rosslyn: Rosslyn Chapel Trust, 1994.

Budge, E.A. Wallis. *The Cult of the Black Virgin*. London: Arkana, 1985.

———. *An Egyptian Hieroglyphic Dictionary Volume 1*. Dover, Dover Publications: 1978.

———. *The Kebra Negast*. London: Gramercy, 1932.

Butler, E.M. *The Myth of the Magus*. Cambridge: Cambridge University Press, 1911.

Callahan, Philip. *Ancient Mysteries Modern Visions: The Magnetic Life of Agriculture*. Austin, Tex.: Acres, 2001.

———. *Nature's Silent Music*. Austin, Tex.: Acres, 1992.

———. *Paramagnetism: Rediscovering Nature's Secret Force of Growth*. Austin, Tex.: Acres, 1995.

Campbell, Joseph. *Transformations of Myth Through Time*. London: Harper and Row, 1990.

Cantor, N.F. *The Sacred Chain*. London: HarperCollins, 1994.

Carpenter, Edward. *Pagan and Christian Creeds: Their Origin and Meaning*. London: Allen and Unwin Ltd., 1920.

Carr-Gomm, Sarah. *Dictionary of Symbols in Art*. London: Duncan Baird Publishers, 1995.

Castaneda, Carlos. *The Teaching of Don Juan*. London: Arkana, 1978.

Cavendish, Richard. *Mythology*. London: Tiger Press, 1998.

Ceram, C. W. *Gods Graves and Scholars: The Story of Archaeology*. London: Gollancz, Sidgwick, and Jackson, 1954.

Chadwick, N. *The Druids*. Cardiff: University of Wales Press, 1969.

Childress, David. *Anti-Gravity & The World Grid*. Stelle, Ill.: Adventures Unlimited Press, 1987.

Churchward, Albert. *The Origin and Evolution of Religion*. Whitefish, Mont.: Kessinger Publishing Ltd., 1997.

Churton, Tobias. *The Golden Builders*. Lichfield: Signal Publishing, 2002.

Clarke, Hyde, and C. Staniland Wake. *Serpent and Siva Worship*. Whitefish, Mont.: Kessinger Publishing Ltd., 1877.

Coles, John. *Field Archaeology in Britain*. London: Methuen, 1972.

Collins, Andrew. *From the Ashes of Angles, The Forbidden Legacy of a Fallen Race*. London: Signet Books, 2004.

———. *Gateway to Atlantis*. London: Headline, 2000.

———. *Gods of Eden*. London: Headline, 1998.

———. *Twenty-First Century Grail: The Quest for a Legend*. London: Virgin, 2004.

Cooper, J.C. *An Illustrated Encyclopaedia of Traditional Symbols*. London: Thames and Hudson, 1978.

Croker, Thomas Crofton. *Legend of the Lakes*. N.p., 1829.

Crooke, W. *The Popular Religion and Folk-lore of Northern India*. Whitefish, Mont.: Kessinger Publishing Ltd., 1997.

Cumont, F. *The Mysteries of Mithra*. London: Dover Publications, 1956.

Currer-Briggs, N. *The Shroud and the Grail; a modern quest for the true grail*. New York: St. Martin's Press, 1987.

David-Neel, Alexandria. *Magic and Mystery in Tibet*. London: Dover Publications, 1929.

Davidson, H. R. Ellis. *Myths and Symbols of Pagan Europe*. Syracuse, N.Y.: Syracuse University Press, 1988.

Davidson, John. *The Secret of the Creative Vacuum*. London: The C. W. Daniel Company Ltd., 1989.

Davies, Rev. Edward. *The Mythology and Rites of the British Druids*. London: J. Booth, 1806.

De Martino, Ernesto. *Primitive Magic*. Dorset: Prism Unity, 1972.

Devereux, Paul. *Places of Power: measuring the secret energy of ancient sites*. London: Blandford, 1999.

———. *Secrets of Ancient and Sacred Places: The World's Mysterious Heritage*. Beckhampton: Beckhampton Press, 1995.

————. *Shamanism and the Mystery Lines*. London: Quantum, 1992.

————. *Symbolic Landscapes*. Glastonbury: Gothic Image, 1992.

Devereux, Paul, and Ian Thompson. *Ley Guide: The Mystery of Aligned Ancient Sites*. London: Empress, 1988.

Dinwiddie, John. *Revelations—the Golden Elixir*. Writers Club Press, 2001.

Dodd, C.H. *Historical Tradition of the Fourth Gospel*. Cambridge: Cambridge University Press, 1963.

Doel, Fran, and Geoff Doel. *Robin Hood: Outlaw of Greenwood Myth*. Temous, 2000.

Duckett-Shipley, Eleanor. *The Gateway to the Middle Ages, Monasticism*. Ann Arbor, Mich.: University of Michigan Press, 1961.

Dunford, Barry. *The Holy Land of Scotland: Jesus in Scotland and the Gospel of the Grail*. N.p., n.d.

Dunstan, V. *Did the Virgin Mary Live and Die in England?* Rochester, N.Y.: Megiddo Press, 1985.

Eliade, Mircea. *Shamanism: Archaic Techniques of Ecstasy*. Princeton, N.J.: Princeton University Press, 1964.

Ellis, Ralph. *Jesus, Last of the Pharaohs*. Cheshire: Edfu Books, 2001.

Epstein, Perle. *Kabbalah: The Way of the Jewish Mystic*. Boston: Shambhala Classics, 2001.

Ernst, Carl. *Venomous Reptiles of North America*: Washington, D.C.: Smithsonian Books, 1992.

Evans, Lorraine. *Kingdom of the Ark*. London: Simon and Schuster, 2000.

Feather, Robert. *The Copper Scroll Decoded*. London: Thorsons, 1999.

Fedder, Kenneth, and Michael Alan Park. *Human Antiquity: An Introduction to Physical Anthropology and Archaeology*. Mountain View, Calif.: Mayfield Publishing, 1993.

Ferguson, Diana. *Tales of the Plumed Serpent*. London: Collins and Brown, 2000.

Fergusson, Malcolm. *Rambles in Breadalbane*. N.p., 1891.

Fontana, David. *The Secret Language of Symbols*. London: Piatkus, 1997.

Ford, Patrick. *The Mabinogi and other Medieval Welsh Tales*. Berkeley, Calif.: University of California Press. 1977.

Fortune, Dion. *The Mystical Qabalah*. Maine: Weiser Books, 2000.

Foss, Michael. *People of the First Crusade*. London: Michael O'Mara Books, 1997.

Frazer, Sir James. *The Golden Bough*. London: Wordsworth, 1993.

Freke, Timothy, and Peter Gandy. *Jesus and the Goddess*. London: Thorsons, 2001.

Gardiner, Samuel. *History of England*. London: Longmans, Green, and Co., 1904.

Gardner, Laurence. *Bloodline of the Holy Grail*. London: Element, 1996.

Gascoigne, Bamber. *The Christians*. London: Jonathan Cape, 1977.

Gerber, Richard. *Vibrational Medicine*. Santa Fe, N.M.: Bear & Company, 2001.

Gilbert, Adrian. *Magi*. London: Bloomsbury, 1996.

Goldberg, Carl. *Speaking With The Devil*. London: Viking, 1996.

Gould, Charles. *Mythical Monsters*. London: Senate, 1995.

Graves, Robert. *The Greek Myths: 2*. London: Pelican, 1964.

Gray Hulse, Tristan. *The Holy Shroud*. London: Weidenfeld and Nicolson, 1997.

Grierson, Roderick, and Stuart Munro-Hay, *The Ark of the Covenant*. Detroit, Mich.: Phoenix Press, 2000.

Guenther, Johannes Von. *Cagliostro*. London: William Heinemann, 1928.

Hagger, Nicholas. *The Fire and the Stones*. London: Element, 1991.

Halifax, Joan. *Shaman: the Wounded Healer*. London: Crossroad, Thames and Hudson, 1982.

Hanauer, J.E. *The Holy Land*. London: Senate, 1996.

Hancock, Graham. *The Sign and the Seal*. London: Arrow, 2001.

Harbison, Peter. *Pre-Christian Ireland*. London: Thames and Hudson, 1988.

Harrington, E. *The Meaning of English Place Names*. Belfast: The Black Staff Press, 1995.

Hartmann, Franz. *The Life of Jehoshua The Prophet of Nazareth: an occult study and a key to the Bible*. London: Kegan, Trench, Trubner & Co., 1909.

Heathcote-James, Emma. *They Walk Among Us*. New York: Metro, 2004.

Hedsel, Mark. *The Zelator*. London: Century, 1998.

Heindel, Max. *Ancient and Modern Initiation (1865–1919)*. The Rosicrucian Fellowship International.

Howard, M. *The Occult Conspiracy*. Rochester, N.Y.: Destiny Books, 1989.

James, E.O. *The Ancient Gods*. London: Weidenfeld and Nicolson, 1962.

Jennings, Hargrave. *Ophiolatreia*. Whitefish, Mont.: Kessinger Publishing Ltd., 1996.

Johnson, Buffie. *Lady of the Beast: the Goddess and Her Sacred Animals*. San Fransisco: Harper and Row, 1988.

Jones, Alison. *Dictionary of World Folklore*. New York: Larousse, 1995.

Kauffeld, Carl. *Snakes: The Keeper and the Kept*. London: Doubleday and Co., 1969.

Kemp, Barry. *Ancient Egypt: Anatomy of a Civilisation*. London: Routledge, 2005.

Kendrick, T. D. *The Druids*. London: Methuen and Co., 1927.

King, Serge Kahili. *Instant Healing: Mastering the Way of the Hawaiian Shaman Using Words, Images, Touch, and Energy*. Los Angeles: Renaissance Books, 2000.

Kingsford, Anna. *Clothed With The Sun*. London: John M. Watkins, 1889.

Knight, Christopher and Robert Lomas. *The Second Messiah*. London: Arrow, 1997.

———. *Uriel's Machine: Reconstructing the Disaster Behind Human History*. London: Arrow, 2004.

Laidler, Keith. *The Divine Deception*. London: Headline, 2000.

———. *The Head of God*. London: Orion, 1999.

Lapatin, Kenneth. *Mysteries of the Snake Goddess*. Boston: Houghton Mifflin Company, 2002.

Larson, Martin A. *The Story of Christian Origins*. Village, 1977.

Layton, Robert. *Australian Rock Art: a new synthesis*. Cambridge: Cambridge University Press, 1986.

Leakey, Richard and Roger Lewin. *Origins Reconsidered*. London: Doubleday, 1992.

Le Goff, Jacques. *The Medieval World*. London: Parkgate Books, 1997.

Lemesurier, Peter. *The Great Pyramid Decoded*. London: Element, 1977.

Levi, Eliphas. *Transcendental Magic*. London: Tiger Books, 1995.

Lincoln, Henry. *Key to the Sacred Pattern*. Gloucestershire: Windrush Press, 1997.

Loye, David. *An Arrow Through Chaos: how we see into the future.* Rochester, N.Y.: Part Street Press, 1983.

Lyall, Neil, and Robert Chapman. *The Secret of Staying Young.* London: Pan, 1976.

Maby, J.C., and T. Bedford Franklin. *The Physics of the Divining Rod.* London: Bell, 1977.

MacCana, Proinsias. *Celtic Mythology.* New York: Hamlyn, 1992.

Mack, B.L. *The Lost Gospel.* London: Element, 1993.

Mackenzie, Donald. *Indian Myth and Legend.* Whitefish, Mont.: Kessinger Publishing Co., 2004.

Maclellan, Alec. *The Lost World of Agharti.* London: Souvenir Press, 1982.

Magin, U. *The Christianisation of Pagan Landscapes.* In *The Ley Hunter* No. 116, 1992.

Mann, A.T. *Sacred Architecture.* London: Element, 1993.

Maraini, Fosco. *Secret Tibet.* London: Hutchinson, 1954.

Matthews, John. *Sources of the Grail.* London: Floris Books, 1996.

————. *The Quest for the Green Man.* Newton Abbott: Godsfield Press, 2001.

McDermott, Bridget. *Decoding Egyptian Hieroglyphs.* London: Duncan Baird Publishers, 2001.

Meij, Harold. *The Tau and the Triple Tau.* Tokyo: H.P., 2000.

Michell, John, and Christine Rhone. *Twelve-Tribes and the Science of Enchanting the Landscape.* Grand Rapids, Mich.: Phanes PR, 1991.

Milgrom, Jacob. *The JPS Torah Commentary: Numbers.* New York: Jewish Publication Society, 1990.

Miller, Crichton. *The Golden Thread of Time.* Incline Village, Nev.: Pendulum Publishing, 2000.

Moncrieff, A. R. *Hope, Romance & Legend of Chivalry.* London: Senate, 1994.

Morgan, Gerald. *Nanteos: A Welsh House and its Families.* Llandysul: Gomer, 2001.

Morton, Chris, and Ceri Louise Thomas. *The Mystery of the Crystal Skulls.* London: Element, 2003.

Muggeridge, Malcolm. *Jesus.* London: Collins, 1975.

Myer, Isaac. *The Qabbalah*. Whitefish, Mont.: Kessinger Publishing Co., 2003.

Nilsson, M. P. *The Minoan-Mycenaean Religion and Its Survival in Greek Religion.* Oxford: Lund, 1950.

Oak, P.N. *World Vedic Heritage: A History of Histories*. 1984.

O'Brien, Christian and Barbara Joy. *The Shining Ones*. London: Dianthus Publishing Ltd., 1988.

Oliver, George. *The History of Initiation*. Whitefish, Mont.: Kessinger Publishing Ltd., 1841.

———. *Signs and Symbols*. New York: Macoy Publishing, 1906.

O'Neill, John. *Nights of the Gods*. N.p., n.d.

Opponheimer, Stephen. *Eden in the East*. London: Orion, 1988.

Orofino, Giacomella. *Sacred Tibetan Teachings on Death and Liberation*. London: Prism-Unity, 1990.

Pagels, E. *The Gnostic Gospels*. London: Weidenfeld and Nicolson, 1979.

Paterson Smyth, J. *How We Got our Bible*. London: Sampson Low, n.d.

Pennick, N. *Sacred Geometry*. Chievely: Capall Bann, 1994.

Phillips, Graham. *The Templars and the Ark of the Covenant*. Rochester, Vt.: Bear & Co., 2004.

Picknett, Lynn, and Clive Prince. *The Templar Revelation*. London: Corgi, 1998.

———. *Turin Shroud: In Whose Image? The Truth Behind the Centuries-Long Conspiracy of Silence*. New York: HarperCollins, 1994.

Piggot, Stuart. *The Druids*. London: Thames and Hudson, 1927.

Pike, Albert. *The Morals and Dogma of Scottish Rite Freemasonry*. Richmond, Va.: L.H. Jenkins, 1928.

Plichta, Peter. *God's Secret Formula*. London: Element, 1997.

Plunket, Emmeline. *Calendars and Constellations of the Ancient World*. London: John Murray, 1903.

Powell, T.G.E. *The Celts*. London: Thames and Hudson, 1968.

Price, Randall. *Searching for the Ark of the Covenant*. Eugene, Oreg.: Harvest House, 2005.

Rabten, Geshe. *Echoes of Voidness*. London: Wisdom Publications, 1983.

Radin, Dean. *The Conscious Universe*. London: HarperCollins, 1997.

Randles, Jenny, and Peter Hough. *Encyclodepia of the Unexplained.* London: Brockhampton Press, 1995.

Read, Piers Paul. *The Templars.* London: Phoenix, 1999.

Rees, Alwyn, and Brynley. *Celtic Heritage.* London: Thames and Hudson, 1961.

Reid, Howard. *Arthur—The Dragon King.* London: Headline, 2001.

———. *In Search of the Immortals: Mummies, Death and the Afterlife.* London: Headline, 1999.

Richet, C. *Thirty Years of Psychic Research.* New York: Macmillan, 1923.

Rinbochay, Lati, Locho Rinbochay, Leah Zahler, and Jeffrey Hopkins. *Meditative States in Tibetan Buddhism.* London: Wisdom Publications, 1983.

Roberts, Alison. *Hathor Rising: The Serpent Power of Ancient Egypt.* Rottingdean, East Sussex: Northgate, 1995.

Roberts, J.M. *Antiquity Unveiled.* N.p.: Health Research, 1970.

———. *The Mythology of the Secret Societies.* London: Granada, 1972.

Robertson, J. M. *Pagan Christs.* London: Watts, 1903.

Rohl, David. *A Test of Time: The Bible—from Myth to History.* London: Arrow, 1995.

Rolleston, T. W. *Myths and Legends of the Celtic Race.* London: Mystic P, 1986.

Russell, Peter. *The Brain Book.* London: Routledge, 1980.

Schaya, Leo. *The Universal Meaning of the Kabbalah.* N.J.: University Books, 1987.

Schele, Linda, and Mary Ellen Miller. *The Blood of Kings: Dynasty and Ritual in Maya Art.* New York: Braziller, 1992.

Scholem, Gershom G. *On the Kabbalah and Its Symbolism.* London: Routledge & Kegan, 1965.

Schonfield, Hugh. *The Essene Odyssey.* London: Element, 1984.

———. *The Passover Plot.* London: Hutchinson, 1965.

Schwartz, Gary, and Linda Russek. *The Living Energy Universe.* Charlottesville, Va.: Hampton Roads Publishing, 1999.

Scott, Ernest. *The People of the Secret.* London: The Octagon Press, 1983.

Seife, Charles. *Zero: The Biography of a Dangerous Idea.* London: Souvenir Press, 2000.

Seligmann, Kurt. *The History of Magic*. New York: Quality Paperback Book Club, 1997.

———. *Signs, Symbols and Ciphers*. London: New Horizons, 1992.

Sharper Knowlson, T. *The Origins of Popular Superstitions and Customs*. London: Senate, 1994.

Simpson, Jacqueline. *British Dragons*. London: B. T. Batsford and Co., 1980.

Sinclair, Andrew. *The Secret Scroll*. London: Birlinn, 2001.

Smith, M. *The Secret Gospel*. London: Victor Gollancz, 1973.

Snyder, Louis L. *Encyclopaedia of the Third Reich*. London: Wordsworth, 1998.

Spence, Lewis. *Introduction to Mythology*. London: Senate, 1994.

———. *Myths and Legends of Egypt*. London: George Harrap and Sons, 1915.

Stephen, Alexander M. *The Journal of American Folklore*. January/March, 1929.

Stirling, William. *Canon: An Exposition of the Pagan Mystery Perpetuated in the Cabala as the Rule of All the Arts*. Whitefish, Mont.: Kessinger Publishing Co., 2003.

Stone, Nathan. *Names of God*. Chicago: Moody, 1944.

Sullivan, Danny. *Ley Lines*. London: Piaktus, 1999.

Talbot, Michael. *The Holographic Universe*. London: HarperCollins, 1996.

Taylor, Richard. *How to Read a Church*. London: Random House, 2003.

Temple, Robert. *The Crystal Sun*. London: Arrow, 1976.

———. *Netherworld: Discovering the Oracle of the Dead and Ancient Techniques of Foretelling the Future*. London: Century, 2002.

Thiering, Barbara. *Jesus of the Apocalypse*. London: Doubleday, 1996.

———. *Jesus The Man*. London: Doubleday, 1992.

Thomson, Ahmad. *Dajjal the Anti-Christ*. London: Ta-Ha Publishers Ltd., 1993.

Thomson, Oliver. *Easily Led: A history of Propaganda*. Gloucestershire: Sutton Publishing, 1999.

Toland, John. *Hitler*. London: Wordsworth, 1997.

Tolstoy, Nikolai. *The Quest for Merlin*. London: Little, Brown and Co., 1985.

Tull, George F. *Traces of the Templars*. London: The Kings England Press, 2000.

Turville-Petre, Gabriel. *Myth and Religion of the North*. London: Weidenfeld and Nicolson, 1960.

Uleyn, Arnold. *Reliosteit en Fantasie*. Baarn, Netherlands: Ambo Books, 1978.

Vadillo, Umar Ibrahim. *The Return of the Gold Dinar*. Cape Town: Madinah Press, 1996.

Villanueva, J. L. *Phoenician Ireland*. Dublin: The Dolmen Press, 1833.

Villars, de, Abbe N. de Montfaucon. *Comte de Gabalis: discourses on the Secret Sciences and Mysteries in accordnace with the principles of the Ancient Magi and the Wisdom of the Kabalistic Philosophers*. Whitefiesh, Mont.: Kessinger Publishing Ltd., 1996.

Vulliamy, C. E. *Immortality: Funerary Rites & Customs*. London: Senate, 1997.

Waite, Arthur Edward. *The Hidden Church of the Holy Grail*. Amsterdam: Fredonia Books, 2002.

Wake, C. Staniland. *The Origin of Serpent Worship*. Whitefish, Mont.: Kessinger Publishing Ltd., 1877.

Walker, B. *Gnosticism*. Wellingborough: Aquarian Press, 1983.

Wallace-Murphy, Hopkins. *Rosslyn*. London: Element, 2000.

Waters, Frank. *The Book of the Hopi*. New York: Ballantine, 1963.

Watson, Lyall. *Dark Nature*. London: HarperCollins, 1995.

Weber, Renee. *Dialogues with Scientists and Sages: Search for Unity in Science and Mysticism*. London: Arkana, 1990.

Weisse, John. *The Obelisk and Freemasonry*.Whitefish, Mont.: Kessinger Publishing Ltd., 1996.

Wheless, Joseph. *Forgery in Christianity*. Health Research, 1990.

Williamson, A. *Living in the Sky*. Norman, Okla.: University of Oklahoma Press, 1984.

Wilson, Colin. *The Atlas of Holy Places and Sacred Sites*. London: Dorling Kindersley, 1996.

———. *Beyond the Occult*. London: Caxton Editions, 2002.

————. *Frankenstein's Castle: The Double Brain—Door to Wisdom*. London: Ashgrove Press, 1980.

Wilson, Hilary. *Understanding Hieroglyphs*. London: Brockhampton Press, 1993.

Wilson, Ian. *The Blood and the Shroud*. London: Orion Books, 1998.

Wise, Michael, Martin Abegg, and Edward Cook, *The Dead Sea Scrolls*. London: Harper Collins, 1999.

Within, Enquire. *Trail of the Serpent*. N.p., n.d.

Wood, David. *Genisis*. London: Baton Wicks Publications, n.d.

Woods, George Henry, *Herodotus Book II*. London: Rivingtons, 1897.

Woolley, Benjamin. *The Queens's Conjuror*. London: HarperCollins, 2001.

Wylie, Rev. J. A. *History of the Scottish Nation, Volume 1*. 1886.

Zollschan, G.K., J.F Schumaker, and G.F. Walsh. *Exploring the Paranormal*. London: Prism Unity, 1989.

Other References

Dictionary of Beliefs and Religions. London: Wordsworth, 1995.

Dictionary of Phrase and Fable. London: Wordsworth, 1995.

Dictionary of Science and Technology. London: Wordsworth Edition, 1995.

Dictionary of the Bible. London: Collins, 1974.

Dictionary of the Occult. London: Geddes and Grosset, 1997.

Dictionary of World Folklore. London: Larousse, 1995.

Web References

www.gardinersworld.com

www.serpentgrail.com

www.theshiningones.com

www.philipgardiner.net

www.radikalbooks.com

www.elfhill.com

www.handstones.pwp.blueyonder.co.uk

www.sacredconnections.com

www.pyramidtexts.com

INDEX

About the Author

Philip Gardiner is the best selling author of several books including *Gnosis: The Secret of Solomon's Temple Revealed*, *Secrets of the Serpent*, and *The Shining Ones*. He has made several television documentaries and award-winning DVDs. He speaks around the world on various subjects, including marketing, propaganda, alchemy, and gnosticism. His Website is *www.gardinersworld.com*.

Books of Related Interest

Gnosis:
The Secret of Solomon's Temple Revealed
Philip Gardiner
EAN 978-1-56414-909-1

Hidden History
Brian Haughton
EAN 978-1-56414-897-1

Opening the Ark of the Covenant
Frank Joseph
EAN 978-1-56414-903-9

The Templar Papers
Oddvar Olsen
EAN 978-1-56414-863-6

Knights Templar Encyclopedia
Karen Ralls, Ph.D.
EAN 978-1-56414-926-8

New Page Books
P.O. Box 687
Franklin Lakes, NJ 07417
1-800-227-3371
www.NewPageBooks.com